HOMES

THE FIGHT FOR SOCIAL HOUSING AND

FOR

A NEW AMERICAN COMMONS

LIVING

JONATHAN TARLETON

BEACON PRESS, BOSTON

BEACON PRESS
Boston, Massachusetts
www.beacon.org

Beacon Press books
are published under the auspices of
the Unitarian Universalist Association of Congregations.

28 27 26 25   8 7 6 5 4 3 2 1

This book is printed on acid-free paper that meets the uncoated paper
ANSI/NISO specifications for permanence as revised in 1992.

Text design and composition by Kim Arney

An excerpt from David Graeber, *The Utopia of Rules*:
On Technology, Stupidity, and the Secret Joys of Bureaucracy
(Brooklyn, NY: Melville House, 2015), is printed here with permission.

Library of Congress Cataloguing-in-Publication
Data is available for this title.
Hardcover ISBN: 978-0-8070-1780-7
E-book ISBN: 978-0-8070-1779-1
Audiobook: 978-0-8070-1815-6

To Haleemah, my home.

The ultimate hidden truth of the world is that it is something that we make, and could just as easily make differently.

—DAVID GRAEBER

CONTENTS

A NOTE ON PROCESS

In early fall of 2014, when I was working as an editor and writer at *Urban Omnibus* in New York, I opened our general pitch inbox and found a message from a resident of a large affordable-housing cooperative called Southbridge Towers. He wrote that a vote was soon taking place at his co-op, one that could "privatize" it—that is, remove the rules that kept it affordable and value all its apartments at a dramatically higher market rate. The resident was concerned; the story had gotten little coverage beyond neighborhood publications, and his co-op wasn't the only one in the city facing this threat.

From that email grew the rare *UO* story that I would shepherd all the way from the slush pile into print, and its core questions have stayed with me. Three years later, in 2017, I was a graduate student in urban planning eager to delve back into them: How were the resident-owners of co-ops like Southbridge making the personal and collective decisions that would decide the future of their homes? What factors influenced whether they prioritized individual or collective benefits?

In addition to my work as a writer, editor, budding urban planner, and housing professional, I am also trained as an oral historian, and that lens heavily influenced my approach to these questions. I knew that piecing this puzzle together would require in-depth ethnographic interviews with the residents involved and a nuanced understanding of the debates that had occurred among them. How people explained their actions was sure to be as important to this story as the outcomes themselves. I also sought to compare multiple co-ops undergoing similar processes, each with its own culture. I aimed to identify two co-ops that had recently held a privatization vote and had similar expected "market" values. In the end, it was Southbridge—the co-op that had first sparked my interest—and St. James Towers that fit the bill best.

In early 2018, I conducted interviews with co-op residents, local government officials, and citywide housing advocates. With the residents, I asked a set group of questions, then pursued threads of interest in the conversations that followed. I spoke first with cooperators who'd been visibly involved in their buildings' privatization debates, then identified and reached out to less prominent residents via social media, phone calls, and community institutions (such as churches, community development corporations, parent-teacher associations, and senior centers).

Most interviews were conducted in person, recorded, then transcribed; these transcriptions, along with the field notes I took during and after each conversation, form the meat of what you'll find within these pages. In parallel to these interviews, I also gathered flyers, memos, newsletters, reports, and blog posts produced by Southbridge and St. James residents over the course of their internal debates. Using qualitative research techniques, I identified themes from these data that underlie my arguments. Years later, in 2021 and 2022, I conducted follow-up interviews with various cooperators and also spoke with a smattering of new interviewees for the first time. I supplemented these primary sources with archival research on the two developments to contextualize their histories. It is worth noting that my interviews were all retrospective: they all occurred after the key events portrayed in this book, though they are supplemented by and checked against materials that documented those events in real time.

I have changed the names of the narrators from the two co-ops out of respect for their privacy, even when not explicitly requested to do so. The term "narrators" is employed in the field of oral history to refer to interviewees, a word choice that reflects how individuals narrate their lived experiences in the context of wider historical events. I do not use it lightly: although this book is ultimately and necessarily filtered through my viewpoint, the narrators' voices are the driving force behind the stories. My belief in the importance of not just what they have to say, but also how they say it, is central to my approach. Throughout the book I include direct quotes from my conversations with these residents. Some of their perspectives are unique; others are able stand-ins for widely held ones.

I am grateful to all who spoke to me with such openness, and I have taken the utmost care to render your words and perspectives faithfully.

THE NARRATORS

ST. JAMES TOWERS

PRO-MITCHELL-LAMA
Wenna Redfern
Graham Hales
Tia Ward
Harriet Brighton

PRO-PRIVATIZATION
Lester Goodyear
Deborah Norton
Simon Doran
Miranda Lynch

SOUTHBRIDGE TOWERS

PRO-MITCHELL-LAMA
Daniel Brampton
Chris Hresko
Eva Sacks
Leo Aria
James Szal

PRO-PRIVATIZATION
Harvey Marshall
Jan Naumann
Marissa Heine
Tom Goldhaber
Jacob Villa

BEYOND

NEW HAMPSHIRE
Ian McSweeney
Steve Normanton

MASSACHUSETTS
Kristen Wyman
Pam Ellis

MISSOURI
MAK
Tara Raghuveer
Magda Werkmeister

HOMES
FOR
LIVING

PART I

The Public,
the Goods

INTRODUCTION

A House Divided

"Hey guys, I'm heeeere," Wenna Redfern announces as she and I enter her favorite local diner, just across the way from her home in Bed-Stuy, Brooklyn.* She's a slight, fashionable Black woman, her mischievous grin and tortoiseshell glasses framed by a high, gray hairline that marks her as an elder. We take seats by the front window, from where she can keep an eye on her street. In between teasing asides with the staff, she puts in her regular order: a medium half-orange/half-cranberry juice, a coffee, and an English muffin "for the table." Her grandmotherly prodding suggests that I, too, should prepare to tuck in. "Listen," she says, gesturing to the diner at large, "I probably have stock in this place."

Wenna is used to owning pieces of her neighborhood. For the past six decades, she has been a resident and part-owner of St. James Towers, a high-rise down the street fronted by a concrete playscape in the round. Its twenty-four brown-brick stories contain 326 apartments. Its balconies, one a roost for twin swan statuettes, look onto row houses flanking a grand French Gothic church, their stoops touching down on a spacious sidewalk punctuated with gingko and maple trees.

St. James may appear undistinguished against these surroundings, but it is the product of one of the most successful social housing programs in US history. This program, nicknamed Mitchell-Lama after

---

*Bed-Stuy is short for Bedford-Stuyvesant, a neighborhood with, like many New York neighborhoods, fluctuating boundaries. Today, St. James Place, where this diner sits, is commonly considered part of Clinton Hill, a piece of Bed-Stuy that has been rebranded by the real estate industry. Throughout the book I will refer to the area as Bed-Stuy or Bedford-Stuyvesant, as Wenna Redfern does.

3

the two New York State congresspeople who sponsored its originating 1955 law, funded the construction of 140,000 apartments across 270 developments in New York City (and more across the state). Roughly half of those homes in the city take the form of what's known as a limited-equity cooperative.

"When we moved here, my father said it was nothing but a glorified project," Wenna tells me, looking out at her co-op through the glass. There is, indeed, something special about St. James. As a cooperative, it is owned and governed collectively by its residents. As a limited-equity co-op, resale prices on its apartments (technically, the co-op shares) are determined not by whatever a potential buyer will pay but by an appreciation formula designed to keep the cost accessible to middle- and low-income folks. St. James receives government subsidies for sticking with the inclusive tenets of true co-ops and in support of its endeavor to provide housing to people who need it. Ordinary housing for ordinary people. Bidding wars are of no use here; only a spot toward the front of the lengthy waitlist will help you join Wenna. Residents maintain significant control over their homes but are limited in their ability to profit from them. Social housing is decommodified housing.

It and other forms of "affordable" housing* are outliers in America, especially so these days in Bed-Stuy, a historically Black neighborhood that is now being aggressively gentrified. For decades, Black families like Wenna's forged community here despite racist policies of redlining, blockbusting, and urban renewal. She's since seen their numbers plummet as White families and singles have flocked from the suburbs back to the cities they once abandoned. Now in her eighties, Wenna bestows on herself a telling moniker, punctuated by a halting laugh and a sigh of exasperation: she is a neighborhood "leftover," a title that hints at the racism that courses through American housing and her family's deep roots in the neighborhood, predating their time at St. James. That she owns a share in the co-op is the primary reason why she's able to claim it.

However unique her situation, Wenna regards her home as ordinary, quotidian, banal. As we sip our beverages, Wenna and I express our shared belief that this is what housing fundamentally should be.

---

*Housing accessible to low- and middle-income people is often described as "affordable" or "subsidized." These are imprecise descriptors given that affordability is relative and government subsidies for "market-rate" housing across the country are monumental.

The real focus of a residential structure should be the lives under its roof, not what it can fetch in a sale; its architecture in service to those lives rather than to glamorous shots in real estate listings. We agree: housing should be a functional, accessible container for people, stuff, and experiences. It should shelter us and the meaning that coalesces as we live within it, the proverbial notches—of memory, identity, and family—on the doorframe.

Until recently, this conception of home would have been so commonplace among Wenna's neighbors at St. James Towers that our conversation at the diner would have seemed odd. One rarely discusses givens. But St. James, as Wenna tells me between sips of her juice cocktail, is no longer regarded only as 326 containers in which life can take place. A group of residents have launched a campaign to capitalize on a controversial loophole in the Mitchell-Lama law, one that allows cooperators to vote on whether to privatize their complex. St. James is therefore at risk of losing the "social" qualities that make it extraordinary, of becoming just another piece of real estate: housing for profit, not for living.

Privatization would transform every St. James shareholder into the owner of a market-rate Brooklyn apartment. Those who go on to sell would gain cash in their pocket like they've never had before. But for residents like Wenna, who have no intention of moving, privatization could mean rising costs—higher maintenance fees, higher property taxes—and an eventual forced exit. These local choices have ripple effects: St. James's commodification would presage another blow against the uphill campaign to ensure that New York doesn't become a place where only the wealthy can thrive.

Wenna, allergic to obfuscation and full of snark, identifies the root of this campaign: "It's all about money; it's all about the dollar bill." As the privatization debate among her neighbors has intensified, their tower has become a battleground over what we owe one another, what ownership is, and how to balance competing private and collective interests within a society that venerates individual wealth.

Wenna reaches into her bag, fishes through newspaper clippings and paper-clipped articles, and hands me one. "I printed that out for you," she says, tapping the peak on a still-climbing graph in a news piece. It shows a new record in median New York City rents—the latest entry in the annals of the housing crisis. Such stories that turn homes into news are plentiful and prominent in New York and across the US, often for all the wrong reasons. Let us count (just a few of) the ways. Predatory mortgages and their subsequent repackaging into junk securities brought down the global economy in 2008. Little more than a decade later as COVID spread, laid-off workers under stay-at-home orders regularly faced eviction despite a federal moratorium barring the same.[1] Rents across the country have reached heights never before seen.[2] Homeowners' associations caught the bug for foreclosing on their members' homes over a smidgen of overdue fees.[3] Deeds to family homes in neighborhoods once deemed too risky for capital are now being stolen as an investment strategy.[4] Houses owned by Black families are routinely valued far below comparable—or identical—structures held by White owners.[5]

Indeed, today, if you want a good shot at submitting the winning bid for a home in a "hot" area, you may need to forego a proper inspection and sweeten your offer. A realtor at a recent first-time homebuyers' class I attended recalled that one of his clients successfully sealed the deal on a property by promising to put up the seller at their vacation home in Greece for a week each year over the next five. Needless to say, folks looking to buy their first home don't have an exotic second property to leverage. As I write in 2023, a recent drop in housing prices and corollary halt to building activity will soon add a different flavor to the coverage.[6] By the time you are reading this book, there will have been more twists. Housing across the country, once absent from the national conversation but now animated by speculation and profiteering, has risen to the political and familial forefront.

Of course, for some Americans, housing unaffordability actually brings good tidings. In May 2022, the *New York Times* ran a headline that told that side of the American housing story: "The Extraordinary Wealth Created by the Pandemic Housing Market." In the article, Emily Badger and Quoctrung Bui wrote that "over the past two years, Americans who own their homes have gained more than $6 trillion in housing wealth"—an astonishing rise in valuation that had nothing to do with a change to the housing itself. Rather, it has to do in part with the fact there aren't enough homes that are affordable to those who need them. The reporters, to their credit, did acknowledge this flip side: the increase in home equity is "also inseparable from the housing affordability crisis."[7]

The parallel trends of housing wealth and housing insecurity in the US are not incidental. They're part and parcel, as inextricable as Taco

Bell and indigestion. Wenna, however, eats a different meal than the one served up by the wider American housing system, as she observed between English muffin bits. Because her Mitchell-Lama apartment is decommodified, she has managed to weather the winds of gentrification, even as the diner where we met that lazy Saturday morning has, since that meeting, given way to a new iteration serving $13 pancakes, her proverbial stock in the eatery diluted.

As an owner of social housing, Wenna doesn't directly participate in the dizzying heights or steep risks of the housing market. Her share in the complex and payment of a monthly maintenance fee guarantee her an apartment, as well as the right to vote in co-op board elections and on other major building matters. Unlike the more familiar condo structure, wherein resident-owners hold sole title to their apartments' interiors and own the building's common areas as a collective, a co-op's building(s) and land are owned by the company in which residents own shares. While this is a common approach to apartment living across Europe and in New York City, co-ops are rare beasts throughout the rest of the United States. The term may evoke crunchy twenty-year-olds shacking up in grungy digs, but in New York, co-ops are far more associated with luxury, secrecy, and exclusivity.[8] Horror stories abound of buyers willing to pay big money, only for co-op boards to deny entry on barely veiled grounds of race, family, or profession. Have a baby? Don't count on your million-dollar offer being accepted. Musician? Fuhgeddaboudit.

Mitchell-Lama co-ops like St. James are known citywide for being a great deal on good housing. Their median monthly housing costs were, in 2014 (when the data was last available), $900. This is just about what Wenna pays.[9] In contrast, the city's median monthly rent stood at $1,700 in 2021.[10] Mitchell-Lama owners acquire their units not by purchasing them on the market but by applying to the program, documenting that they are sufficiently low- or middle-income, joining a waitlist, and, when their name comes up, paying an up-front sum that is a fraction of the prevailing market-rate price of a similar apartment (at St. James, the average share in 2016 cost $44,000). When Wenna moves out or passes away, her share and unit will return to the co-op to be offered to the next person on the waiting list.

Despite the insulation this structure provides Wenna, she is still affected by the housing crises playing out around her. Everyone is. One's friends are priced out of the area and move away, grandchildren can't afford to live nearby, nieces from out of town must pass up a promising job in the city, and the health aide Wenna may need one day is likely to arrive at her home exhausted by a two-hour commute from a less expensive part of the region. Reporting on the dire state of US housing has become so repetitive that its illustrative data has joined the unenviable company of other tragic figures to which we are habituated. "A person working full-time at minimum wage cannot afford a standard two-bedroom apartment in any U.S. state; in only 274 counties [out of more than 3,000] can they afford a one-bedroom"[11] is akin to "by 2050, sea levels along coastlines will rise by one foot."[12]

However, in the midst of these crises—sweeping not just coastal cities but the likes of Kansas City, Missouri, and Spokane, Washington[13]—there are also moments of light. Things are so bad that individuals across the ideological spectrum are searching for answers and solutions. The commonly cited culprit, pointed to by policymakers and YIMBY (Yes In My Backyard) activists alike, is an insufficient supply of housing—the result of decades of underbuilding abetted by exclusionary zoning codes, restrictive regulations, and antagonistic neighbors. But simply constructing more buildings does not necessarily lead to more accessible housing, as any nervous tenant who's watched luxury towers rise up in their neighborhood can tell you. One prescription can't cure what is, in fact, many interlinked crises. As all pharmaceutical ads stress, the relevant medicine for a certain illness doesn't always play well with the pills to treat another.[14]

In this context, efforts have rightfully gained steam to not just build more housing but to restructure its relationship to markets. Rent control is back on the mainstream policy table despite having been unjustly pilloried by economists for years.[15] Shared equity models, which include limited-equity co-ops and en vogue community land trusts, are popping up beyond their traditional stomping grounds in New York and DC. Long Island—known for the sprawling, suburban, single-family Levittowns that embody the US' history of speculative homeownership—is gearing up to add co-ops like St. James to its housing mix.[16] Midsize cities across the country, from Eugene, Oregon, to Pittsburgh, Pennsylvania, are also exploring this time-tested method of insulating a basic human need from the caprice of the market.[17] Implicit in these new initiatives is a renewed understanding that when we prioritize housing's exchange value (what it can fetch in dollars) over its use value (the shelter and home it provides), we erode the basic structure needed for society to function.

Housing is, in a word, infrastructure. Like all infrastructure, it requires maintenance. The physical and financial side of this necessity is easily recognizable. At St. James, Wenna's monthly maintenance fee includes her share of the buildings' costs, be they a mortgage payment, water bill, or repairs to the parking lot sinkhole that, if unaddressed, could expand into a portal to hell. But beyond the physical and financial aspects of St. James are organizational and cultural pillars that hold everything together: the bylaws, the norms, the gatherings to mark the passing of a neighbor. In order to maintain St. James as a decommodified public good, residents like Wenna must ward off attempts to extract profit from their homes, a feat made more difficult by the wider, hyper-commodified housing landscape.

Now that the co-op has paid off its government-subsidized mortgage and stayed in the Mitchell-Lama program beyond the legislatively required time frame, precisely that kind of extraction is today possible through privatization. Residents can decide, over the course of three votes, to remove the limited-equity provisions that keep this housing from being sold for whatever the market will bear. The call, in other words, is coming from inside the co-op. That decommodified, social housing is in the air is a consequential and heartening shift. But what good are these approaches if we cannot even maintain such housing that already exists—if the people who live in it, those Americans best positioned to understand the importance of insulating housing from the speculative market, are behind its very undoing?

That residents of social housing may nonetheless treat their homes as a commodity is nothing new. As urban geographer Amanda Huron points out, these homes become desirable as commodities precisely *because* they are rare beacons in a sea of unaffordability. Paradoxically, the ability of someone to purchase them for a reasonable, non-market price creates the conditions under which people will go to extreme lengths to get at this otherwise hard-to-come-by resource.[18] Meet scarcity, the mother of commodification. And say hello to one of its eternal grandchildren, corruption.

In Lower Manhattan, across the East River from St. James, stands a nine-building, 1,651-apartment, limited-equity co-op known as South-bridge Towers. Like St. James, Southbridge is a part of the Mitchell-Lama program. With its vast concrete courtyards and utilitarian balconies, it plays the role of ordinary housing well, appearing almost mousy next to Lower Manhattan's icons: the Municipal Building, One World Trade Center, the stone towers of the Brooklyn Bridge that rise over once-active piers of yore. But through its warren of cinderblock hallways, stories circulate of fishy apartment transfers. One, dating back almost twenty years, is particularly notorious.

Jody Wolfson, often clad in black, enjoys the company of toy dogs (mi-kis are a favorite), the concerts of Italian crooners, and co-op board politics. She served as Southbridge's treasurer—that is, until her term came to an ignominious end on December 27, 2005, when she was in-dicted on federal fraud and conspiracy charges. Wolfson had schemed to illegally sell her apartment for (a paltry, in New York real estate terms) $150,000 to a buyer posing as her live-in boyfriend. She did so alongside her neighbor and colleague at the New York State Division of Housing and Community Renewal (DHCR), Mark Marcucilli, in the process also crafting lies that would have allowed her to move into her mother's apartment on the same floor.[19] Needless to say, the facade that she—a board member *and* an employee of the State agency tasked with supervising such co-ops—had Southbridge's best interests at heart swiftly crumbled.

The scheme touched a nerve throughout the city. New Yorkers fund the Mitchell-Lama program precisely to protect their low- and middle-income neighbors from the perils of a voracious speculative market. Wolfson invited that market—in this case, an illicit one—inside, taking a bribe from a prospective resident in exchange for letting him cut to the front of the waitlist. In other words, she operated as a savvy real estate professional, turning a limited-equity co-op into a run-of-the-mill condo, where selling a home to the highest bidder is business as usual.

Allegations of this kind of graft are rife within other Mitchell-Lama co-ops in New York, but they're not what keep folks like Wenna up at night. Privatization does. It is an even more pernicious version of such commodification—a legal way to reap personal benefit by commodify-ing social housing. Some Southbridge residents had bought their homes for as little as $3,000 in the 1970s, thanks to public subsidy. Now, as at St. James, Southbridge residents have the opportunity to remove the resale restriction that keeps it affordable for people like them, thereby creating a new asset potentially worth $1 million per unit.

To Wenna, the legality of this change, sometimes more opaquely but less controversially referred to as "reconstitution,"[20] doesn't matter. She may own her apartment, but as a piece of vital infrastructure, its value is not hers to reap alone. She's willing to fight to maintain St. James as social housing, as are many of her like-minded cooperators at home and at Southbridge who see such maintenance as their responsibility. They face an equally staunch opposition: their neighbors and now-former friends who see privatization, and the profit that could come with it, as a right.

This feeling of entitlement did not arise in a vacuum. Americans often elevate the financial aspect of home above and beyond its emotional dimensions. This is the country where government-subsidized homeownership after World War II created the White middle class; where colorful shows that venerate housing speculation (think *Flipping Virgins* and *Zombie House Flippers)* have displaced the relatively staid renovation stalwart *This Old House.* Investing in American real estate can be recast as self-care and elevated to an art.[21] On the online service Masterclass, Compass Real Estate CEO Robert Reffkin offers courses alongside Gary Kasparov teaching chess and Penn & Teller modeling magic. In that light, fighting to commodify St. James and Southbridge looks quintessentially American. Unlike almost all other housing in the US, however, this social housing is *not* a commodity to be swapped for the largest bag of cash from first occupancy. Instead, it is—as two-thirds of respondents to a national survey regard *all* housing to be—a public good.[22]

"Public goods" is a tricky term, in large part because it's been co-opted by economists into a larger categorization question, one that seeks to divide "goods" into those that should and should not be (according to certain, reductive theory) provided by government.[23] Moreover, the traditional economic definition of public goods frames not only housing but the biological bases of life—air and water—as resources to be commodified. To use that framework is to adopt its underlying ideology: almost everything is a commodity to be bought or sold at any price, regardless of the social consequences.

There is, however, a more intuitive definition of public goods, one more in keeping with the term's usage in common conversation. Public goods, one could say, are those things that contribute to *the* public good and are thus necessarily defined by what a society decides is important and necessary.[24] The "public" here refers not to government ownership but to beneficiaries. St. James and Southbridge are private companies, owned and operated by their resident shareholders, but they have been funded by the public, via government, to provide housing accessible to generations of ordinary people. One may not occupy the apartment today, but one could do so in the future. Everyone needs housing, and society benefits from that vital need being met. Teachers can guide the next generation without spending their free periods scouring listings or, worse, their evenings in their cars. Folks who've fallen on hard times can focus on getting help or moving forward rather than losing their homes and then engaging in a perverse dance with police over where to pitch a tent. Accessible housing, and especially social housing like limited-equity co-ops, is a public good that benefits us all, even if we aren't the bodies occupying it. Here is another sense in which housing should be common: it should contribute to our commonwealth, as legal scholar Jedediah Purdy puts it, to "the well-being of the whole community—the flourishing that is shared and open to all."[25]

The essential nature of public goods also makes them particularly vulnerable to capture for profit. One need look no further than our public health system in the midst of the pandemic, when lifesaving (and economy-saving) vaccines were withheld on shallow grounds of intellectual property—knowledge that's been commodified. Or, consider education, another public good, where profiteering in the form of predatory, for-profit technical colleges has mired millions in debt. St. James and Southbridge are clear examples of public goods whose futures are threatened by attempts to privatize their value. Should those efforts succeed, the future is foretold. Most of us live with it in the present, within housing crises born of speculative actors failing to provide a basic human need that all people can access. It's clear: our current system, where housing is treated primarily as a commodity, does not work. St. James and Southbridge, however, do—if they can be maintained in the face of privatization campaigns from some of their own residents.

Under mainstream economic thought, such uninhibited pursuit of cash may seem "rational," even inevitable. But residents like Wenna are willing to forgo the lure of wealth to maintain a public good that can benefit future generations. To ask why cooperators choose either to emulate Wenna or to opt for profit is to open a window into a larger, pressing matter: how we as a society are able to maintain the public goods that make things tick.

The stories of the privatization fights at St. James and Southbridge Towers that follow—seen at eye-level from Wenna and many more residents—reveal themselves to be deeper than simple morality tales of profiteering vs. altruism, more complex than a battle between selfish privateers and idealistic defenders of the public realm. Rather, the sides that cooperators take in these community-shredding debates, how they construct their arguments—how they justify their positions to themselves and the pitches they make to sway others—all hold key information on the fervent contest over space across the country. The human perspectives of Southbridge and St. James serve as a prism through which to better distinguish the consequences of how we govern, the language we use, and the rights we feel entitled to—and what they mean for our ability to create and sustain cities that approach the ideal of equity, which, though increasingly invoked, remains painfully out of reach. These stories are parables, in the term's actual meaning: they don't tie up neatly. They are, in the words of poet and theologian Pádraig Ó Tuama, an "irritant" that "gets under the skin" and "leaves all kinds of tendrils at the end."[26]

What does it mean when the people who are the primary beneficiaries (and, in this case, owners) of a public good are also the biggest threat to its survival? What kind of belonging do we venerate: belonging to a community, a collective, a public, a place—or something belonging to you, as property? How do these logics of ownership intersect with divisions of race and class, access to opportunity, and virtues of empathy and mutual support? Whose good are we working toward, and who are "we"? The crucibles of the fiery debates that consumed these two co-ops as residents like Wenna argued for and against privatization of their homes offer answers.

At their center lies a fundamental American tension between collective and private interests. Homes, once emblematic of the promise of the American Dream, are now the site of its reckoning. Many Americans will no longer brook a persistent racial wealth gap or a dwindling middle class, and they are hungry for new or expanded approaches to repair these wounds—decommodifying housing, regulating rents, and establishing community land trusts. People across the country and the ideological spectrum are appropriately questioning what ownership means, what rights are inherent within it, and what responsibilities owners have to our communities. They—we—also need to be asking how to maintain the solutions that will be, or are already, put in place. The later chapters in this book look beyond New York to other contests and campaigns: new agricultural commons, the LANDBACK movement in Indigenous communities, and tenants' rights organizing. Together, they form a broader picture of the cultural and political changes necessary to assert a renewed ethic of ownership that can help us maintain our public goods.

The fight is fierce, but as for Wenna, she's resolute before the struggle. "I'm going to kick ass," she tells me, a glint in her eye.

CHAPTER 1

Social Homes

When representatives from Tishman Realty & Construction Co. tossed a ceremonial shovelful of dirt on June 26, 1962, marking the plot where St. James Towers would eventually rise at the corner of St. James Place and Lafayette Avenue, they did so on already broken ground. On that day, the famed developers began to realize a vision for Bedford-Stuyvesant first advanced a decade prior. In 1953, the City's Committee on Slum Clearance, wielded by the heavy fist of master builder Robert Moses, had deemed the mostly Black area blighted. So the City seized it—forty acres emanating north and east from the corner—and told the 1,100 families living and working there to get lost.[1] Their sacrifice was required to make way for new buildings and different people. The City's vision included an expansion of the Pratt Institute—the renowned arts and architecture university then scattered along the neighborhood's public ways—and two new clusters of high-rise, modernist apartment buildings. Such displacement, and replacement, was often the outcome of this kind of public-private endeavor, termed by turns urban renewal, slum clearance, or, for its basis under the first section of the federal Housing Act of 1949, a Title I project.

That muggy summer Tuesday may have been one of mixed feelings for Wenna Redfern's father. As an architect for Tishman's chosen design firm on the project, Kelly & Gruzen, he'd helped draw the plans for one of the residential clusters, then called University Terrace. The project was meant to revitalize an urban neighborhood and build affordable homes for the middle class. But the dense fourteen-block supposed slum that was cleared to make room for the project had been a center for Black life in Brooklyn. Its destruction, and that of other neighborhoods like it, gave urban renewal another colloquial name, the implication likely to tinge Wenna's dad's pride in his work with bitterness: "Negro removal."[2]

Under Moses's plan, the neighborhood's standard blocks would be transformed into three "super" ones running parallel to the avenues. Pratt Institute would fill the middle chunk with grassy quads, sculpture gardens, and private sports facilities. On either side, new residential towers would insulate the institute, which was then "being encroached upon from the south by deteriorating and substandard neighborhoods, and from the east by commerce and industry."[3] These towers were also envisioned as a fire break, a barrier to the supposed blight sweeping the neighborhood. The area's decline had elements real and imagined that combined in a vicious cycle. The "prevalence of first floor stores in otherwise residentially occupied buildings" was enough to justify their demise.[4] The area's occupants, especially the "Negro" population that rose from 28.5 percent of the area in 1950 to 47.7 percent a decade later, was another strike against these blocks.[5] To the White establishment, Black and Brown residents meant risk, crime, and poor housing quality. The accompanying disinvestment in the area, born of discrimination, then gave this bias credence. The powers behind the urban renewal plan, among them Pratt's administration, hoped the new towers set to rise around their expanded campus would be home to a different sort of resident: the faculty and administrators required by the growing institute.[6]

University Terrace was the last of the three superblocks to be developed. It would consist of three identical twenty-four-story apartment buildings, neat rectangles oriented perpendicular to Lafayette Avenue, all their units reserved for middle-income families. Wenna Redfern's would be one of them.

Moving there hadn't been the Redferns' original plan. Wenna's father had initially put money down on land in the Bronx, only to have the owner ("Her name was Mrs. Wheeler. I remember that," said Wenna) back out of the sale once she learned that Mr. Redfern was Black. When Wenna's mom found the plans for University Terrace on her husband's desk, she cajoled him into shelving the drawings for the Bronx dream home he'd designed. They should instead construct a life and community in that "glorified project," she argued. Two years before the groundbreaking, Wenna's mom was fourth in line at the sales office to put down $2,900 for their share—the same share her daughter, then a student at Curry College outside Boston, would fight to keep out of the speculative market over five decades later.

A MOST AMBITIOUS PROGRAM

That Black middle-class families like the Redferns would soon make up the majority of the residents in St. James Towers both fulfilled and subverted the intentions behind the Limited Profit Housing Companies Law of 1955, supported by New York City Mayor Robert Wagner and sponsored by State Senator MacNeil Mitchell and Assemblyman Alfred Lama. Those two legislators, now immortalized in the alpaca-evoking nickname for the housing program created by that act, saw the Mitchell-Lama buildings as gap-filler and counterweight in the housing market. Middle-income folks living in the state's urban areas were too well-off to gain entry to public housing and too poor to afford quality apartments on the speculative market. The Redferns fit this bill.

They did not, however, fit another. The program's supporters had hoped that this new affordable housing would attract the White families then being wooed by the expanding suburbs.[7] The Mitchell-Lama program sent a message to those families: We'll see your cookie-cutter homes financed by cheap, subsidized mortgages tied to the city by interstates, and we'll raise you a new kind of subsidized housing within city limits, close to jobs and transit. Unlike many exclusively White neighborhoods in the sprawling burbs, these buildings did not have racial covenants and redlining to regulate their demographics. Instead, some of these buildings became havens to families like Wenna's who otherwise faced discrimination in the market.[8]

The approach wasn't altogether novel, but the scale of Mitchell-Lama would soon make it what housing historian Matthew Lasner calls "the most ambitious program of its kind in U.S. history."[9] Between 1955 and 1974, ground across New York City broke under the weight of almost one hundred co-ops with sixty-nine thousand apartments and over 170 rental developments with more than sixty-nine thousand additional homes. This outlay includes the largest cooperative development in the world, Co-op City in the Bronx—its thirty-five towers, seven townhouse clusters, and 15,372 units housing fifty thousand residents in a former marsh once home to the Freedomland amusement park.[10] Hip-hop was born in a Bronx Mitchell-Lama building: 1520 Sedgewick Avenue, where DJ Kool Herc made his authoritative debut on the ones and twos in a community room rented for $25 for his sister's back-to-school party. The likes of Alicia Keyes, Larry David, Samuel L. Jackson, and Timothée Chalamet laid their heads on the West Side in artist housing at Manhattan Plaza. And in Coney Island, thrill chasers rattling up the

Cyclone rollercoaster's wooden tracks can look out on Fred-developed Trump Village and contemplate Donald's origin story before the drop.

Mitchell-Lama sought to address a severe housing crisis. Underbuilding during the war had left New York City, and much of the country, in a crunch. In a turn soon to sweep the rest of the country, New York policy-makers also jettisoned direct public delivery of low- and middle-income housing in favor of ventures led by private developers like Tishman. Some of these developers were mission-driven, like the union-backed United Housing Federation (UHF) behind Co-op City. Others were largely out for profit—the potential for which was, as the official name of the Mitchell-Lama act stated up front, supposedly limited. The cap on a developer's return on investment started at 6 percent and was later increased to 7.5 percent. That for-profit developers jumped at the program is not a testament to their commitment to building a public good. Rather, their eagerness speaks to the public largesse of the program. It vastly reduced developers' risks and costs, and the limited government oversight that accompanied it unintentionally permitted that largesse to line many individual pockets.[11] The program provided developers with low interest rate mortgages that covered up to 95 percent of costs; the builders had to risk relatively little cash of their own. The City also gave the projects a tax break of between 40 percent and 100 percent, drastically reducing operating costs. And in some cases, the projects came with a ready-made site for their undertaking, already assembled and occasionally prepared with federal urban renewal funds. This was the case at St. James.

In addition to limiting a developer's profit, state and city government exacted other requirements in exchange for such generous financing. When families like Wenna's began to flock to the sales office that realtor Herbert Charles set up at the corner of St. James Place and Lafayette Avenue, their income would be vetted. No one earning more than six or seven times the monthly maintenance (their share of the co-op's mortgage and other expenses) was allowed to put down a deposit on a share. In 1963, maintenance on the Redferns' three-bedroom would cost just $132 a month. Freshly built and inexpensive, their new home also benefited from its proximity to Pratt, the G subway line, and the fervent Black culture of the larger neighborhood. As these residents took the mantle of co-op ownership from the developers, they too took on a "limited-profit" measure: the limited-equity provision that meant an eventual sale of their share would return to them their initial purchase price plus very limited appreciation.

The program was designed to maintain these limited-profit restrictions permanently, thus keeping the housing affordable to middle- and low-income individuals in perpetuity. There was no way to remove them. Privatization was not even a possibility at the start. This was of little concern to co-op developers, whose role in the buildings was largely done and dusted by the time all the units were sold. On that corner in Bed-Stuy, they could just roll their profits, their backhoes, and their workers into the next building down the avenue, St. James giving way to Ryerson Towers, and Ryerson to Pratt. Given the origins of the program, the limited-profit provisions were far from controversial—they were expected. The developer got paid for work with minimal risk, the cooperators got stable, quality housing at a reasonable price, and city and state governments fulfilled a mission to provide basic shelter for an underserved segment of the populace considered a bulwark in the larger democratic endeavor.

The pedestrian nature of the model at the time, and its exotic status today, speaks to an inversion of exception and rule. Now, one must tag the unwieldy modifier "limited-equity" onto a co-op to clarify that the topic of conversation isn't the kind of expensive buildings that crowd Central Park, inhabiting and inhabited by the upper crust of Manhattan. When St. James began its dimensional transition from financing agreements and blueprints into brick and concrete, limited-equity co-ops were the norm.

OF ANTECEDENTS AND ADVANCES

That "speculative co-ops" suggested a contradiction in terms was due to the influence of a cooperative movement that had made landfall in the American housing space almost a half century prior, one that paved the way for Mitchell-Lama. In 1916, just inland from the sprawling docks of South Brooklyn, a group of Finnish immigrants chose an apt name for the modest four-story walk-up they built together: Alku, or Beginning.[12] Today, you'll find precious little to differentiate Alku and its successor next door, Alku Toinen, from their neighbors. One of red-brown brick, the other tan, each with fire escapes zigzagging up their center and a haphazard arrangement of AC units poking from white-trimmed windows, these cooperative siblings exhibit the same physical unremarkableness of St. James. Only the plaques beside the buildings' simple entryways affirm their spots on the National Register of Historic Places. And yet, these two were trendsetters, built not by for-profit developers but by members of the Finnish Home Building Association who'd pooled funds to provide five-room apartments for themselves rather than crowding together in subpar tenements. This approach to providing accessible and affordable housing to the working class was so novel, this side of the Atlantic, that the two Alkus had to register with New York State's Department of Agriculture, the regulatory body deemed most likely to understand cooperative arrangements.[13]

The Scandinavian American community would do much over the ensuing decade to mainstream the form in New York, building upward of fifty similar limited-equity co-ops across Brooklyn and into Manhattan.[14] They were accompanied by a boom in speculative, luxury cooperatives targeting the upper classes, who had only recently begun to live in multi-family housing. Their homes, in contrast to the ordinary elegance of the Alkus, sported lobbies and doormen to preserve high society's retreat and protection from the wider city. The two varieties of housing co-op may have sported the same corporate form, but the physical and psychological distance between the industrial shoreline of Brooklyn and the tony edge of Central Park East was matched by the gap in intentions and principles that underlay them. The distinction between the two is so stark that the Department of Agriculture's purview over the Alkus made some sense. Those limited-equity co-ops arguably shared more in common with a small food co-op in northwest England started some seventy years prior than with a speculative housing cooperative that could have sprouted next door.

The Alkus' ancestry can be traced back to twenty-eight residents of Rochdale, England, who banded together in 1844 to sell oats, butter, sugar, and flour from an old wool warehouse. They'd had enough of profit-obsessed traders exploiting the city's breakneck, industry-driven growth with their subpar goods: chalk that ruined their dough, sand adding grit to sugar stores, and the I Can't Believe It's Not Butter of the day (spoilt green bars turned yellow again with a dash of copper). Instead, the Rochdale Pioneers created an alternative for themselves, contributing a pound each to start a collective business and the world's first modern co-op.

Today, northeast of Manchester, pressed between the A158 heading to Bury and Bolton and the sprawling Rochdale Exchange Shopping Centre, sits the remains of the street where it all started: Toad Lane, named not for the animal but for the fusion of "the" and "old" in the

Lancashire accent that rang through the mills during the Industrial Revolution. Old it indeed looks, the Pioneers' redbrick building with slate roof and stone lintels bounding broad windows of many panes across a cobblestoned street from an abbey and parsonage. To look inside is to glimpse the simplicity of the co-op's operation: the scales hung from the ceiling, the mixing bowls on wooden tables, the meeting minutes inscribed on broad, bound books in flowery script. It is now a museum. Talk to any of the docents, and you'll hear that the starring act of the Rochdale Pioneer Cooperative Society is not the food, the business, or the individuals and their impressive neckbeards but the co-op's rules.

These governing precepts are now known as the Rochdale Principles. They undergird the cooperative businesses, and many of the cooperative housing schemes, that have flourished since these individuals organized against exploitation by unchecked capitalism. They bind Rochdale to Alku, to St. James and Southbridge, across space and time. They are the foundation of true cooperatives. As revolutionary as they were when promulgated, and as antithetical to prevailing corporate status quo as they remain, the principles are relatively simple, summarized as "Voluntary and Open Membership; Democratic Member Control; Member Economic Participation; Autonomy and Independence; Education, Training, and Information; Cooperation Among Cooperatives; and Concern for Community."[15]

These boil down to the following: Anyone can join if they accept the responsibilities of membership, without regard to their identity. Co-ops are governed democratically—all members' votes hold the same weight, no matter the scale of an individual's economic contribution to the corporation. All members, however, must contribute some capital, on which dividends are equitably distributed. Co-ops should maintain their independence from outside entities while also cooperating with peers to broaden their movement—one that works for the benefit of the communities beyond the co-op. And co-ops should work to educate those communities on the benefits of cooperation, while also ensuring the necessary training of their members to carry on the co-op's work in keeping with the principles.

When the Rochdale Principles were first created—in a country enthralled with monarchy, in a metro area bursting with forced migration as common lands in Europe were enclosed, among a populace laboring in peril in the factories turbocharging capitalism, within a political system that only afforded the right to vote to landed men—they were radical, and their deployment transformative. The pioneers' co-op boomed, growing into the Cooperative Wholesale Society and its current manifestation, the Co-op Group. A Cooperative Union, Cooperative Press, and Cooperative College grew up around it. The principles spread worldwide, facilitated by the International Co-operative Alliance that would bind together the co-ops that employed them.[16]

In early twentieth-century New York, housing activists like Catherine Bauer and progressive Jewish unionists carried forward what the Finns had made of Rochdale's innovation, founding housing co-ops like Sunnyside Gardens in Queens in 1924 and the neo-Tudor Shalom Aleichem Houses just west of the Bronx's Van Cortlandt Park in 1927.[17] There, artist studios, lectures, performances, and a common cafeteria sought to cultivate a secular Yiddish culture within affordable, accessible homes.[18] Their ideals of openness and empowerment melded with those of labor unions, who would soon extend their reach beyond the workplace. Of particular significance would be their collaboration with a Ukrainian socialist-turned-anarchist, Abraham Kazan, and his behemoth United Housing Foundation.[19] The UHF grew steadily to become a major player in the city's housing-development scene and a keystone of a wider era of social democracy in New York City post–World War II. It was guided by an explicit commitment to limited-equity cooperatives, serving union members and the working class and imbuing their dwellings with the sense of solidarity that unions cultivated on the shop floor.

Without Kazan and the UHF, it's hard to imagine limited-equity co-ops making the jump of scale from a smattering of 16-unit Alkus to 326-unit St. James Towers, 1,651-unit Southbridge Towers, and 15,372-unit Co-op City.[20] Kazan is credited with helping to realize forty thousand homes still lived in today, thanks to the huge labor base of his federation and the political and economic power that it carried. He worked closely with the City of New York and New York State (including infamous power broker Robert Moses) to push projects through and create the funding streams that enabled those scalar jumps.[21] Under the State's Limited Dividend Housing Companies Law of 1926, Kazan combined tax abatements with cheap, cleared former "slum" land. This recipe cooked up the predecessors to Mitchell-Lamas: Penn Station South in Manhattan's Garment District and the Seward Park Houses on the Lower East Side.

Despite the UHF's best efforts, other developers weren't interested in following suit, and the State and City were eager to bring more private money into the middle-income housing endeavor. The Limited Profit Housing Companies Law of 1955—Mitchell-Lama—was an attempt to woo that private money in. Mitchell-Lama provided even more generous and direct support of private companies' construction of middle-income co-ops and rental buildings, adding mortgages provided by the State and City and backed by government bonds to the Limited Dividend mix. Middle-income rental projects were an attractive asset class to a different variety of developer and its investors. They were also more likely to serve relatively lower-income individuals than the co-ops. That form, of course, remained preferred by the likes of Kazan, who saw housing not just as shelter but as a place of social transformation. Kazan may not have been pictured on April 18, 1955, as Governor Averell Harriman signed the bipartisan bill, but his influence was present nonetheless. It was a law that bred real hope. "For the first time," wrote the New York State Joint Legislative Committee on Housing and Multiple Dwellings, "the Committee has found it possible to make dents in the housing shortage within the middle-income, white collar field" and to fill the "no man's land" between luxury and public housing.[22]

PRIVATIZATION, UNLEASHED

Before the construction of St. James got underway, the wider urban renewal endeavor in Bed-Stuy peppered the neighborhood with construction cavities throughout the mid-1950s. It also brought scandal. The Pratt Institute portion of the project had proceeded according to plan. Crowds cheered the excavation that would lay the groundwork for a new campus building with a sign ordering workers to "Dig That Crazy Ground!" Bulldozers carved troughs in street walls of row houses, exhibiting rubble before a grab bag of wallpapers. Former front doors stood repurposed as construction fencing, jagged teeth fronting a pit in progress.

Elsewhere in the district, little had changed since the plan was hatched. Before Tishman, the original developer overseeing the urban renewal area had been the private firm Hall Developers. The City had taken the hundreds of existing structures in the area's footprint by eminent domain, then transferred their ownership to Hall. Those properties' former owners were transformed into temporary tenants, with Hall Developers as their landlord. But instead of relocating occupants, demolishing the buildings, and putting up modern housing on the site as promised, Hall sat on the land for almost three years. They milked it for rent, running a commercial parking lot on cleared land in defiance of federal rules barring such use.[23] They neglected uncleared portions, letting ninety-year-old residents freeze in unheated buildings.[24] If the area hadn't been a slum already, Hall Developers ensured it became one, playing slumlord in the process. A series of exposé articles in 1956 and 1957, which found similar practices by Hall Developers in the Manhattantown urban renewal area on the Upper West Side, forced the City's hand.[25] Come June 1957, Hall was removed from the project and replaced by a Chicago builder. The death of the new developer's figurehead in an airplane crash would stall the project further.[26] And come 1959, there was nothing to show in the way of new middle-income housing in Bed-Stuy. More broadly, after four years of Mitchell-Lama, the program's overall effect on the state's housing shortage was also deemed insufficient. Under the directive of the new, swashbuckling governor Nelson Rockefeller, the same committee that had introduced the original Mitchell-Lama bill rushed to tweak it, with consequences that reverberate today.

The implementation of the Limited Profit Housing Companies Law had largely gone according to plan for cooperative developers like the United Housing Federation. They had been quick to snap up the initial $50 million in bond funding. Less eager were the rental developers that the bill had also hoped to target. Despite the ample public funding that had made initial construction of Mitchell-Lama housing a low-cost endeavor for private developers, the economics after occupancy for co-ops and rentals were quite different. Cooperative developers could largely disappear from the financial and governance scene of the buildings once all the shares had been sold to lucky new homeowners. The permanent affordability of this housing made no economic difference to them— their financial stake was terminated once people had moved in.[27] As an anti-privatization Mitchell-Lama cooperator would point out decades later, "the developers got their benefits upfront."

For rentals, on the other hand, the developer continued to own the buildings after they welcomed their first tenants. The developer was responsible for paying down the mortgage and was also, by design, stuck with regulated rents and low- to middle-income residents for as long as it (or its successor) owned the building. This changed slightly in 1957, when Mitchell-Lama was modified to allow for a rental development to be rid of all obligation to affordably house middle-income residents after thirty-five years, if it paid off its State or City mortgage and reimbursed the municipality for previously exempted taxes. The change created the theoretical opportunity for a rental development to leave the program—but on such onerous terms as to make it exceedingly unlikely.

Everything changed when Rockefeller came along. On March 18, 1959, seventy-six days after he took the oath of office, the governor fired off a special message on housing to the State Legislature, encouraging a revision of the Mitchell-Lama law designed to increase profits for the participating private companies. Rather than holding companies to the program's original restrictions of perpetual affordability or the recently implemented thirty-five-year time frame for rentals, companies would now only be bound to the program for fifteen years (almost immediately after changed to twenty) if they paid off their mortgage. The companies would no longer be on the hook for paying back the tax breaks they'd received.

On April 21, 1959, the change went into effect after passage by the legislature and signature by Rockefeller—a monumental alteration by way of only sixty-eight words.[28] The Pandora's box of "privatization" was opened, and our current model of affordable-housing development launched: public investment, private execution, and ultimately public loss and private gain after a determined period of time.

The report of the Joint Legislative Committee on Housing and Multiple Dwellings described the revision thus:

> The Limited Profit Law was amended to permit the voluntary dissolution of the housing company, whether aided by a State or municipal loan, after a period of 20 years, upon repayment in full of the outstanding mortgage indebtedness and the accrued interest. This amendment has the dual advantage of placing the property on the tax rolls at an earlier date, as well as permitting capital gains advantages for *the entrepreneur*. The Committee earnestly hopes that this revision will serve to encourage additional *rental projects* in the City under the Limited Profit program.[29]

Limited-equity proponents like the UHF were scandalized that the State's housing program had chosen to prioritize for-profit, speculative builders over nonprofit co-op sponsors like themselves.[30] But, at the time, no one was concerned about the affect the change would have on the actual co-ops developed under the program. The legislators, and the incentives, were fairly clear that this change was intended for rental properties, not co-ops. The revision would make developing rental buildings more attractive to developers. Most co-op developers could not have cared less. They weren't planning to be the owners of the buildings twenty years from then; the co-op residents would be the owners. When the Joint Legislative Committee referred to "advantages for the entrepreneur," they were decidedly not referring to cooperators.

However, despite the stated intent of the revision, the text of the Mitchell-Lama law never specified that the change only applied to rentals. Whether this was due to imprecise legal drafting or legislators' lack of familiarity with the distinctions between rental and co-op developments, the legal ambiguity that prevailed meant co-ops intended to remain limited-equity in perpetuity would eventually be able to vote to privatize once a specified amount of time had passed and the mortgage had been paid. It also gave birth to the myth that privatization was the goal of Mitchell-Lama, a revisionist understanding that some cooperators now use to justify their quest for profit. MacNeil Mitchell, the eponymous, former State Senator behind the legislation, responded to this argument when the first stirrings of co-op privatization began in 1986: the "Legislature never intended to convert the developments to private ownership. . . . They were designed as something the public enterprise could handle and something that would continue. . . . In hindsight, we should have looked at what would happen in the future. Frankly, we didn't give it much thought."[31] Wenna said essentially the same thing a bit more colorfully years later when asked if privatization had been expected at St. James's founding, her laugh turning to a scoff: "Fifty-five years ago? I don't think so; they're all dead!"

What Wenna's family had seen in St. James, finally rising above Bed-Stuy in the early '60s, was not a possible windfall in the future but rather an opportunity for a stable home and community in which their vote—one share per household, no matter the family size or what they'd paid—was equal to others'. They saw a housing option free from the kind of White control that had thwarted their attempted purchase of land in the Bronx, restricted their rental options to certain neighborhoods, and made access to mortgage financing difficult. As one cooperator described St. James and other Mitchell-Lamas to academic and organizer Kavita Kulkarni, "They were pretty decent. They were clean. People that lived in here were not wealthy, but they were hardworking—basically working-class people. It was definitely a step or two above the projects."[32]

When the building opened in 1963, the racial split between White and non-White cooperators inverted legislators' expectations—the co-op was about 70 percent people of color.[33] One can imagine how the new construction looked against the adjacent, disinvested row houses as the cooperators moved in. While, today, the worn beige bricks of St. James appear slightly tired next to the refurbished facades of million-dollar brownstones, the occasional decaying property reveals the twenty-four-story co-op with its bright, blue awning as solid, even regal.

At St. James, the Redferns sought stability and refuge. They expected to save money that could be put toward life's aspirations. While they were foregoing the prospect of more substantial wealth building through speculative homeownership, the level of racism against Black families in real estate—despite new fair-housing laws—made that look like a shaky prospect. They opted instead for a community where they had a say and one where they knew they could stay put regardless of what transpired in the wider market.

The same was on offer for other families across the city, including those who would occupy Southbridge Towers. But, as the 1960s wore on and the '70s began, the wider fiscal environment in New York City began to buckle. Inflation soared and interest rates rose. The City flirted with bankruptcy amid outright hostility from financiers and the federal government. The same macroeconomic factors in part at fault for higher-than-expected costs meant many Mitchell-Lamas fell behind on their mortgages—deficits that their State and City supporters had to unexpectedly plug as the backing bonds came due.[34] It was a wake-up call for a program that had perhaps given over too much control to private developers and exercised too little oversight while still holding the financial bag. The crisis also put to bed the expectation that Mitchell-Lamas would become economically self-sufficient and that no future infusions of public support would be necessary. By 1974, Mitchell-Lama ceased commitments to new projects and effectively ended as a program to construct new housing.[35] The law remains on the books, and New York State and New York City continue to support and oversee the buildings erected under its auspices. Every recent mayoral race and many an op-ed has called for a Mitchell-Lama 2.0, making clear that the program, despite its bumps in the road, remains a success. St. James and Southbridge are two of its shining examples.

A SELF-CONTAINED COMMUNITY

When I visit Harvey Marshall, a retired teacher ensconced in the management office at Southbridge, he sits near a photocopier used to produce his monthly co-op newsletter that's distributed throughout the complex's nine buildings. His family had moved into Southbridge in the mid-1970s, and his memos often touch on the supposed intention of the Mitchell-Lama law to not just permit the privatization of co-ops but to encourage them to do so. This was a message he'd received from an early age and, he says, from the very inception of Southbridge: privatization had always been the goal, the natural evolution of the limited-equity co-op. Harvey Marshall's father had been intimately involved in his co-op's early days. He'd been president of the advisory board representing new cooperators before the co-op's full turnover to resident governance. After they took control, he told his son, "This place: we can own this in 20 years." It's an odd and revealing statement. The residents already owned the co-op; they were its sole shareholders. But the notion that they were somehow not homeowners would become an influential idea under Harvey's leadership years later.

Southbridge's beginning has much in common with St. James's: same program, same legal structure, same architect, same developer, same process to clear the neighborhood that had existed before to make way for the one to come. However, the distinctions between the two are just as numerous: a different neighborhood with a different history, a different political moment, and a different racial composition.

Many of the first Southbridge residents had come from the Lower East Side as it existed before real estate filleted it into new neighborhoods for sale: a big, burly chunk of Manhattan bordered on the east by the river and on the west by Broadway, running from the Manhattan Bridge and Canal Street all the way north to Fourteenth Street. The Italian, Irish, Jewish, and German families moving into Southbridge in February 1971 hadn't had to go far. But the shift from dense tenement-filled neighborhoods to the complex just south of City Hall, part of the grand plan to erect a Civic Center, could still be jarring. They'd traded ball in the streets for courtyard playgrounds, fire escapes for balconies, landlords for homeownership and self-governance, and the bustle of Grand and Houston Streets for the eerie quiet of the Tannery District and a short walk down Gold Street to Wall Street, where financial markets that whirred from daybreak were deserted come nightfall.

Some shareholders had registered their down payments years before, putting a deposit on a blueprint in a storefront where, a decade prior, the shopkeeper had sold mariners nautical instruments of all kinds. In the sales office adjacent to the cleared 7.5-acre plot from which their new cooperative apartments would sprout—where the Harper brothers once printed the magazine that still bears their name today in an iron-beamed building "prophetic of the skyscraper"—middle-income New Yorkers laid plans to fulfill a dream of owning a home.[36] They'd been promised "a pleasant residential environment; a nicer place to live . . . to bring up children . . . to make new friends," "dramatic views of the bridges," "automatic elevators," and affordable purchase prices of $1,625 to $4,200 ($14,228 to $36,774 in 2023 dollars): a neighborhood of quality and stability.[37]

The Brooklyn Bridge Southwest Urban Renewal Area in which Southbridge would be built was what Mayor Robert Wagner termed a "neglected backwater."[38] Lower Manhattan may not have been a thriving mixed-use neighborhood, but the area certainly appeared to have been productive. In order to make room for Southbridge and the Civic Center, over 191 existing buildings home to 675 businesses were demolished. Getting a sense of their scale can be difficult, but flipping through survey data prepared for the City's Housing and Redevelopment Board helps: page after page of the inventory lists industry, rent, square footage, and personnel of the city's historic Newspaper Row and its center of leather manufacturing and distribution.[39] These industries all expected to grow,[40] and analysts would acknowledge that no one knew if there was available space elsewhere in the city to absorb the businesses to be displaced and the printing presses that required specially reinforced floors.[41] Yet, the City deemed the buildings "obviously obsolescent,"[42] and with memos claiming that "there appears to be no opposition"[43] to their destruction, the plan went forward.

The neighborhood as it was may have been adequate for the 9-to-5 needs of the blue- and white-collar workers who commuted there, but it was so devoid of the amenities of a residential neighborhood that they had to be built into the co-op itself. So, Southbridge's designers sought to embed the entire non-job life of the community within its boundaries. Harvey Marshall remembers that the ample commercial space owned and leased by the cooperative contained a diner and a small supermarket, a Chinese hand laundry and a card store. With 1,651 households to serve, many with young children, the new businesses had plenty of potential customers, and the design of the buildings made it clear who the businesses were for.

Original plans for the urban renewal area called for pedestrian bridges that would bypass local traffic, permitting workers to walk seamlessly between their home and the job centers of finance and government. What got built is rather different. While the apartments' utilitarian balconies look out on the Brooklyn Bridge and onto gleaming towers designed by starchitects, most of the stores look inward across interlaced courtyards, their backs turned to passersby on the streets. Southbridge curls up, shielding its amenities from the surrounding neighborhood in its attempt to create a village in the city. In this familial outpost, amid offices and aging storefronts, Southbridge residents quickly came to regard themselves as trailblazers in an inhospitable landscape, eventual tamers of an urban wild who paved the way for the animated mix that surrounds the buildings today.

CHAPTER 2

Living Cooperation

As it turned out, Harvey Marshall's father didn't stick around for the twenty-year horizon he'd drawn for his son. He departed for Florida just three years into Southbridge's life and turned his share over to Harvey. Marshall's certainty about the intentions of Mitchell-Lama and Southbridge are, in a sense, hard-won. He's been there through most, if not all of it: rifts, tragedy, togetherness. The early days were marked with growing pains severe (or, at least, dramatic) enough to land the cooperative in the Sunday edition of the *Daily News* in 1973. "Residents of Southbridge Find It Hard to Cooperate," the headline read, above descriptions of fraught debates over proposed playground improvements.[1] Harvey had followed the shifting winds of the co-op's dog policy, a recurring matter that monopolizes the flyer space on the complex's common doors to this day. In 1977, one of the New York State Assembly's longest serving members, Louis De-Salvio, and his wife Elvira, came close to eviction due to their illicit black-and-white, wire-haired terrier Brandy.[2] In 2018, the question remained as to whether co-op staff should be responsible for picking up after Brandy's successors.

Marshall also weathered 9/11 there. When the Twin Towers were felled in 2001, the residents of Southbridge were showered in the soot and debris that wafted through their windows, leaving inches-high deposits on sills and long-term health issues for residents young and old. While the rest of Lower Manhattan evacuated, Southbridge, as its residents tell it, was forgotten. They sheltered in place without power, cooperators cooperating like never before. Medicines were fetched for the infirm. As the elevators languished, meals were delivered up flights of stairs to the elderly. In 2012, Hurricane Sandy forced a reprise. With Lower Manhattan plunged into darkness under surging waves that flooded basements and some of those same elevator wells, residents again rallied to assist one another and their wider Seaport neighborhood.

Such was the stability of Southbridge that, despite this external tumult reaching inside, Marshall is one of many near-lifers in the development. Family trees branch up its towers and intertwine, fed by the fertile ground of the community courtyards and rooms, by the traditions and sponsored activities that have long marked it as a sought-after place to raise a family. This is a place "where everybody knows your name" in true *Cheers* fashion, resident Daniel Brampton tells me. He mixes sliced bananas into his oatmeal, his milky blue eyes and heavy brows directed past the booths and out the window of Squires Diner, a community standby inside the complex. This seventy-seater, nicknamed the Gold Fishbowl, is seemingly doubled in the mirrors along its back wall, making it appear as expansive as the Breakfast-Lunch-Dinner-Brunch menu. Brampton recalls how "Joe, who used to be head of the board, said when he had little kids, he would say 'I'm gonna go to the store.' And he said his daughters would say 'No daddy, don't go,' cause they knew he would meet people on the way and they would want to talk." With a slightly jaded, ironic tone of someone burned by the community's closeness, Brampton summarizes: "Here, people know each other. They may not like each other, but they know each other."

Jan Naumann, a lawyer and, unlike Brampton, a friend of Marshall's, is among the residents who's come to know her neighbors quite well. She moved into the brand-new complex with her parents at thirteen and met her future husband on the co-op's youth committee. "I had my doors open when we first moved in. . . . People had parties in the halls!" Jan's adult kids now comprise the third generation of her all-Southbridge family. Unlike their parents, Jan's children weren't able to avail themselves of the matchmaking potential of the since-disbanded youth committee—the ski trips, the bowling league, the junior board of directors have all been retired. But Southbridge still boasts a famous Halloween party, Christmas tree– and menorah-lighting ceremonies, a photography club, five-days-a-week card-playing seniors, and a bevy of free classes—tai chi, yoga, even psychic/intuitive development that promises "fun, easy exercises which develop the 'extra' sensory perception innate in everyone!" Something for all, perhaps, though Marissa Heine, a real estate agent and resident who speaks with a languid mix of Long Island accent and Valley girl cadence, is less convinced of the advisability of some. Belly dancing used to be on Thursdays at 7 p.m. in the community room, within eyeshot of the diner's LED sign proclaiming COFFEE! above a cup flashing with steam. "Sometimes I walk by . . . I'm like, well, I don't know if I really want to be in a leotard in the middle of the community room with the blinds up."

Across the Brooklyn Bridge, the co-op community at St. James Towers is similarly stable, though its community room is decidedly less hopping. Tucked into the end of the ground floor closest to the defunct playground, past the grid of small, clear mailboxes inset in white, painted-brick walls, it mainly serves for meetings, gatherings upon a resident's passing, or the occasional birthday party. No belly-dancing class here. The relative dearth of events at St. James itself has less to do with how active the community is and more with its location within lively Bed-Stuy.

Wenna Redfern remembers the luminaries who have lived at 21 St. James Place, many when the anachronistic Mr. Zip sign above the mailboxes still made sense. "We had doctors, lawyers, and Indian chiefs in here!": Ron Brown, chairman of the Democratic National Committee and Secretary of Commerce under Bill Clinton; Vernon Jordan, another Clinton advisor and civil rights activist; and Charles Lawrence, justice of the Appellate Division of the New York State Supreme Court. Many, like Wenna's family, had laid roots in the neighborhood prior to St. James's construction. "We all lived in Bed-Stuy," said Wenna. "We children were all in the same kind of clubs. . . . We called them the upper limit of the Brooklynites. . . . We call it being bougie." When summer in the city got hot, many St. James residents fled to the historically Black beach enclave of Sag Harbor, Long Island.

Matriarchs like Wenna's mother presided over the middle-class community that grew in St. James, keeping kids like Graham Hales, now an even-keeled middle-aged board member of the co-op, in line. "My mom would go after you in a minute, but they always respected her," Wenna recalls. Graham was a toddler when his family arrived at Southbridge from a rental townhouse, and he was a college graduate when he moved back to St. James after his mother's passing. Now a leader with slightly graying hair donning business casual wear on any given day, Graham checks in on Wenna as she ages. He is part of a family that endured and grew in the building, the likes of which he calls "dynasties."

As steady as St. James may be, the neighborhood outside has changed dramatically. Wenna describes the visual manifestation through a ritual she undertakes as consistently as her Sunday trips to the movies: "I have friends down there, and we sit on their porch. . . . And we begin to count the Blacks. And we don't see the Blacks anymore." Many have been displaced by the ongoing wave of gentrification: the rising rents, predatory landlords, and flood of new, often White residents attracted to the neighborhoods' culture, location, architecture, and charm. Many others did not survive the preceding, intersecting waves of economic collapse, disinvestment, crime, and public health emergencies. St. James resident Tia Ward, between openly flirting with the wait staff at the Southern joint down the street and answering calls on three phones, remembers those times by substances and their victims. "I grew up around here with crack vials, dope fiends, and drug addicts"; now she's a full-time caretaker for her centenarian mother. It wasn't always bad right near St. James, but if you fanned out into the wider neighborhood (let alone the wider city), you'd be bound to encounter the fruits of organized neglect.

Tia and Wenna's neighbor Lester Goodyear, often seen in a leather cowboy hat with his gray goatee popping against his dark brown face, recalls when "drugs, prostitution, and muggings were so rampant in the neighborhood that, for several years, we had to hire building guards with attack dogs." A small guardhouse at the Lafayette Avenue entrance to the co-op parking lot, once staffed, now uses the same security system that my grandmother in Nanticoke, Pennsylvania, employed: a uniformed shirt, hung to suggest a bodily presence that isn't really there. Goodyear, a fifty-plus-year resident and former board president, perhaps rightfully feels some responsibility for the upward turn in fortunes for the neighborhood. He calls it "a stable College Community," a term that evokes the kind of brochure-ready images of the Pratt Institute's annual kite-flying competition that bygone urban renewal proponents like Robert Moses might have dreamt of. The area's appeal is not the only thing that Goodyear—his affect one of a wise, easygoing old-timer eager to drop knowledge and a ready chuckle on newcomers to his haunts—would like to own. He'd like to own his apartment at St. James, he says. Because to Goodyear—one of the loudest pro-privatization voices in the complex—ownership of a share in a limited-equity co-op isn't really ownership at all.

WHAT OWNERSHIP?

Before Goodyear settled at St. James in his late twenties, he made his first Brooklyn home in Crown Heights, kitty-corner to the opulent conservatory of the Brooklyn Botanic Garden. When he arrived, he was the block's only Black resident. After his move to St. James, Goodyear became a neighborhood stalwart. He is a longtime member of Community Board 2, the appointed advisory group to his local district. He signs off each letter to fellow cooperators with a quote from FDR—the all caps, a bit of poetic license: "WE HAVE NOTHING TO FEAR BUT FEAR ITSELF." So when I reach him by phone for the first time, I'm surprised that little of his passion, born out in flyers with headlines like "We Should Be Very Alarmed by This Latest Attempt to Steal 21 St. James Pl.," comes through in his gravelly voice. If anything, he sounds uninterested—that is, until I ask him if he believes he should be able to sell his share in St. James Towers for whatever the market will bear.

"I deserve to own this apartment!" Goodyear yells. A coughing fit quickly takes over. At eighty-two, he tries to avoid getting worked up. His central role in the privatization campaign at St. James is thus outside the realm of spoken conversation. He prefers the pen for his arguments, which he's collected in a twelve-page dossier of manifestos on the American Dream and its connections to citizenship, homeownership, capitalism, and personal wealth. His response to my question, a kind of non sequitur from a question on selling at market-rate to an answer about ownership, says quite a bit. He may be a shareholder in his cooperative, and therefore a homeowner in principle, but to Goodyear, unless he can sell that share for whatever amount he wants, he's no owner at all. To boot, he deserves that ability and the profit that's likely to come with it should he ever exercise what he sees as a right.

My question elicits his fury, followed by an indignant appeal to my intellect: "You're a rational man, you know what I'm saying." Goodyear understands the drive for personal profit to be part and parcel with basic reason. His tone matches his flyers' all-caps FDR quote. Goodyear dates the quote, incorrectly, to December 7, 1941—the day of the attack on Pearl Harbor that spurred the US' entrance into World War II. The phrase evoking "fear itself" actually comes from FDR's inaugural speech almost nine years prior in the depths of the Great Depression. It's a telling error: Goodyear is not referencing that call for social solidarity via public investment in new safety-net programs and infrastructure. Rather, he signs his neighborly missives with a battle cry.

Goodyear's argument—that ownership in a limited-equity cooperative is not *true* ownership—resonates in the stairwells of St. James and warren-like courtyards of Southbridge. The debates within both are, in one sense, definitional. What is ownership? What rights does it guarantee? What responsibilities, if any, does it carry? No one is pulling out a pocket *Merriam-Webster's* to better hurl insults across elevator lobbies, but every resident involved carries a personal conception of what it means to own a share in their cooperative.

Ownership, put simply, is possession. But possession of a house or apartment is rarely simple. For many, the space of home is the most important physical realm of an individual's or family's life—if you're one of the lucky ones to own such a space at all. Where that home stands determines the future, from where children go to school to how long they are likely to live.[3] What that space is worth to others has become the primary mechanism by which Americans accrue wealth—or lose a life's savings. An apartment or house is the biggest, most expensive, and most influential thing you will ever own. And owning one is distinctly different than owning, say, a Matchbox car: the complexity of the former is vast; the latter, according to my six-year-old nephew Asher, is a straightforward matter of his universal domain.

Lester Goodyear dispatches with much of that complexity when his coughing fit abates. "I don't think of us as owners, because I can't function as an owner." He lists the disqualifications:

> I can't take out a mortgage on my apartment. If I have a relative that lives here for more than a certain number of days, I have to add them to the occupancy. I can be surcharged. We don't have the opportunity to alter [certain things in our apartments] without the approval of the Board of Directors. If I move out or even if I die, I have nothing to say about what the value of my apartment is.

Rules, for Goodyear, equate to infringements, which in turn violate "true homeownership." Such a regulation-less ideal, as many a homeowner can tell you, hardly approaches reality. As scholar-activist Matt Hern notes, "We are all renters in the eye of the state. All you homeowners—try not paying your taxes . . . and see how that goes."[4] The bundle of rights that come with homeownership also come with responsibilities and requirements. There are pesky city zoning codes, condo-association bylaws, mortgage terms, utility rights-of-way. If you're in the path of a proposed project that a government wants to build, eminent domain may move you and rid you of your ownership altogether—just like it did to the folks who once lived where Goodyear does now. When I was a middle-schooler visiting a friend in a suburb of Athens, Georgia, I wondered aloud why his neighborhood looked so uniform. My dad then gave me my first lesson in homeowners' associations, which often stipulate everything from the content of yard signs to the design of the windows. Even that pales in comparison to the regulations with which owners of some historic properties must comply, which touch on everything from paint color to the preservation of slanting stairwells.

The ideal that Goodyear sketches also conveniently omits American real estate's varied forms. You might own the structure of your home but not the land: that's the case for roughly 12.4 million Americans who live in manufactured housing (more commonly known by the misnomer mobile homes).[5] Or maybe you own the structure and the land but only at its surface, like the growing number of Americans living above oil and gas deposits that are owned or leased by prospectors through the category of subsurface rights.

Goodyear, as a decade-plus member of the land-use committee on his community board, would also be familiar with the peculiarity of owning the sky above certain buildings that are not built as densely as zoning allows. These "air rights," typically the purview of only the most sophisticated and monied real estate developers, can be transferred to nearby parcels to birth larger buildings than otherwise permitted. In comparison, ownership of a share in a cooperative with limits on resale value starts to look pretty banal.

But Goodyear is hardly alone in promoting a Matchbox version of homeownership. Over a century of public policy and real estate propaganda has succeeded in planting a particular vision of the owned home in the American mind. This ideal has aesthetic and ideological elements. It's created the illusion that ownership is something narrow and immutable. And what that looks like is so pervasive, virtually any American can describe the color and style of fence that guards it.

Though now a signature of the American suburb, the most famous home bounded by a white picket fence in 1934 stood a few blocks south of Grand Central Terminal in Manhattan. "America's Little House," as it was known, was an aspirational model that stood on Park Avenue at Thirty-Ninth Street across from the luxurious Griffon condos and in the shadow of the neo-Gothic Lincoln Tower. No single American owned this home, and no one lived there. The Bowery Savings bank held the deed, and the New York branch of the national campaign Better Homes in America sponsored the erection of the two-story, three-bedroom, Georgian-style spectacle. If America's Little House was a monument to any president, it honored Herbert Hoover. Hoover, during his tenure as Secretary of Commerce in the 1920s, had played an outsized role in pushing homeownership as both a financial and moral good for all Americans, though he will be forever associated not with tasteful shutters and dormer windows but with the Hooverville shantytowns of the Great Depression.

The Little House was a far cry from those encampments of the unhoused. It featured terraces, "play" and "drying lawns," and a bird bath surrounded by dogwoods and pin oaks, maples and crab apples. During its year in the city, two hundred thousand visitors would come through the house to view its layout, which sported a nursery, "clothery," and a bedroom conspicuously labeled "Owner's Room." The only permanent occupants of the property resided in the garage, where a CBS broadcasting studio took to the airwaves to promote homeownership and the specific ideal of homemaking embodied in the Little House across "the world's largest radio network."[6] The use, if not the form, was fitting. Midtown Manhattan was and is, after all, an office district; the plot today is home to 99 Park Avenue, a twenty-six-story, six-hundred-thousand-square-foot premium office space for everything from real estate brokerages to hair-transplantation clinics.

Better Homes in America was ostensibly a private-sector campaign—a product of realtor lobbies, building trades, lumber and brick producers, mortgage lenders, and architects. But it amplified federal propaganda on the virtues of homeownership, namely the Own-Your-Own-Home campaign of the 1910s. Hoover had his hands in both. During a campaign conference in 1931, he extolled that homeownership:

> makes for happier married life, it makes for better children, it makes for confidence and security, . . . it makes for better citizenship. There can be no fear for a democracy or self-government for liberty or freedom from homeowners no matter how humble they may be.[7]

Messages like this, pushing the idea that homeownership was for everyone, spread throughout the country. It was found in songbooks, essay competitions, and articles published in the likes of *Better Homes and Gardens* (run by Hoover's former Cabinet-mate Edwin Meredith). This construction of the idea of Americanness, of the physical markers of the American Dream, did not just promote; it also tore down. Renting was anathema—as housing historian Lawrence Vale puts it, "clearly, the 'better' home needed to be an *owned* home."[8] This home also needed to be as private as possible: apartment buildings were undesirable, and cooperative ownership, according to none other than etiquette pundit Emily Post, was "beset with far greater danger than is possible to one who merely buys a house."[9]

The implied danger here was moral as well as financial. If dense urban housing and cooperative arrangements evoked the supposed contagion of socialism and communism, the single-family home was the antidote. According to the National Association of Real Estate Brokers, renting in apartment buildings was "'anti-family' since it allowed 'others the control of the place that is the center of your whole personal and family life.'"[10] Another organization of realtors touted single-family homes over collective housing arrangements with the rousing appeal that "socialism and communism do not take root in the ranks of those who have their feet firmly embedded in the soil of America through homeownership."[11] True to the capitalist messaging, single-family homeownership was also framed as the financially sound decision—a vehicle for savings due solely to the owner, who could be either Black or White, as long as their neighborhoods remained segregated. (Real estate professionals and government employees would ensure this.) Policies to promote homeownership would follow in the 1930s and formed "part of the largest expansion of the welfare state in American history" alongside Social Security. Notably, these efforts did not promote homeownership as a way to build wealth through investment and appreciation but as a way to save money through what was essentially government-subsidized rent control.[12] With a down payment, families got access to a fixed monthly payment for housing that, at the time of purchase, they technically owned very little of thanks to a government-backed mortgage.

Homeownership thus became the marker of true citizenship, an ideology as evident in Goodyear's pamphlets as in the *Better Homes* cookbook that has sat on my mother's shelf since 1977. This ideology, embodied in the Little House, offers a straightforward story of private property and personal control, pushing cooperative housing firmly outside the norm. Against this backdrop, the Mitchell-Lama model of a public good governed cooperatively by its resident shareholders looks abnormal and, to some, downright un-American.

OF FAMILIARS AND FOILS

By some standards, limited-equity co-ops like Mitchell-Lamas are indeed foreign. Shared-equity models like limited-equity co-ops and social housing generally are far more prevalent outside the US than within its bounds. The situation says far less about its viability in the American context than it does about Americans' conceptions of ownership and home.

In the Swiss capital of Zurich—no slouch when it comes to nerve centers of global capitalism—one in five homes are owned by a nonprofit cooperative. By municipal law, cooperators' monthly maintenance charges are limited to amounts that only cover operating and capital costs. The lack of income restrictions on the co-ops means that a wider range of society benefits from social housing and supports its aims. Switzerland's comprehensive social safety net—healthcare, education, financial support following retirement—removes the pressure that Americans put on housing appreciation to fund life's aspirations and necessities. And while it's theoretically possible for these co-ops to "privatize" and enter the speculative market, not one has left the municipal program over the last century, thanks to municipal policies that encourage retention, economies of scale as co-op promoters continue to build new developments, and a nonspeculative ideal built into the co-ops' very identity.[13]

Beyond Zurich, there is no shortage of successful social housing models in Europe. Vienna's is chief among those that inspire the envy and awe of American progressives, who visit to snap selfies in front of decommodified apartment blocks designed with panache by the continent's up-and-coming architects. A constellation of policies (including rent control and just-cause eviction protections) and the lack of stringent-means testing (80 percent of Viennese residents qualify) ensure that nearly all segments of society enjoy the benefits of social housing. This makes the Vienna model—one focused on renting rather than owning—politically untouchable.[14]

However, Americans needn't always look elsewhere for decom-modified housing strategies. Mitchell-Lama remains the American gold standard, but there are other models worth studying. In 1970, two former voting-rights organizers of the Student Nonviolent Coordinating Committee, Shirley and Charles Sherrod, along with peace activist Robert Swann, grew their own co-op near Albany, Georgia. They took inspiration from the *moshav* model in Palestine and established the first community land trust—dubbed New Communities, Inc.[15]

Although the community land trust (CLT) model is now best known for its potential to provide affordable, stable housing to low-income folks, Swann and the Sherrods originally developed it for agricultural purposes, seeking a way to build power among mostly Black sharecroppers vulnerable to eviction and suffering from disenfranchisement. They did so by decoupling ownership of property built on land ("improvements" in real estate speak) from ownership of the land itself. By holding the land in trust, the landowner—usually a nonprofit entity with a specific mission, à la New Communities—is able to require things of the property built upon it while also lowering costs for the people who lease it for farming or living. A home built in a CLT can carry the same kind of resale restriction as limited-equity co-op shares: they can't be sold at market rates. The price is determined by a set formula accounting for inflation and, sometimes, owner investments.

You may have heard of CLTs; they are the model du jour of decom-modified housing, trotted out in the press as an exciting alternative, then pilloried for being difficult to scale. Their appeal might stem from a sense of familiarity they elicit in Americans: while the divorce of land from property may seem unusual, owners within a community land trust still often lay claim to a physical home—not immaterial shares in a corporate body. The CLT model is also attractive for its emphasis on self-determination, particularly among marginalized communities and individuals who have historically had little control over their surrounds, among them renters, people of color, and the unhoused. CLTs are, after all, political projects that go beyond providing affordable housing to imagine a radically different way of governing in community, the art of which urbanist Cassim Shepard regards as "the contemporary practice of citizenship."[16] As much as they would like to separate themselves from the speculative market that surrounds them and the governing bodies that promote it, however, community land trusts remain heavily reliant on public or philanthropic dollars to get going and maintain themselves.

This is not a knock on the model but rather describes an aspect of almost all strategies to provide housing for low- and middle-income residents in our cities. Such has been the case for generations. Public dollars go into their creation and maintenance—as they also do with mansions, luxury towers, and modest suburban homes. Whether through tax incentives, subsidized mortgages, insurance, or direct grants, public funding is an ingredient in all American housing. Sometimes this public investment carries stipulations meant to achieve a policy goal; sometimes few strings are attached—a different path to a different policy goal. In that sense, all American housing is public.[17]

Yet, an association with "publicness" arises only when it comes to housing for lower-income folks. Public housing—rental apartments wholly owned by government housing authorities, a form of decommodified housing distinct from limited-equity co-ops and community land trusts—is the paradigmatic example. Popular conceptions of such housing have been distorted by the racist stigma and fearmongering of "big" government cultivated throughout the second half of the twentieth century, from McCarthy's Red Scare on through to Reagan's welfare queens. When we think of government-associated housing, these messages claim, we should think of undeserving people of color on the public dole and heavy-handed communists controlling the minutiae of our residential lives.

The "publicness" of public housing is predicated on government ownership. But there is another association between the public and home based instead on purpose. That is, the intent to provide a public good. Though speaking of "privatization" at St. James Towers and Southbridge Towers is technically a misnomer—these are owned by private corporations with private shareholders, after all—the shoe fits. To dissolve them as limited-equity co-ops would be to privatize a kind of housing meant to serve the public. Privatization then allows for their treatment as a commodity for sale to the highest bidder.

Though Lester Goodyear may contend that his variety of homeownership at St. James is somehow not "true homeownership," and though the predominate narrative in the US marks social housing as somehow anathema, it's evident that neither position is accurate. They are the products of a certain ideology, one that Harvey Marshall's father carried within him upon moving into Southbridge. This is the source of Marshall's assertion that the goal of privatization has walked the maze of Southbridge's interlinked corridors since their very creation.

If these dreams of privatization did exist from the start, Southbridge's demonstrated commitment to protecting its affordable nature more than outweighed them. "Preserve Southbridge," reads the first line of the co-op manual from 1979. The guide emphasizes Southbridge's affordability and its status as a Mitchell-Lama, as well as "everyone's responsibility" to help the co-op survive difficult economic times and create a good place to live. These messages, too, take pride of place, preceding the nuts-and-bolts sections of the manual—the details of the co-op board, the trash compactor, and balcony rules ("If there are toddlers in the family, you may not be aware that they are discarding items from your terrace").

Thirty-something resident Chris Hresko missed out on toddlerhood at Southbridge, moving in at age eight in 1997, but he may still have been tempted to unleash aerial assaults on passersby as the fourth grader who roamed the complex, hopping between the game room and the Burger King, between his friends' units and his parents' and grandparents'. He remembers his family preaching a cooperative mindset, instilling in him the importance of maintaining Southbridge as an affordable redoubt in a city of capital. Hresko didn't recall whether his elders had received similar lessons from co-op leadership, but it had once been common for new Mitchell-Lama residents to receive some political education in cooperativism. In the '60s, the State's Division of Housing and Community Renewal distributed a pamphlet titled *The ABCs of Ownership in State-Aided Cooperative Housing.* The nonprofit Play Schools Association published another called *Learning to Live in a Middle Income Cooperative.* At the mammoth, UHF-sponsored Co-op City, moving in included orientation sessions to instill the "meaning of cooperation." Residents' welcome packets included a pamphlet titled *Co-op Living: A Guide for Members.*[18]

Regardless of their original genesis, the lessons from Hresko's forebears stuck. When I meet this data whiz and community organizer in 2014, he's engaged in projects to distribute maps of the City's vacant public land to the masses and to document redlining's lasting effects. His ruddy, round face flushes upward toward his widow's peak as he contemplates the stakes involved in possible privatization. Such is his inheritance, both from the family he was born into and the family he chose.

Eva Sacks, one of Hresko's chosen kin, also comes by her commitment to social housing honestly. Her cluttered Southbridge apartment shows off dual interests in preservation: posters for Puerto Rican bomba and plena concerts—mementos of her vocation as a folklorist—coexist with copies of the pro-Mitchell-Lama flyers she's authored, a series dubbed *Just the Facts*. She's taken up the mantle of her mother, remembered as a "communist" organizer by pro-privatization Harvey Marshall, in a red-baiting tone reminiscent of Hoover-era propaganda.

Southbridge resident Leo Aria remembers Sacks's mom as well. She was the elderly woman who took him, a young activist, under her wing—"You come up here. You sit at this table"—at a meeting she'd called to staunch Southbridge's first flirtation with privatization in the 1980s. Aria is not so young anymore. The prominence of his ears and nose are a marker of his age, as is his now-decaffeinated espresso, swamped in a packet of sugar and half-drunk. He is known for his outspoken activism on the Lower East Side and for the verbal sparring he undertakes with the owner of the Italian café where we meet. But Leo recalls that when he first met Eva's mother, he quietly stood at the back of the room, "very reluctant. . . . I didn't know anyone." Eva's mother "was holding this meeting with this other guy who was very loud and annoying people by how loud he was speaking, and how emphatic he was against privatization." Leo took the seat he'd been offered—both at the table and on a committee to counter stirrings of privatization at the co-op. He ran for the board. He won. He eventually became board president, a role he held for years across multiple terms and described as akin to being "the mayor of a small city."

Aria's deep involvement in the co-op coincided with the first privatizations among other Mitchell-Lamas. The program had stopped building new developments amid the City's financial crisis, and the 1980s saw jostling at the state level over how to effectively support existing co-ops. In 1984, a bill was introduced that encouraged the privatization and sale of co-ops in order to feed a state-wide fund for distressed buildings and cash for cooperators. The bill was killed after significant backlash but not before normalizing the notion of privatization as a possible outcome for the limited-equity co-ops. The same year, the first rental Mitchell-Lama left the program. Five years later, in 1989, the Anthony J. Contello Towers in Gravesend, Brooklyn, became the first Mitchell-Lama co-op to privatize after it had remained in the program for the requisite years and paid off its government mortgage. It is now known as Waterview Towers.

That co-op's pursuit of privatization required the creation of new processes and new regulations for how this never-intended transition should take place. The fundamentals of those processes and regulations remain in place today. They largely stem from business and securities law. Co-ops are, at their most basic, corporations with shareholders. Privatization, in those terms, means destroying the old company with its limited-equity restrictions and forming a new one without them. The sale of shares in a new co-op (be it limited-equity or speculative) is interpreted by the State's attorney general to constitute an offering akin to companies selling their shares on the stock market. Such sales must therefore include extensive offering plans to outline what exactly is being sold and what the risks of purchasing a share are. Developing these plans costs a lot of money—many lawyers, accountants, and government professionals are involved—and to expend that money, the company (the co-op) needs its shareholders (the cooperators) to approve those expenditures before then approving the resultant offering plan.

Working backward, a process, eventually codified in Mitchell-Lama regulations by the State and City housing agencies, took shape. The cooperators had to hold a series of three votes: the first to approve spending cash on a study to determine the feasibility of privatization, the second to approve the development of the offering plan, and the third to approve the offering plan itself. The first vote would require a simple majority to pass, while the second and third required two-thirds of residents to approve. Only then could the old, limited-equity co-op be replaced with the new, privatized one. These votes would become the central battlegrounds of all Mitchell-Lama privatization battles to come.

The privatization question was in the city's air, and as the 1980s wore on it would waft toward Southbridge, much to Leo Aria's chagrin. Between the governor and legislature debating the role of privatization in co-ops, regulatory agencies contending with the how, and the cottage industry of property managers, lawyers, and accountants specializing in Mitchell-Lamas all chewing on what this would mean, there were many vectors through which the question may have first arrived there. As Aria became aware that some residents were interested in privatization, he honored his commitment to representative democracy and encouraged the curious to study leaving Mitchell-Lama through a co-op committee. His support ended there. The board, with Leo at the helm, opposed privatization, and a separate group of like-minded residents formed, calling themselves Southbridge Towers Cooperators for Mitchell-Lama. Together, throughout the '80s and early '90s, the board and the committee parried attempts by some of their fellow residents to pursue privatization—a process they expected to be lengthy, expensive, and fraught, if not explosive. The pro-privatizers didn't have the votes to kick off the privatization process to begin with, and the pro-Mitchell-Lama board kept the votes from even occurring.

By the 2000s, though, Aria & Co.'s decades-long efforts to keep Southbridge's privatization at bay began to show cracks. "I was very powerful. That doesn't last, that fades away," he reminisces. The city's industrial economy had given way to a base dominated by FIRE—the very finance, insurance, and real estate companies that surrounded the complex. New York's policies followed the trends of the neoliberalization, privatization, and public austerity sweeping the nation and beyond. The decimation of the UK's social housing stock via Margaret Thatcher's Right to Buy policy* continued to reverberate, as did wider privatization of public goods: water in Bolivia, telecom infrastructure in Mexico, and education, well, everywhere.

Southbridge residents were both different and the same. Some were older with new priorities and needs; some were younger, and the copies of the co-op guide that they received no longer included the section stressing the need to "Preserve Southbridge"—that had been removed by 1993. Harvey Marshall was among those pro-privatizers, some of whom were veterans of previous attempts in the 1980s and '90s and were ready to try again. With real estate values in New York ascendant, the lure of profit had never been stronger, and the political environment reinforced the belief that profit from all varieties of real estate was uncontroversial. So the question loomed: You can take the building out of the market, but can you keep the market out of the building? Chris Hresko, now wan and not a little demoralized, recalls how Southbridge had once operated "like a close-knit family." The privatization debate would cut families—both cooperative and nuclear—"down the line," with atomic repercussions.

---

*Beginning in the early 1980s, Thatcher's Right to Buy program allowed tenants of council housing (what would be termed public housing in the US) to purchase their apartments at a steep discount. Though it allowed many tenants to become homeowners, the policy decimated the country's social housing stock and often left vulnerable tenants-turned-owners holding the bill for the long-term disinvestment of the units. Many would eventually lose those homes or sell them off, beginning a cycle of former decommodified housing becoming progressively commodified and out of reach of the low- and middle-income people it had been built to serve.

PART II

Southbridge
Towers

CHAPTER 3

Let's Explore Our Options

In 2005, autumn in New York—true to Ella Fitzgerald and Louis Armstrong's trilling—brought "the promise of new love." Post-9/11 redevelopment schemes for Lower Manhattan were in full swing, along with the cranes and backhoes tasked with bringing them into being. The neighborhood, once regarded as an office district only—Southbridge Towers the exception that proved the rule—had already begun its transformation into a place for monied residents. A bevy of incentives and federal dollars was now supercharging the process. It was in with the new and capitalize on the old: the South Street Seaport would be mall-ified for tourists, preservationists would be mollified with the protection of low-rise warehouses that had once served nearby docks, and the old Fulton Fish Market and its piscine smell would be relocated to the Bronx. The season was also, as "Autumn in New York" promises, "often mingled with pain": the trauma of four years prior, the growing ones of a district remade. And, at Southbridge, the reopening of a tear in the cooperative body. The question of privatization, once seemingly sewn up in the early '90s, was broached again, this time prompted in part by the remaking of the co-op's surrounds. Harvey Marshall's hoped-for comeback was on.

As with most co-op politics, the matter was the purview of the fifteen-member board of elected cooperators that governs Southbridge and carries a fiduciary duty to the co-op. For most of the co-op's four-thousand-plus residents, the board's workings served as good diner gossip when annual elections rolled around but were otherwise not something they followed. Residents' ability to check out from the co-op's operations is the beauty, and perhaps a pitfall, of a well-run operation like Southbridge: one needn't worry whether, say, the London planetree leaves that'd begun to fall on the pedestrian thoroughfare would be collected. The management company hired by the board would handle it. Even when things went wrong with such mundane operations, as they inevitably do, the board would field the complaint. Yes, the board also promulgated rules that shaped co-op life, but most cooperators were just happy to let the board do its job as long as their maintenance charges stayed low, their complex safe, their apartments functional.

Other residents, however, formed the small groups who peopled the board and scrutinized its minutes. With another window for privatization approaching in the middle distance after the complex's mortgage was refinanced with a private lender and existing affordability terms were met, a segment of these co-op heads, including Harvey Marshall, organized in 2004 to counter the Southbridge Towers Cooperators for Mitchell-Lama. They called their new group Southbridge Rights, Inc. It was "an independent organization" and self-described purveyor of "Unbiased Information for Southbridge Shareholders," positioning itself as an all-purpose political party for the complex's mini-government. It had its own party mouthpiece, the *SouthBridge Owners Shareholder News*, and a PO box at the local post office. More importantly, it had a sure-fire strategy for bringing privatization to fruition: take over the board.

Southbridge Rights had already won seats in the spring elections, but it remained in the minority. So it turned to another strategy, and another campaign, to move its cause forward. The organization presented the board with a petition signed by six hundred shareholders calling for "a referendum on beginning a study to investigate our options to reconstitute the co-op as a normal, regular apartment co-op," as reported in their newsletter's "Special October Election" issue. The argument for proceeding with such a study was simple. Combined with the show of broad interest by way of petition, it was also potent: it's just a study; we want to explore our options. As a pro-Mitchell-Lama blogger would put it, "'We Just Need More Information,' the Trojan Horse of Mitchell-Lamadom."[1]

For Southbridge Rights, the study was merely the first move in a larger plan. It would kick off the three-part process required by the State for privatization to take place. First, a feasibility study had to be funded by a vote of the cooperators. Second, on the basis of the feasibility study, cooperators had to vote to fund a draft offering plan that would detail what privatization would look like. Third, cooperators had to vote to approve the final offering plan, thereby authorizing the legal transformation of the co-op: its privatization.

The feasibility study would assess the complex's financial and physical health, while also giving cooperators a sneak peak of a privatized future. One can't fault them for wanting to understand the possible paths ahead. The buildings were getting old. Major investments in maintenance would be required. A report the year prior had put a figure to this immutable future—$21 million over the next three years—and shareholders expressed concern about where the money would come from. An increase in their monthly maintenance charges? A special assessment that had cooperators pay up for a specific need? A new subsidy from the State? Privatization could provide a fresh funding source for the complex in the form of the "flip tax" taken from the first sale of each share at market rates. But costs, property taxes chief among them, would also rise. The prudent thing, many agreed, would be to contract someone to work the numbers.

The board responded to the petition put before them by scheduling a vote on a feasibility study to take place on October 19 and 20. In an unusual maneuver, it also scheduled another vote for the week following, that one a referendum on whether or not the co-op should take advantage of a state tax break. Spacing out the two votes obscured their interplay. If Southbridge elected to receive the tax break, the co-op would be locked into the Mitchell-Lama program for another fifteen years. Even if cooperators turned out in favor of commissioning a feasibility study, the referendum a week later could make its projections useless. Privatization would be off the table. This did not go unnoticed by Southbridge Rights. The second vote, they said, was a bad-faith trap laid by pro-Mitchell-Lama board members and the State.

As it turned out, cooperators ultimately had no option to test this snare. Their first vote on the supposed Trojan horse, the feasibility study, had proven so decisively in favor that the board called off the second. Studying privatization passed with 741 yeas to 350 nays. Perhaps more persuasive than the prospect of exploring options and getting information, though, was Southbridge Rights' canny refrain of what privatization would bring beyond cash: "a normal, regular apartment co-op." Their bulletin's columns, alongside "news" indistinguishable from editorials and the party's latest slate of candidates for co-op elections, repeated this characterization. One article proposed an alternative to the politicized word "privatization": "We still think 'normalization' is a more accurate term—becoming a normal apartment co-op—but this is no time to quibble over language!"

Of course, they were already quibbling. Southbridge Rights was setting a narrative, using language to shape perception, seeking to frame
how cooperators would understand the complex question of privatization and what it meant for the nature of their home. The message
was clear: their current form of homeownership, the limited-equity arrangement regulated by government, was an aberration. They couldn't
turn Southbridge into 1,651 single-family homes surrounded by white
picket fences, but there was still room to strive toward Herbert Hoover's
ideal enshrined in the Little House, still opportunity to achieve what
Goodyear across town at St. James call "true homeownership." The
only way to excise abnormality from Southbridge was to abolish its
resale restrictions and remove any hint of publicness from its grounds.

INEPT, CORRUPT, EXPENDABLE

Next door to Southbridge, hemmed in by the complex on two sides and
an on-ramp to the Brooklyn Bridge on another, sits 100 Gold Street.
The chunky building with a rather bold orange lobby houses New York
City's Department of Housing Preservation and Development. HPD, as
it's known, is one of the governmental agencies that oversee Mitchell-
Lamas. Despite their buildings' proximity and shared history as crea-
tures of the Brooklyn Bridge Southwest Urban Renewal Area, HPD
doesn't have much, if anything, to do with Southbridge. It oversees
only those co-ops, like St. James, to which the City provided the initial
subsidized mortgage. Southbridge received its mortgage from the State,
and so the State's housing agency—the Division of Housing and Community Renewal, or DHCR—is Southbridge's regulator.

When I met to discuss DHCR with Harvey Marshall, we conversed in
the management office, the hub of Southbridge's private government. He
sat me beneath dueling rectangles of an LCD screen and whiteboard at
a long, glossy table. This understated, paunchy White man with slightly
receding salt-and-pepper hair then described what DHCR proverbially
brought to it: nothing.

His statement was somewhat undercut by the fact that Southbridge is
governed by volunteers who, like him, may or may not have experience
relevant to managing a massive development with complex finances.
That DHCR would have a seat at the table would make sense. The
State has skin in the game as the mortgagee, is charged with fulfilling
the public purpose of Mitchell-Lama co-ops, and can provide expertise

that folks like Marshall—he, a retired elementary school principal—may lack. DHCR, in theory, is there to make sure regulations are followed and prudent financial decisions made. It oversees bidding on major contracts, such as replacing the boilers or the roof. It makes sure residents whose income has risen above the entry threshold pay the extra surcharge they are supposed to. It is tasked with ensuring the waitlists to join the co-op are properly administered. Resident Tom Goldhaber, who as former treasurer of the board often had close contact with the State agency, got the intent of their role: "I understand that the concept of it was for the DHCR to more or less monitor what's going on here and make sure things don't go wrong, make sure expenses are being done properly, make sure there's a proper budget. The problem is they did none of that."

In short, the DHCR's execution was lacking, and everyone knew it. The agency's ineptitude or disinterest was, oddly enough, something pro-Mitchell-Lama and pro-privatization cooperators agreed on, even as they came to the same conclusion from different angles. Folks like Goldhaber thought government oversight inhibited good operations by way of policies that required acceptance of the lowest contractor bid—a formula for low-quality work. Eva Sacks, the communist's daughter, held onto the idea that "as long as [Southbridge] remained a Mitchell-Lama, there would be, as pitiful as it was, some kind of oversight" from DHCR. But she acknowledged that the agency's approach amounted to "benign neglect. . . . I think the person we worked with at DHCR was probably waiting for his moment to retire three weeks after he got the job." Harvey Marshall pointed to staffing cutbacks as an indication that the State's interest in Mitchell-Lamas just isn't all that strong.

Southbridge residents weren't alone in their critique of the agency. From the outset of the Mitchell-Lama program, DHCR came under fire for failing to properly supervise construction by private sponsors, often signing off on subpar designs and execution that burdened co-ops with costly fixes for years. Reports from the likes of the state comptroller display some of the agency's shortcomings over time. One such report had, DHCR explained:

> captured the period immediately following the departure of DHCR's entire data-entry and verification group. . . . This group entered and won the Lotto jackpot. They simultaneously left DHCR's employ in the space of a single pay period and retired. Thereafter, DHCR was left

with an extraordinary staffing issue and, more importantly, a knowledge gap that DHCR could not have anticipated.[2]

Pity any government agency whose workers win the lottery and quit
en masse; pity also certain government agencies who are almost invari-
ably denied the funding they need to properly do their jobs—especially
the kind of oversight and maintenance that often is the first duty to fall
by the wayside.

DHCR's reputation wasn't helped by cooperators' misunderstanding of its role. Some residents would send staff mundane complaints
that are far outside their purview. Mark Colón, then the president of
DHCR's Office of Housing Preservation, told me that "We get claims
that the person downstairs is smoking, that they have an illegal service
animal. We have to refer them back to the process: have you asked the
property manager about this?" Eva Sacks told me, "People moved in
here and didn't know what Mitchell-Lama was." But if some of DHCR's
shortcomings are outside its control, it has only itself and its employees
to blame for its sullied name in another respect. As James Szal, pro-
Mitchell-Lama cooperator extraordinaire, put it, "DHCR was a joke. . . .
The only time we really heard about it was when the shit hit the fan,
pardon my French, or when they found corruption." Corruption, that
is, that implicated both the co-op board and the agency itself.

Two months after the vote on the feasibility study and either side of
Christmas, Southbridge Rights received two gifts. The first, as reported
before the co-op board elections the following April, was that "One of
the most vocal opponents of SouthBridge Right's efforts to reconstitute
SouthBridge Towers as a normal, private co-op was arrested . . . and
accused of illegally selling her apartment shares." They spoke, of course,
of the dog-loving board member and DHCR employee Jody Wolfson.
The second: "In a related development, Wolfson's supervisor at The
New York State Division of Housing and Community Renewal, Mark
Marcucilli, was also arrested and charged with both conspiring with
Wolfson to sell the apartment, and defrauding [the Lower Manhattan
Development Corporation's] post-Sept. 11 grant program."

The *SouthBridge Owners Shareholder News* went on to quote one
of its own publishers:

> "Perhaps this begins to explain why some members of the Board
> have been so opposed to our efforts," said Jared Brown, president

of SouthBridge Rights. "Until now it didn't make sense why anyone would be so against something that was so clearly in everyone's self interest. But if people are making illegal money under the table, you can see why they wouldn't want things to change around here. The involvement of DHCR is quite significant, because they are the agency that sets the voting rules regarding our efforts to reconstitute. These indictments are like a breath of fresh air."

Wolfson and Marcucilli's grafting allowed the pro-privatization caucus to bend the narrative in their favor. Not only was DHCR inept, they claimed, but its employees were also corrupt, and the removal of its oversight by means of privatization would be a boon to the co-op. They were also now able to smear their pro-Mitchell-Lama peers as hypocritical, given that Wolfson, one of their own, had been caught doing illegally what pro-privatization cooperators wanted to carry out aboveboard.

While the indictments and eventual convictions of Wolfson and Marcucilli may have come as a surprise, the existence of corruption at Southbridge did not. Jan Naumann, who was advocating for privatization in part for the personal profit it could bring, described corruption as "a problem. There are always people in it for what they can get for themselves." Rumors abounded of residents lying about who was living in an apartment in order to get a bigger place or circumvent rules on succession. When a resident leaves an apartment, a family member can only take over the unit if they are already living there—otherwise it goes to the next person on the waitlist. Marshall spoke of past board members getting apartments for their relatives. Another resident claimed that the current management company had paid off a past board president to get the lucrative contract for the complex.

That was just at Southbridge. At co-ops throughout the city, allegations abound and stretch back in time to implicate even the legislators for whom the program was named. State Senator Mitchell's private law firm made bank from an unusually large share of legal work on major Mitchell-Lama projects; State Assemblyman Lama's architecture practice thrived in a similar manner. In the '60s, Fred Trump was accused by a State auditor of overcharging on construction and land costs, pushing the limits on his profits at his eponymous village in Coney Island.[3] A bit farther down the boardwalk, three cooperators at the Luna Park Housing Corporation pocketed $874,000 in exchange for delivering eighteen apartments to recipients not on the waitlist, a scandal dubbed

Handbags for Housing due to the perpetrators' expensive taste in designer clutches.[4] In the Bronx, the management at Tracey Towers is rumored to have been paid off by residents from West Africa in order to jump ahead on the co-op waitlist—one explanation for how the development became New York's "Little Ghana."[5]

With every deal struck to reap money or favor from these public goods, this social housing gets commodified. Whether a current cooperator jumps ahead on the waitlist for a better view and an extra bedroom, or a prospective one seeks to bypass long lines of fellow strivers, they're participating in an illicit market. The irony is that this decommodified housing is being commodified precisely for the affordability and stability that it provides, thanks to its insulation from the speculative market—the same market that creates an incentive for such corruption by failing to provide the housing that people need.

Pro-privatizers were keen to stress the legality of their approach versus the illegality of Wolfson's. The latter is by no means admirable and remains a threat to the provision and maintenance of social housing. But it's worth noting that Wolfson's scheme to sell her Southbridge share didn't remove it from the Mitchell-Lama program; it didn't change the housing from social to speculative. The kind of commodification inherent in privatization, however, is permanent. The courts can remedy the injustice of an illegally transferred Mitchell-Lama share, but a privatized complex will stay that way forever.

THE GAMBLE

Southbridge's accounts were in the red as May 2006's board election approached—or so a Southbridge Rights talking point had it. The reported budget shortfall made the headlines in the *SouthBridge Owners Shareholder News* alongside Wolfson's arrest, privatization's promise, and the slate of six candidates endorsed by the organization. The complex's deficit presented Southbridge Rights with another opportunity to tout the apparently all-purpose funds that privatization, apartment sales, and resultant flip taxes would proffer. Sussing out just how those gains would interact with the increased expenses of privatization—millions in property tax abatements lost, no more offers of subsidized financing from the State—was precisely what the feasibility study was supposed to do. If the true ramifications of privatization remained somewhat muddied, the political picture at Southbridge was clearer. Southbridge

Rights had momentum, and as it grew, so too did the opposing chorus of pro-Mitchell-Lama shareholders.

James Szal is one such cooperator. He is a silver-haired retired special-ed teacher with a flair for political theater that extends into other realms of his life. Szal's apartment screamed personality when I visited, a stark contrast to the sterile lobby and concrete block hallway I'd walked through to get to his door. His home is painted a bright red and filled with black furniture, including a signature plush chair in the shape of a gargantuan high-heeled shoe. As he bent down to pick up his shih tzu Gucci, then 105 (in human years), I glimpsed across the back of his T-shirt the white plumage of a bald eagle, crisp before a faded American flag. Szal's slicked-back hair and sharp eyes mimicked those of the nationalist raptor, one who would surely have a different kind of affection for the shih tzu than Szal. He dismissed his whining dog lovingly—"Stop being such a pain in the ass, Gucci."

Szal carries a cemented reputation of being just that to pro-privatization cooperators. He served on the board for twelve years before losing his seat as privatization gained ground. But even without an official position, he continued to raise his voice on co-op matters. When it comes to privatization, Szal does not skirt what he sees as the ethical questions at hand. "It was unconscionable to me to make a profit and deny other people that right" to access an affordable home through Mitchell-Lama. Southbridge's departure from the program would not only reduce the number of limited-equity apartments available to other New Yorkers. It would also send the complex's waitlist—on which hundreds of aspiring cooperators had placed their names and hopes—to the shredder. Szal understood that this ethical argument—one rooted in an altruistic concern for unknown future shareholders—was hard for certain neighbors to grasp:

> When you bring up the issue about the consequence of taking away the same opportunity from other people that you have, it was, "Well, what is that about?" It's like trying to explain chocolate to someone who never tasted chocolate. You either get it or you don't. People say to me, "Why do you do your community work?" And I say, "Well, if you need to ask me that, I can't explain it to you."

However, the potential blow to social housing was not the only concern of the pro-Mitchell-Lama side. Like their pro-privatization opponents, they had financial motivations. And while folks like Szal acknowledged that privatization might benefit them financially, they also saw privatization for the grand gamble that it was.

If Southbridge privatized, two major financial changes would occur. First, the complex would no longer benefit from what was known as "shelter rent," a much-reduced property tax payment to the City saving it 75 to 90 percent relative to a speculative co-op. Under privatization, Southbridge would have to pay full price.[6] That tax burden would also likely rise further as the valuation of the property increased in the overheated market.

The second major change would be sales of shares: with the waitlist in the shredder and the price restrictions lifted, cooperators could hawk their stake in Southbridge directly to any interested party for whatever price they'd pay. These sales would not only generate cash for the seller. The co-op would also get a cut through the flip tax. The first post-privatization sale of any share would carry a hefty tax of between 20 and 30 percent. Any subsequent sales of the same share would be taxed at a much more modest 2 to 3 percent.

As complex a scheme as it appears, the math of privatization is a relatively simple matter of addition and subtraction. Would the flip tax revenue cancel out the increased property taxes and the various other costs that pro-privatization advocates said it would cover? Or would Southbridge be, well, in the red?

That was the gamble. Southbridge Rights saw little risk: we're in Lower Manhattan, they reasoned, and the market is booming. Cooperators will sell, and buyers will buy. Flip taxes will cover everything, and cooperators who choose not to sell their newly valuable share and stay put instead will not have to pay any more in maintenance than they do under Mitchell-Lama. As Szal's partner in pamphlets Eva Sacks put it, "I think even people who were pro-privatization at some level thought of this as affordable housing and rationalized that privatization would keep . . . it affordable, but it would keep it affordable just for them." Affordable, that is, if you already owned a share—not if you were seeking to buy one.

Szal, Sacks, and their allies weren't convinced that this is how things would play out. What if the market collapsed? What if not enough cooperators sold their shares and thus not enough flip tax revenue was generated? What if, due to the existence of asbestos in their apartments, prospective buyers had issues getting the mammoth mortgage they would likely need to purchase a privatized share? Without DHCR in the picture as a guardrail and advocate, what if the complex's insurance providers dropped them or jacked up their rates? Getting proper coverage had been a struggle since 9/11. Or what if the projections for capital needs proved too optimistic? And, arguably the biggest question of them all, what would happen when flip tax revenue petered from a torrent to a trickle? The co-op's big cut would only apply to the first post-privatization sale of a share, so once all the cooperators eager to leave cashed out, what then?

The answer to each of these scenarios was the same: cooperators would have to reach into their own pockets to cover costs to replace the elevators or finally sort out why the solar panels on the roof had never properly worked, raising carrying charges, levying special assessments. The families who wanted out of Southbridge would get cash. They could take the money and run, though their proceeds might not be significant enough to purchase anything close to comparable nearby. Urban geographer Amanda Huron observed that phenomenon among privatized limited-equity co-ops in Washington, DC:* "When this housing becomes a commodity, and [the residents] are able to trade it in for cash, they often receive far less than the home is really worth. . . . Many co-op members end up losing out."[7] Profits were eaten up either by taxes or external actors—the lawyers and accountants, sometimes developers, pushing privatization for their own benefit.

Meanwhile, the folks who remain at the co-op—those who want to continue living in their home rather than move and profit from it in the short-term—would be on the hook for rising housing costs. The question of when those costs, so alluringly reasonable for decades, would rise was not so much an "if" but a "when," the answer not scientific but speculative. Southbridge Rights saw that time frame as far off; Szal thought it might come sooner than expected and devastate the most vulnerable

---

*Washington, DC's ecosystem of limited-equity co-ops has a very different history from New York's. It was born of the passage of the Tenant Opportunity to Purchase Act in 1980, through which tenants of co-ops were given a right to buy their homes from their landlord upon the latter's intent to sell. With support from the District of Columbia's municipal government and various nonprofit groups, some such groups organized themselves into limited-equity co-ops.

residents in the process. Those on a fixed income might be shoved out of Southbridge if they were unable to pay the climbing maintenance. Szal himself was not in such a situation. He had consulting gigs on top of the community work that his wife liked to remind him was unpaid. But even Szal feared the hardship of a privatized future: "It still does not seem to me that it's tenable over time. So, I think I will reach a point where I will need to sell." Not because he necessarily wants to leave, to be clear, but because he might not be able to afford to stay.

Privatization presented a difficult decision to cooperators, and the feasibility study was meant to provide an initial read on the situation, including the complex's future affordability. The board contracted Stuart Saft—a spectacled and suited real estate lawyer who counts among his honors a listing in *Who's Who in the World* since 1995—to conduct it. This wasn't his first rodeo: in the early 2000s he'd conducted studies for a potential Co-op City privatization, ultimately counseling the Bronx behemoth against it. He'd been quoted in the trade magazine *The Cooperator* in 2001: "Each time we do the economic analysis on behalf of one of these boards, we come up with the fact that if they buy out, the housing no longer becomes affordable."[8] However, Saft's Southbridge study, released to cooperators in October 2007, came to a different conclusion. The study's bottom line: Southbridge could privatize, maintenance for cooperators who remained would stay low, and those who wanted to sell could clean up.

The *SouthBridge Owners Shareholder News* played up the last bit: "GET *YOUR* COPY, including such tantalizing details as the estimated value of each and every apartment at SouthBridge Towers, 'The Study' is must reading for all cooperators." In Southbridge's courtyards, murmurs about its contents joined the soundscape of humming AC units and low-grade ambient city, punctuated by the occasional yelp from a scootering kid, who, rounding the corner on a bank of concrete benches, takes a spill. The Southbridge Towers Cooperators for Mitchell-Lama—Eva Sacks, Leo Aria, and Daniel Brampton among them—combed through the study and responded, with a deeper but no less aggrieved howl: "It is built on quicksand!"

It was the necessary assumptions underlying the analysis, the substance of the what-ifs, that caused pro-Mitchell-Lama cooperators to cry foul. They took issue with how future sales were estimated, noted inconsistencies on mortgage projections, and highlighted the inadequacy of the capital-needs study that only looked five years into the future.

Southbridge Rights called these criticisms "scare tactics" and proceeded with attempts to debunk what they saw as their opponents' myths. The fact remained, however, that only one scenario was presented in the study. There were no sensitivity analyses to show what would occur if certain assumptions were not borne out by reality. As Saft's accountants were quick to admit, such deviations were almost certain to occur.

That hardly seemed to matter to most of the cooperators who picked up the unlikely paperback thriller from the management office downstairs. They'd been given their first quasi-official taste of what selling without restrictions could look like. There it was, their own proto-Zillow listing, showing at least one more zero on the end of their apartment's value than they were accustomed to seeing, ranging from the mid-$200,000s to over $1 million. The local newspaper *Downtown Express* ran a story on the study preceding its full release: "Big bucks at Southbridge—residents will be rich, study says." "It's worth $10,000 now," one shareholder said of his apartment. "Whatever it's worth will be more."[9]

JUST SAY WHAT'S WHAT

Around the same time of the study's release, an additional argument for privatization began to make the rounds, one based not on levels of profit but types of people. One must make below a certain income to be eligible to purchase a share in a Mitchell-Lama, and to some, the threshold, $150,125 for a household of three in 2022,[10] now felt too low. People in professions that residents thought should be served by the housing—teachers, the paradigmatic example—sometimes made too much to qualify. Privatization would mean that such folks could theoretically access Southbridge again, and residents like Jan Naumann planned to roll out the welcome mats for them, eventually going so far as to apply for a real estate broker's license in preparation. "People were asking me a lot of questions about real estate, which wasn't my forte before, but just because I'm a lawyer, they ask me questions. So I figured I'd better brush up on this stuff."

If Naumann's office is any indication of her sales style, tchotchkes will be involved. Thirteen stories above an expansive, marble-clad lobby in Manhattan's Financial District, we huddled in her cramped room, surrounded by files, straw-filled coffee cups, and mediocre reproductions of classic paintings. On top of one cabinet, a cabal of Minions figurines—bright yellow, mostly bald, goggle-eyed—stood next to the voluminous ridges of a wigged-judge statuette. Elevated on a pedestal behind me were the thick, red pigtails of fast-food icon Wendy, bestowed in honor of Jan's work on restaurant-chain compliance.

Her excitement about potential new co-op arrivals was palpable as we talked, though whether she was jazzed about the new neighbors themselves or the sales commissions they would bring is as hazy as her transition lenses, which had failed to lighten once we stepped indoors. She's among the pro-privatization faction that sees the process of leaving Mitchell-Lama as cooperative in and of itself—that is, it's good for her *and* good for everyone else. Tom Goldhaber, a resident since the '70s, believes the same. His involvement in the privatization campaign was motivated in part by an opportunity "to improve the neighborhood and improve the way the co-op was being run."

As Tom saw it, a privatized Southbridge, liberated from waitlists and open to the market, would allow for more turnover of apartments:

> Younger people [could] come in and . . . purchase basically a starter unit in New York City. . . . It's offering an opportunity for people who could not afford to live in Manhattan, and they now have an opportunity . . . to live in an affordable place in, really, a cool place in the world to live.

Goldhaber insisted that privatization would actually be a win for access to housing and that the housing would remain affordable. Asked if he thought it would be more affordable than under Mitchell-Lama, Goldhaber responded: "Does it cost you more to buy in? Yes, but if you're a person who wants to own something, it gives you an opportunity to buy an asset now."

Participate in any public discussion on "affordable" housing, and you're likely to hear a chorus of "affordable for whom?" The question is apt, the answer often dredged in an alphabet soup heavy on the letters AMI, for area median income. Its percentages (60 percent AMI, 80 percent AMI, etcetera) are used to designate different tiers of affordability. A certain affordable home might be restricted to people making 60 percent AMI or below. In short: affordability is relative. This relativity can make the term "affordable housing" meaningless, so who exactly would a privatized Southbridge Towers be affordable to?

Goldhaber put the value of his "asset" at Southbridge, should it privatize, at $500,000 to $750,000; other residents quoted sales expectations that were much higher. At the time, the *total* (not down pay-ment) up-front cost for a two-bedroom Mitchell-Lama apartment ran around $35,000. At Goldhaber's valuation, the same apartment post-privatization would require a $100,000 to $150,000 down payment and a mortgage. That may be cheaper than other cooperatives or condos in Lower Manhattan, but coming up with such a sum remains far out of reach for a vast number of New Yorkers and unfathomable for many of the people who were waiting their turn on the co-op's waitlist. A report from real estate website StreetEasy estimated that it would take eighteen years for a twenty-five- to forty-four-year-old New Yorker making the median annual income to save up for a down payment on a home at the city's median sales price of $637,250.[11] A privatized Southbridge share would be unaffordable to most.

While Goldhaber claimed that privatization would be more inclusive of young families making home in Lower Manhattan, Jan Naumann's take on privatization preached the exclusion of certain individuals that didn't meet her standards:

> We started to go very downhill because the government's definition of what constitutes middle-income wasn't valid anymore. It became low-income, and that was a real problem. People were not dressed nicely anymore. People were walking around in pajamas. People were embarrassed to bring people there. The upkeep wasn't quite as good, just because people weren't that interested. There was just a different feel from when we had first moved in from the people to where it be-came. It was going to mid-, lower-income, and that was a real prob-lem, at which point it was getting very much an us-and-them kind of thing, and that was not good for the co-op.

The supposed decline of Southbridge was a matter of opinion. Pro-Mitchell-Lama Leo Aria told me, "It wasn't getting worse, it was pretty nice." But privatization, Jan believed, is about "keeping up our area, . . . going up instead of spreading the projects."

Southbridge sits near the confluence of the Hudson and East Rivers at the lower tip of Manhattan. Continue walking along the latter's wa-terfront, and you'll pass a wide swath of high-rise, tower-in-the-park housing developments. These cousins to Southbridge are owned by the New York City Housing Authority (NYCHA) and are rented to low-income New Yorkers. This is public housing: the Alfred E. Smith Houses,

Rutgers Houses, La Guardia Houses, Vladeck Houses, Baruch Houses, Gompers Houses, Wald Houses, and Riis Houses. These brick homes have their own strong histories of community and organizing, their own community rooms occupied with classes, their own untread green grass behind hedges or fences peppered with plantings under mature trees. To Jan, however, these are just "projects" to be contained. Her concerns actually have little to do with who owns and operates the buildings and more to do with who lives in them:

> As [residents] got to the lower end [of the income spectrum], unfortu-
> nately, things that come with that were crime, drugs. There was more
> of a drug problem. People letting people in and out through the base-
> ment buying and selling, there was some of that. . . . Projects have been
> shown—they clearly don't work. They just become areas of crime and
> fear and you know. They brought neighborhoods down rather than
> incorporating people into safe, clean neighborhoods.

Residents of public housing in New York are overwhelmingly people of color. Less than 5 percent of NYCHA's 350,000 official residents identify as White. Naumann may not know that most scholars of public housing would contest[12] the conventional takes on "the projects" that she spouted. But she is almost assuredly aware, as a lifelong New Yorker, that evoking the "projects" as a stand-in for a neighborhood of crime is a not-so-silent, racist dog whistle. In Jan's opinion, Southbridge was "teetering," with only two ways to tip: (1) privatize, and the co-op gets to decide who is welcome there, or (2) remain affordable and regress. To her, avoiding decline meant excluding the people associated with public housing: low-income Black and Brown families.

Marissa Heine, a fellow real estate agent and Southbridge resident, blew that dog whistle a bit harder when she recalled a problematic tenant in her building:

> I'm not trying to discriminate here but, I mean, it's a socioeconomic
> thing. I mean there are more people with more problems in South-
> bridge. It was more diverse. . . . There was one person who had an
> apartment there, and this guy brought unsavory people in, he actually
> was evicted. . . . Scary thugs. Matter of fact, when he left, . . . I was
> offered his apartment. It was a bigger apartment. I was on a waiting
> list for one. I was like, "Oh God, I could never take that apartment,"

because people would be coming out of jail and ringing that door-bell at two o'clock in the morning. I'm not going to be like, "Oh, you know, Dave hasn't lived here in five years. Sorry you're doing 10 to 5 or whatever."

The references to the projects, prison, "thugs," and discrimination all carry strong racial overtones. Pro-Mitchell-Lama cooperator Eva Sacks said of Southbridge: "Racism is sometimes quite overt here and other times subtle, the way White people can be subtle about racism. It goes beyond 'some of my best friends are. . . .'" Heine's and Naumann's comments mostly opted for the overt, save for one of Jan's that initially left me scratching my head. As we wrapped up our conversation, I asked her if she supported the government building affordable, subsidized housing, like the kind she's just maligned (and lives in). "Yes," she said, fiddling with the cross on her necklace, her transition glasses finally untinted. "You just have to say what's what." I got what she meant by that a bit later: that the government has to say which complexes are low-income housing and which are middle-income housing, and ne'er the twain should meet. While in theory low-income residents could buy into a Mitchell-Lama co-op, the up-front purchase of shares is a steep barrier to most residents of public housing, who average $24,600 in annual income.[13] (Mitchell-Lama co-op homeowners citywide average more than double that at $58,400.[14]) The term "low-income" seems to operate for Jan as it does for many, as a euphemism for Black folks.

There are good arguments for relaxing the income limits attached to social housing or eliminating them altogether. Doing so can expand the political constituency for social housing that, in the US, has been deliberately narrowed through means testing. The more people that can and want to live there, the more support social housing is likely to have. Relaxing income limits could also create communities with less stigma and, arguably, greater stability. Jan's argument, however, does not stem from either of those rationales. In the light of her desire for income-segregated communities, Jan's reminiscences about early days at Southbridge, among the Italian, Irish, Jewish, and German originals from elsewhere in Lower Manhattan, feel less like pure nostalgia and more like a claim to Southbridge by the almost entirely White cast of original cooperators. She expressed concern with a growing East Asian presence in the co-op, spillover from Manhattan's nearby Chinatown. Of the pro-privatizers she said, "We wanted it to be like what we remembered it being, more like the co-op our parents had moved into." Privatization maybe couldn't fully restore that past, but it could keep the wrong people out and allow the co-op to decide who the right neighbors were.

Southbridge isn't the first Mitchell-Lama co-op where this kind of exclusionary argument held sway: in 1989, the *New York Daily News* reported that at Forest Park Crescent in Glendale, Queens, "Proponents of privatization have been circulating flyers warning that if the buildings don't go private, homeless people will take up residence and begin urinating in the halls." The *Daily News* article quoted Frederick Mehlman, an assistant attorney general at the State's Real Estate Financing Bureau, who wrote that the allure of eliminating waitlists for co-op units through privatization is often rooted in racism: "This way, you don't have to admit blacks and Hispanics in the building. That's what happened in a Brooklyn building (Contello I in Bensonhurst, the only Mitchell Lama co-op in the city that has gone through the conversion process). It's a very important reason for going private, but they don't like to mention it."[15]

Controlling the racial makeup of Southbridge could also temper Jan's own embarrassment with her home, a shame stemming from how certain other New Yorkers saw her affordable housing. I sensed only pride in Southbridge from Jan, until she described a conversation with a fellow parent who branded Southbridge "an economically undesirable location." Jan took issue with an outsider criticizing Southbridge in this way, even as she herself questioned her complex's desirability and socialized with many neighbors who regarded Southbridge as just "one step up from the projects." This latent sense of inferiority had, as Marissa and others told it, crept up in recent years as Lower Manhattan had turned into a neighborhood catering to tourists and the rich. "We used to be able to go to the Gap and actually buy stuff. Now, I just walk down the Seaport, and [see] $600 pairs of shoes."

They felt the neighborhood gentrifying around them, felt that they were becoming "an island in the middle of the island." Income is, like affordability, relative. Even as folks like Leo Aria could see that "we had money; we had everything going for us," other Southbridge residents didn't want to be the poor kids on the block next to the new bank vaults masquerading as glassy, residential towers. Southbridge's beige bands of concrete and gray aluminum balcony railings mark the complex as more closely related to public housing than those sheer jewel boxes. With privatization, at least the people would be different. It could be a cleansing bath, a chance to wipe away stigma by setting Southbridge dramatically apart from other forms of affordable housing in the city—and making the likes of Jan and Marissa feel less out of place in a rich district.

Their desire to exclude people of color stemmed from concerns about not only appearances but also money. With the prospect of privatization on the horizon, they saw the arrival of lower-income and "more diverse" residents as a threat to their future property values. Southbridge would become another installment in the long history of White homeowners excluding racial others and low-income individuals from their neighborhoods to supposedly preserve the property values they claim to have earned.[16] As Jan said, "There's still that neighborhood element that can bring down property value. I mean, I'm lucky I'm on a good floor."

Harvey Marshall would later tell me that his pro-privatization campaign got a boost when people like Jan saw the demographics of Southbridge changing. She and Marissa championed privatization not only as cooperators looking to add to their personal ledgers but also to help other people buy and sell those assets—duel motivations that hearken back to another torrid episode in the history of racialized real estate in the US—blockbusting. The term refers to the practice, at its height in the '50s and '60s and technically outlawed in the Fair Housing Act of 1968, of real estate agents urging White homeowners to sell at low prices before Black residents moved into the neighborhood, warning them that those future Black neighbors would ultimately depress the value of their homes. (Agents would often then sell the same homes to new Black residents at significantly higher prices.)[17]

At Southbridge, a similar if less overt message seemed to circulate: privatize soon or watch your home's potential privatization value fall as undesirable neighbors move in. You can take the building out of the market, but you can't take the market out of the building. Or racism out of the market.

In 2007, with the first hurdle toward privatization—the feasibility study—cleared, Southbridge Rights and its supporters began to believe that their goal was within reach. This hope was also paired with a vigilance born of past experience. Some who'd been involved in the privatization push in the '80s knew that without sustained board control their progress could be easily undone. If the votes on the next two hurdles—the creation of a more in-depth plan for privatization and then a decision on whether to implement it—were to stall or fail, they'd be right back to where they started. They'd have to start over with a new feasibility study, and they'd likely have a less motivated crew of supporters to give them the governing power required to push things forward again. The May 2007 board elections were crucial: if the pro-privatizers could gain control of the co-op board, the next obstacle would be scalable; if not, they could lose everything they'd gained.

Tom Goldhaber had up until then largely avoided board politics. The feasibility study spurred a new interest in co-op governance. "I saw an opportunity to put a nice asset on my balance sheet," he told me. So he decided to run for the board. He secured a Southbridge Rights endorsement, alongside five other pro-privatization candidates. It was clear that the organization was asking people to vote not for their candidates per se but for their stance on one issue. "SOUTHBRIDGE RIGHTS SAYS BOARD ELECTION IS CRUCIAL TO CONTINUED PROGRESS TOWARDS RECONSTITUTION," their newsletter shouted. When the ballots were counted on May 1, 2007, pro-privatizers, Goldhaber included, claimed four of the five seats available. For the first time, pro-privatization cooperators held a majority on the Southbridge Board.[18]

Their pro-Mitchell-Lama opponents took heart that it hadn't been a full sweep. They comforted themselves with a derivative of the same idea that Southbridge Rights had used to sell the feasibility study: the vote only showed people wanted more information, more exploration of their options. It didn't mean they necessarily supported privatization, right? But now the trend was set. The possibility of privatization was not going away anytime soon. On the contrary, it would become the chief focus of the co-op's governance.

Harvey Marshall, who would soon ascend to the board presidency, recalled that the outcome of the vote cast a kind of chilling effect on other co-op issues. Pro-privatization cooperators subordinated other co-op concerns—where their dog could pee, the aesthetic of the hallway—to the cause of privatization. Myopia, in a word, set in.

Leo Aria, who prides himself on the comprehensive governing approach he'd taken as board president in the '90s, knew that privatization was now the be-all and end-all: "For some it was their singular purpose, almost to the degree that they fail to recognize that we are also a human community with many other broader concerns." The pro-privatizers' capture of the board, ostensibly licit, was reminiscent of the allegations of corrupt board governance of yore. Both sought one thing: an extraction of profit from a public good. That profit was the goal of privatization was not disputed; whether it was deserved, however, was another story.

GIRL, YOU EARNED IT

I first encountered Marissa Heine via one of the mailers she'd sent out to her fellow residents when privatization was gaining steam. On the glossy postcard—depicting Southbridge at the fore, 1 World Trade Center and Frank Gehry's sail-inspired 8 Spruce Street in the back—she announced her qualifications as a future speculative apartment owner's ideal advisor: "agent of BOND New York Real Estate, New York's largest independently-owned real estate broker," "neighborhood expert," and, most prominently, "a Southbridge Towers homeowner for 20+ years."

When I walked into her BOND office just west of the Flatiron Building and Madison Square Park, she was wrapping up a call with a "keep me in mind for Paris." She then ushered me up a floating staircase to a light-filled upper story. She briefed her manager on my interest in Southbridge, who called on me to "publish Marissa's name many, many times."* As Heine and I discussed her early support for privatization, she cryptically stated, twice, "I believe in real estate."

I took that to mean that she believed in real estate as a financial asset. She'd been selling it for seven years and had been acquainted with it, as most Americans are, for her entire life. The precise weight of the statement, however, is still hard for me to grasp. It is rare to hear anyone firmly state their belief in something that most people already agree with. And hers is a pithy enough formation—"I believe in real estate"—that it conjures up many a song, from Hot Chocolate's disco hit "I Believe in Miracles" to the *Space Jam*-famous "I Believe I Can Fly." Indeed, some reference to the ascendant is common in such statements; Marissa's tune was less soulful but not far from a firm "I believe in God." Marissa, judging by the cross that hung from her neck, does.

---

*As explained in "A Note on Process" at the front of the book, Marissa is a pseudonym.

Marissa had been banking on the value of real estate since 1994, when she moved from a rent-controlled apartment in Stuyvesant Town to Southbridge. StuyTown, a sprawling, iconic city-within-the-city rental complex on the east side of Manhattan, had for decades been a bastion of rent-regulated affordability for middle-income folks until it was further thrust into the speculative market in 2006 as part of "the biggest real estate deal of all time."[19] Marissa had already traded rent control for her share in the limited-equity co-op by that point, but she didn't want to remain sheltered from the market's whims. Trumpeting the mistaken idea that Mitchell-Lamas were meant to be privatized, she told me, "I knew that someday it would go private. I mean it was designed for that, and it could have happened a lot sooner. I thought it was inevitable."

As a single mother "living close to the edge" when the prospect of privatization arose in 2005, Marissa had initially been worried that she would not be able to afford a market-rate Southbridge. This concern, however, appears to have been fleeting. She described herself as an early supporter once she realized privatization was for the "greater good." With "the gap between the uber-wealthy and middle class just widening and widening in New York City," Marissa told me, "it's just that more difficult to achieve the American Dream. I mean, it is an American tradition, right? Like pioneers—Move west. Get land."

Her American Dream is in fact linked to the American tradition of settler colonialism, where land is taken by force, and the individuals who have usurped it come to feel entitled to their ownership. It's Manifest Destiny, wherein settlers set out to fulfill their intuited duty to develop "barren" territory and reap economic blessings in the process. Pro-privatizers and their opponents both use this language. If Southbridge had its own high school, the mascot would be the Pioneers. The argument goes like this, in the words of pro-Mitchell-Lama Leo Aria:

> You're creating the community by living there. . . . Now maybe these people earned their right to acquire whatever the market will say they should get after privatization. . . . These people built this community, they built Southbridge Towers, and now they want to profit from it. I saw nothing radically wrong with that.

That folks like Aria have poured their lives into their communities cannot be denied. But did they actually build them? Aria's pro-Mitchell-Lama ally Daniel Brampton characterizes the pioneering argument—one he rejects—by employing a myth used to justify Israeli colonialism: "'There was a desert here. We made the desert bloom. Before us, there was nothing at all.'"

Many cooperators have served on the pro bono board, managing the budget, negotiating telecom contracts, keeping the landscaping tamed—the kind of labor commonly understood as implicit in homeownership. Many also contribute to the community beyond Southbridge. Aria is, for one, the longtime leader of a community development corporation, and Heine, a volunteer at the South Street Seaport Museum. But Aria's claim that little of value existed in Lower Manhattan prior to Southbridge is suspect—not the least because the same argument has been used for centuries to justify the displacement of marginalized communities. Recall the census of the area prior to its "renewal": hundreds of businesses, centers of the city's printing trade and more, lined these streets. Reach further back, and you'll uncover the oldest remnants of what was then called New Amsterdam: the tip of Manhattan is, after all, where the colonial outpost was first established.

However, there are uncanny parallels between this value-creation argument and the rhetoric of activists fighting the displacement of longtime residents in gentrifying neighborhoods across the country. Both these groups are pointing to residents and saying that those individuals *are* the community, they contributed to the shape it takes today, and they should be able to benefit from it. While both Marissa and Leo believe that they are creators of value in Lower Manhattan, they disagree on a key point: what that entitles them to. Folks like Leo regard the ability to live in an affordable community that one shaped, in part, to suit oneself as something to cherish and maintain. But pro-privatizers see their contributions to community as investments that deserve a monetary return. Not only have these cooperators earned this profit by creating the value that underlies it; they claim that this was all part of the plan. Minion maven Jan Naumann carried the same tune: "When we moved in, it was '70, '71, that was part of the deal. It was like a contract, you know? You live in this lousy area, the area hopefully will get better, and in return for you being a pioneer in this area, you will be able to purchase it and actually own it outright down the road." In other words, the profit they would reap from privatization was both promised and earned.

As privatization became more and more plausible, pro-privatizers saw the need to construct such justifications for it. Among them, this variety of entitlement to profit would prove particularly powerful.

THE RED HERRING

As Southbridge took steps toward privatization, State regulators tiptoed around the conflict inside. They spoke of having little latitude to insert themselves into the debate. Although DHCR's stated policy preference was to keep Southbridge in Mitchell-Lama, the agency employees tread carefully in advocating for it. The possibility of privatization was provided for (however mistakenly) under statute, after all.

DHCR was used to being buffeted back and forth by cooperators or politicians who saw its oversight as either too heavy-handed or not heavy-handed enough. As DHCR's Mark Colón put it, "If there's something going wrong, they want more involvement. But other times when they have a plan to do something . . . they all of a sudden want to be treated more independently." Pro-Mitchell-Lama residents expected more support from the agency; pro-privatizers wanted DHCR to stay the hell out of their business.

DHCR did have one potentially transformative carrot with which to entice developments to stay in Mitchell-Lama: money. Not exactly free money, but a subsidized mortgage that could go toward window replacements and brick repointing, heating system upgrades and sustainability improvements. In return, the co-op would commit to staying in Mitchell-Lama for another fifteen to thirty years. That exchange of cheap money for years of affordability is familiar. It is a trade that underlies most if not all affordable-housing programs in the US, from the Low-Income Housing Tax Credit to the original formulation of Mitchell-Lama.

To be eligible for privatization in the first place, co-ops had to pay off their original subsidized mortgage provided by the State or City. Southbridge had already done that, refinancing its mortgage with a private lender. The new pro-privatization board wasn't about to go back. It rebuffed DHCR's advances, untempted by lower interest rates. Pro-Mitchell-Lama types like James Szal saw this as another example of the board's myopic approach. They only had eyes for privatization. Pro-privatizers, though, saw the State's offer as a kind of entrapment. One false step, and they'd be stuck with the State. Board control was not only crucial to continuing to move their campaign forward; it was also necessary to prevent pro-Mitchell-Lama cooperators from brokering a deal that would put privatization out of reach for another couple of decades.

Politicians also weighed if and how to get involved. Many observers and advocacy groups, including the Southbridge Towers Cooperators for Mitchell-Lama, expected them to. Not one election cycle has gone by in New York over the past decade without a prominent politician calling for the creation of Mitchell-Lama 2.0. Such is the respect and popularity of the OG program. But intervening in privatization fights operates under a different political calculus than promoting new developments. This was the problem that then Manhattan borough president, future City comptroller, and perennial mayoral hopeful Scott Stringer had to solve in real time.

It was common for politicians to come to Southbridge. The complex boasted a huge voter base, and its community room made for an ideal campaign spot. Stringer's visit to the co-op just prior to the feasibility study's public release in 2006 was run-of-the-mill in that sense. That is, until he started to speak of the importance of preserving Mitchell-Lama and urging the cooperators before him to play their part in doing so. "About three quarters through the meeting someone challenged him," Eva Sacks recalled. "He backpedaled so fast I thought he was going to bump into the wall. He mid-stream changes his tune. . . . It was like whiplash." The *Downtown Express* reported that Stringer then "made it clear that residents have to look at the issues closely and decide together what is the best action to take."[20]

From then on, politicians stayed away from the issue. According to James Szal, they did so out of the stated rationale that Southbridge residents "have the right to vote and decide their fate." It was a democratic take in a sense but one that assumed that the only people who had a stake in these co-ops were the cooperators themselves. The logic narrowed the frame, leaving the larger neighborhood and the city as a whole, already suffering from a chronic shortage of affordable housing, on the outside. The majority of shareholders were, indeed, at least privatization-curious. As Szal said, "If you were looking for votes, would you piss them off?" Leo Aria, however, was unsympathetic. He regarded politicians' neutrality as "almost immoral."

Had DHCR decided to oppose privatization more aggressively, it would have been doing so without political cover. The very scale of Southbridge had made privatization politically radioactive. Elected officials had seen the power of Mitchell-Lama voters before. The mammoth population of Co-op City gave it leverage not just in local elections but in negotiations with the State over ballooning mortgage payments resulting from construction defects. This led to the largest "rent" strike in US history, lasting from June 1975 to July 1976 and nearly bankrupting the State's housing-finance agency. Politicians with little skin in the game were keen to associate themselves with the strike, popular as it was with such a large voting bloc. In that case, however, the cooperators' cause had been to keep a Mitchell-Lama's maintenance affordable to its residents, current and future.[21] The movement at Southbridge was decidedly different.

With politicians and the State taking a hands-off approach to Southbridge's privatization, the whole process took on a bureaucratic, technical air. The residents' dueling sides focused their arguments not on social impact but on money: the profit to be made, the carrying charges that could rise. When the State made its occasional statements, it followed suit. There was no lobbying for preserving this public good, no discussion of how the public's investment in this housing might eventually go to line the pockets of a mere few. Southbridge's decommodified homes were discussed with dollar signs, and DHCR offered only financial incentives.

With the feasibility study complete, the Southbridge Rights–controlled board now needed cooperators to vote to clear the second hurdle to privatization: funding the creation of a "Black Book." This hundreds-of-pages-long offering plan would detail the ins and outs of what leaving the Mitchell-Lama program and converting to a market-rate co-op would mean. The specialized labor involved in creating the Black Book would cost the co-op an estimated $300,000. That was in part because the offering plan had to take on a very particular form, given how the State's attorney general's office interprets privatization. To the AG, the privatization of a co-op's shares constitutes an offering of financial securities, just like shares in Apple or Boeing on the stock market. As such, Southbridge's offering plan would be laden with a surfeit of disclosures, and the AG's office would be scrutinizing the assumptions and promises it made regarding the co-op's and cooperators' financial prospects before approving the plan for distribution.

This promised scrutiny came as a relief for pro-Mitchell-Lama cooperators who'd been harping about just these issues in the feasibility study. But, like the State's offers of cheap debt, the AG treating Southbridge's bid to "go private" just as it would a company going public also unintentionally branded the complex as just another financial scheme. The process adopted the lingo of securities trading, including the term for the draft version of the eventual Black Book. In finance-speak, this document was called a "Red Herring." Like the origins of that term—the pungent, dried fish rubbed across a trail to confuse a hunting dog—the State's approach to privatization via DHCR and the AG's office distracted from the key ethical issues at hand. That pro-Mitchell-Lama co-operators soon chose to follow a similar line, arguing for Mitchell-Lama on purely financial terms, proved a pivotal surprise.

CHAPTER 4

An Offering

For the pro-Mitchell-Lama cooperators at Southbridge Towers, 2007 ended much as it had begun: in defeat. The co-op-wide vote on the second step toward privatization—whether to finance the draft offering plan, known as the Red Herring—had resulted in a definite "yes," leaping over the majority threshold needed with room to spare. If they were to prevent privatization, they would need to hone their strategy, bring in reinforcements, or both. By this point, they knew winning a majority in the third and final vote in the process—on accepting the offering plan and thus officially privatizing—was unlikely. Fortunately, they didn't need to. Privatization would only pass if more than two-thirds of cooperators voted for it. The hurdle loomed, and the pro-Mitchell-Lama side sought to do just enough to keep Southbridge in the program: grounded, stable, fundamentally unchanged.

The Southbridge Towers Cooperators for Mitchell-Lama were not the only ones fighting such a battle. Theirs was but one front in a larger war against the privatization of Mitchell-Lama co-ops and rentals across the city. On rentals, the citywide Mitchell-Lama Residents Coalition was bringing together tenants to lobby their corporate landlords to remain in the program or to secure fair treatment and avoid eviction should their development go private. Many of the co-op battles were being waged collectively under the umbrella of the Cooperators United for Mitchell-Lama (CU4ML), a loose alliance supported by the nonprofit Urban Homesteading Assistance Board (UHAB) that had led anti-privatization groups to victory at other cooperatives.

So to UHAB and CU4ML, some of the pro-Mitchell-Lama cooperators turned. Daniel Brampton was one. A retired public employee, he was a relatively new cooperator who had nonetheless quickly become embedded in co-op politics once privatization raised its head. Early on in the debates, a pro-privatization board member with whom he was "cordial" had initially sold him on cashing out. That lasted about as long as it took him to get home to his wife, who, as he told me, set him straight, pointing out

> how unfair it was to the people who were on the list to get an apartment, how unfair it is to the people who are of moderate income and here we were, people who had benefited by getting these apartments. . . . As soon as my wife said that, not for the first or the last time did I understand that I was lucky to be married to her, because she broke it down for me.

That Brampton then looked to involve a wider coalition in the co-op's debate is on brand. He attributes his anti-privatization stance not just to his wife but to his university days at Providence College, where he "got known in the civil rights community."

> When a group of people were starting the first Rhode Island chapter of [Congress of Racial Equality or] CORE, I was invited to become a charter member . . . I went into the Peace Corps in Ethiopia. After Peace Corps, I got involved in a whole lot of peace demonstrations and stuff like that.

He ended up a case worker in New York, then a supervisor, and retired in 1995, earning $41,000 in his last year before a pension and social security kicked in to pay his bills. Like Harvey Marshall and James Szal, two other retired public employees living at Southbridge, Daniel was keeping busy. When he saw the well-oiled machinations of Southbridge Rights that the pro-Mitchell-Lama side was up against, he felt compelled to jump into organizing once again. He was frank about the fissures among the pro-Mitchell-Lama cooperators and the fact that privatization didn't follow the formula of a superhero plot, good guys vs. bad: "It wasn't just the terrible people against the wonderful, ethical people, considering some of the wonderful, ethical people were not even that wonderful or that ethical." But he cared about the issue, and before long, he had joined the board of CU4ML.

Unlike Brampton, others in the pro-Mitchell-Lama camp weren't so sure about bringing such "outsiders" into the Southbridge debate. This was one of many strategic points on which ostensible allies disagreed. Brampton recalled the fractious early meetings he'd organized, keen to "find the generals" for the pro-Mitchell-Lama faction:

> They all start arguing with each other. Everybody has a different version of what went on in the past, and people start saying "When I ran for the board in 1992, you opposed me" or whatever. . . . It's like all of a sudden meeting this dysfunctional family . . . and everybody says "Don't trust him" or "You know what she did when I . . ." I came home, and I literally had a really bad headache, but I said okay, you know, we're gonna go ahead with this thing.

Despite the disagreement, they called in CU4ML to give an open-invitation presentation to residents, based on the organization's experience at other co-ops. CU4ML's spokesperson would be Dick Heitler, an unabashed Mitchell-Lama adherent. He was board president of another Mitchell-Lama co-op, a former assistant commissioner at the City's Department of Housing Preservation and Development, former vice president at community development powerhouse Local Initiatives Support Corporation, and a day-in, day-out professional supporting low-income co-ops across the city through UHAB. For pro-privatization cooperators, these credentials read not as evidence of his expertise but as a series of threats. An anonymous flyer shoved under doorways prior to Heitler's presentation in May 2008 warned:

> Mr. Heitler *will not* be giving a factual, *non-partisan* speech. Mr. Heitler represents low-income people from undesirable housing situations (otherwise known as slums). He could be the prime source of your future neighbors under Mitchell-Lama. He advocates that [Southbridge Towers] should be an extension of a social agency, by providing housing for the very same people who do not meet the minimal requirements for NYC housing projects, such as former prisoners, drug users, and convicted felons.

In truth, Heitler's talk largely stressed the financial risks that privatization would present to current cooperators. But he did also argue that there were nonfinancial reasons to say no to privatization—the same reasons that animated the Southbridge Cooperators for Mitchell-Lama: to maintain social housing for folks like them who needed it. He invoked the Rochdale Principles developed outside Manchester, England, so many years ago and urged cooperators to be true to Mitchell-Lama's original intent: to provide fair, democratic homes that serve a public purpose. These nonfinancial arguments, however, gave pro-privatizers the opportunity to brand Heitler and CU4ML as "ideological." This charge would sour some of Southbridge's pro-Mitchell-Lama folks on making any such nonfinancial arguments at all.

YOU SAY IDEOLOGY, I SAY ETHICS

Leo Aria of the espresso was one such soured. Indeed, by the time we spoke, he'd decided that some of his supposed anti-privatization comrades were not just "ideological" but "crazy":

> They were obsessed. Much of it was ideologically based. Socialist, communist, whatever the hell they were. They could not conceive of a family wanting to prosper, and I was more family-oriented. . . . The non-privatizers are crazies. They're crazy. They span the spectrum of ideology, and some of them are very hard to tolerate because they're closed minded and naïve about who they're living with.

Despite his pro-Mitchell-Lama stance, Leo not only believed that he and his neighbors had earned the profit that could come with privatization; he also implied that such a belief was nonideological, natural, beyond the realm of politics.

It is true that the typical American would think of commodified housing as a given. Federal policy has for decades financialized housing and painted profit and wealth from homeownership as normal. Leo, though, isn't your typical American. Not only did he live in social housing; he had an established reputation as a fighter for affordable housing—the result of his past activism in a nearby neighborhood. Still, profit via housing, even social housing, has become so normalized that it has taken a vaunted place in unquestioned culture. Ideas in opposition to that dominant culture were thus "ideological."

Aria's opinions aside, the question remained of what the pro-Mitchell-Lama side's future strategy would be. He avoided calling his fellows, Brampton and Eva Sacks among them, "crazies" to their faces.

Instead, when it came time to debrief about Dick Heitler's presentation, he claimed that moral arguments wouldn't work. Sacks remembered: "His position was you can't put your values out there. People don't care about values. People care about money; they care about what's gonna be in their pockets; they care about what they can 'own.'" She and Brampton were inclined to agree.

"The ethical, while it motivated me, didn't seem to motivate a lot of people," Brampton explained. One neighbor had been moved enough to write letters to a local weekly newspaper about the economic risks associated with privatization. "But when I tried to talk [to that neighbor] about the ethical problems," Brampton recalled, "he laughed in my face. He said 'Listen . . . if there's a million dollars on the ground and I have to stoop down to pick it up, I'll do that.'" Pro-privatizers like Harvey Marshall were willing to admit the validity of the argument that future generations should have access to Mitchell-Lama housing, but they just as easily brushed that off as ideological, as if that was somehow disqualifying. Another pro-privatizer, Jacob Villa, went so far as to say that, "ideologically, I'm with [the pro-Mitchell-Lama shareholders] 100 percent." But in the nonexistent realm beyond ideology, he clearly wasn't.

Ethical, "ideological," arguments were out. The debate around privatization at Southbridge would be waged strictly on matters financial. Chris Hresko, the third-generation cooperator in his twenties who liked to evoke the Zapatistas in Mexico and the need for "praxis" in his work, began to engage more in the larger privatization debate at this stage. He "really felt that we were losing part of what the soul of this complex was." He saw the peril in dropping his side's ethical stance for the purely financial, especially as they were finding it difficult "to sell someone on what they have [rather] than the lure of what they can have." Ethical arguments, however, had become associated with "socialism and that kind of red scare mentality." So the Southbridge Towers Cooperators for Mitchell-Lama chose the same course the State had: the privatization debate would be conducted on Southbridge Rights' terms, centering the question of how either course of action would economically benefit the co-op's current residents. The "Let's get rich!" argument for privatization could go unquestioned as normal, while the ethics of doing so would be confined to the negatively connoted realm of ideology. Money, one way or another, would rule the day.

Organizing experts, however, would observe that the pro-Mitchell-Lama faction had committed a cardinal sin of political messaging.

In allowing their opponents to set the framework of the debate, they reinforced a narrative that worked against them. Groups like Race Forward, the Narrative Initiative, PolicyLink, the Culture Group, and Community Change have for the last decade been advocating for social movements to devote greater attention to cultural strategy and narrative design. They explicitly counsel against making the very move that the pro-Mitchell-Lama side had made.[1]

Many campaigns make this mistake. It's born of the simplistic view that we make decisions strictly out of self-interest and that organizing for change requires appealing only to that self-interest. As the organizers of Race Forward's Butterfly Lab put it, "People are complicated and, by nature, hold contradictory beliefs and values. They react to stories, which activate these beliefs and values. Stories, then, are the basic unit of change. Messages are reminders of what we think and how we might choose to act. Narrative is the level at which society moves." The narratives evoked in a debate like Southbridge's, then, matter quite a bit, especially when they do battle with meta-narratives often regarded as common sense, among them the dominant American one that housing exists to build wealth. As the Narrative Initiative explains, such a narrative "reproduc[es] itself as we unconsciously repeat and reinforce it. Their invisibility makes them that much more potent."[2]

Southbridge Towers Cooperators for Mitchell-Lama and the State—both of which desired to preserve this social housing—failed to question that meta-narrative of housing as commodity. Instead, they bought into it. In doing so, they banished the narrative that housing is for living and that social housing should be available to future generations. It can be tough to thread the needle between appealing to individuals' interests and avoiding the unintentional bolstering of a damaging narrative. A group of funders for affordable and social housing have even encouraged its messengers to avoid using the term "affordable" when speaking about housing crises: "Overemphasizing 'affordable' can push people toward a commodity frame with attendant individualism leanings. . . . The central dimension for housing in people's mind is cost—which reinforces the idea of housing as a commodity."

The narrative at Southbridge was thus set in favor of the privatizers. Only one way of seeing home, and the relationship between people, society, and their homes, was espoused. Narratives "provide us with frames of reference that determine how we comprehend complex realities and define the important boundaries between what we imagine to be possible, probable, or practical," the Narrative Initiative writes. "They facilitate interpretation of the past, understanding of the present, and a vision for the future."[3] The people who hoped to preserve social housing had watered the seeds, planted by their opponents, of its potential undoing.

ALL QUIET ON THE SOUTHERN FRONT

On June 23, 2009, the first iteration of the Red Herring was submitted to the attorney general's office for review. The six-hundred-plus-page document was made available to cooperators as well, though fully grasping the density of its projections and caveats was beyond the knowledge and desire of most.

The draft offering plan was a feasibility study on steroids. It featured lengthy descriptions of all the steps to privatization, delineations of certain risks in doing so, and outlines of the benefits offered by the potential paths ahead. It included schedule after schedule of financial projections under both privatization and the continuation of Mitchell-Lama. It incorporated close to thirty exhibits: appraisals, bylaws, regulations, laws, advisory opinions, and sample ballots and leases. Lots of words, lots of numbers, across lots of pages.

Despite this submission, to the average Southbridge resident, nothing of much consequence on privatization seemed to be happening. The lack of hubbub was partially by design. Because Southbridge's board was the governing body for the company technically offering the privatized shares, they were prohibited from providing any information on that offering beyond the official plan. This "quiet period" came from securities regulations and practice, just like the fishy nickname for the draft plan. Like the review of the Red Herring itself, the gag order was overseen by the State's AG's office. Of course, unlike a traditional stock offering, Southbridge was awash in whole organizations beyond the co-op board advocating for and against privatization, all with a stake in the outcome. The quiet period would soon turn not so quiet after all.

The Southbridge Towers Cooperators for Mitchell-Lama were the most vocal. They turned their megaphones primarily to the AG's office. In doing so, they forewent the opportunity to appeal to their neighbors and engage in pivotal political education, efforts that might have been more effective. Eva Sacks, over the course of the historic presidential campaign the year prior, had stocked up on new metaphors for why privatization was downright wrong. She was particularly fond of a proverb from First Lady Michelle Obama's Democratic National Convention speech: "When the door of opportunity opens, we don't pull up the ladder behind us." These quotes went unused; the Mitchell-Lama lovers instead focused on the myriad ways the Red Herring was incorrect or misleading. Like the moral arguments they kept sheathed, the group also shielded support they were receiving from CU4ML from public view. Together, the two groups combed through the draft offering plan, flagging everything from mistakes to what they saw as willful lies, and fired off letters to the AG detailing the defects. Brampton recalled that they had "a huge number of criticisms":

> Apparently, the assistant AG read them because the first time . . . the board got an answer, it had over 300 objections. 300 criticisms of what the [Red Herring] said and did not say; what was accurate, what was not accurate. Then the board . . . had to redo the Red Herring to answer the objections.

The deficiency letter the Southbridge board received from the AG on March 31, 2010, numbered precisely 328 items needing correction. Pro-privatizers like Jan Naumann brushed off the deficiencies: "262 were typos, you know? They were totally insignificant." They were hardly typos. The substantial revisions took months to address, and the momentum that Southbridge Rights had built up with win after win was now finally starting to flag. The cogs of bureaucracy and the reasonable time it took the board's consultants to put together the offering plan gave the impression of a process that may never end. Half a year after the deficiency letter, the board submitted a revised Red Herring, dubbed the "Black Lines" in securities speak.

Almost five years had elapsed since the first feasibility study in 2005. Co-op members had passed away while waiting for privatization. Kids had grown up, and like Chris Hresko, started to get involved in co-op politics. Southbridge Cooperators for Mitchell-Lama figured that the longer they could keep the offering plan in draft phase, the more unlikely its transformation into the Black Book would become. More delay also meant more board seats up for grabs. There was more time to sow doubt. They launched a newsletter called *Ponder This*, releasing the first issue in January 2011. Below the mind-numbing details on the changes to the Red Herring following the AG's deficiency letter—the mechanics of gift transfers of apartments, an increase in projected real estate taxes, and the cost of a proposed interest-only "balloon" second mortgage—the pro-Mitchell-Lama faction hammered home their argument: "Remember: We cannot un-privatize. If you have doubts, vote NO. The issue can be revisited at a later time."

As Southbridge Rights waited for the AG's approval, it not-so-subtly expressed its feelings about the "quiet period." "Wish We Could Say More," a headline read in their newsletter. "It's a bit complicated, and unfortunate, that our opponents feel free to say whatever and distribute whatever they want, while we observe this quiet period," they complained. The pro-privatizers were aware of their disadvantage. So they called on those not hobbled by securities regulations to speak on their behalf under the banner of a new group, the Concerned Shareholders for Transparency. They soon let bold headlines beckon to their readers—"$15,000 or $350,000? Which Would YOU Prefer"—from foyer floors and hallway bulletin boards. Jacob Villa remembers that he was one of "between eight and twelve of us who got together, and for about eight months planned and set up meetings, and did all kinds of things: went door to door, made up pamphlets, handed those out, put them on doors." His involvement would be felt not just at Southbridge but at other Mitchell-Lamas as well.

GET MINE

There are six Pret A Mangers within a fifteen-minute walk of Southbridge Towers, and Jacob Villa and I ended up at one of them on a rainy Thursday night. He'd been a hard man to pin down. Between his job, tai chi classes, jam sessions, and weekend ski trips, our conversation was hard to fit in. Villa grew up in Southbridge. His parents still lived there, as did his cousin, a Southbridge Rights–affiliated board member. Villa, now about thirty, had since flown the coop: after ten and a half years on the waitlist, he has his own studio apartment in the Mitchell-Lama cooperative East Midtown Plaza. Much like his former home, East Midtown was in the midst of a privatization debate, and his new blood and past experience were tapped by members of its board.

> Somehow, they found out about me. I don't know how. No, seriously! I get a phone call about a year and a half ago: "Are you Jacob?" "Yes." . . . They're like, "we're trying to push [privatization] here, we

need your help, we need information you can give us." Luckily, I kept all of the pamphlets that we wrote out, I had copies of them, and I gave them to him like, "these will all work. Just change the names and whatever." I gave them ideas. They said, "you should run for the board." . . . I said "no, that's the worst thing to happen, because you want me to be able to talk to people, I would have a gag order if I was on the board, so I'm not going to run."

Why someone would desire Jacob as a spokesperson was easy to see: he's conventionally good-looking. His groomed stubble and wavy black hair went well with his green Polo sweater. And he was friendly, smiling under a newsboy cap that evoked a different time downtown. Jacob was also notably younger than most other individuals deep in the Mitchell-Lama privatization debates. He still knows the ins and outs of the waitlists and lotteries:

My mother, right when I turned 18, started clipping out the newspaper things like "oh, here's one, here's one." And not even just Mitchell-Lamas, but the 80–20 apartments*—like okay, here's low-income, middle-income, blah-blah-blah. Just sign up for everything. I signed up for dozens, and I went to interviews for a lot of them.

His mother, one of the original Southbridge cooperators, had moved in to one of the co-op's two-bedrooms with a friend in 1971, then got married and had two kids while living in the complex. Jacob's grand-parents had lived there as well before passing. Then there's the cousin, who came to Jacob to spread the pro-privatization message when the "quiet period" set in. This is the kind of family entrenchment that one cooperator likened to "empire building." Though Jacob now lives at East Midtown Plaza, with Southbridge's privatization he could poten-tially be an heir to his parents' piece of that empire. And if all goes as planned and East Midtown Plaza privatizes as well, he could count two former Mitchell-Lama co-ops in his private domain.

As indicated by Jacob's decade-long wait to get into East Midtown, the odds of a New Yorker actually getting access to social housing are

---

*Jacob is referring to a housing program in which the State provides tax-exempt fi-nancing to multi-family buildings in which at least 20 percent of the apartments are set aside for low-income residents. The remaining 80 percent are rented at market-rate.

long. When I spoke to him, a recent lottery for three hundred new, permanently affordable rental apartments in Brooklyn's Prospect Heights neighborhood had drawn over ninety thousand applications. Regardless, Jacob appeared irked that he hadn't gotten an income-restricted apartment sooner, on account of having too much money to qualify:

> One time I was perfect. This apartment: I had the right salary, I had everything, and this was the only time they did it. Like I would give them my savings information and checking in the banks and stuff just to see. And they added my savings to my salary, and they were like "oh, you make too much." I'm like, "hold on a second. That's not right! I'm making this; that's what I've saved over the years, but that's not what I'm making."
>
> "Well, we combine them, and the percentage is too high."
>
> I said, "so you're punishing me for being fiscally responsible. I don't understand. Like, what if I put this money in a bond or a CD? You wouldn't even know it's there. This doesn't make any sense." And I lost out on that. I lost out on probably 20 apartments over the ten years, and I had basically given up.

Despite this frustration, Jacob championed the benefit that the Mitchell-Lama program has provided him personally. He was among the many pro-privatization residents who were quick to voice their support for government provision of affordable housing. Unlike the majority of his peers, he was also willing to acknowledge that privatization would dissolve the very public good that he claimed to support. "There's a part of me even now that says, [privatization does] kind of get rid of some middle-income housing. But then I remember that we should've had much more built over this span, and it's not on us to preserve it. It's on the City and the State."

In short, he wants to have his co-op and eat it too. As good-natured as Jacob appeared, the entitlement he brought to this debate left an unpleasant aftertaste. He felt entitled, first to ownership of a rare, income-restricted, stably affordable apartment, and second to the value he could reap for himself, should his proselytizing lead to privatization. He thinks the State and City should provide more housing like Southbridge, but he absolves himself of any responsibility to maintain such public goods. The contradictions abound. Such is one way that pro-privatization folks like Jacob have managed their competing ideas of what and who their housing is for, dominated by the conviction that profit is the norm and anyone who seeks it need feel no responsibility for casualties suffered along the way. After all, Jacob said, profiting "is not bad. Everybody's a little greedy. . . . We're humans; who wouldn't?" According to this view, greed isn't just rational; it's all-natural, containing no trace of ideology.

Jacob's working of the system may be unsavory, but it is hardly unique. A cottage industry of blog posts offers tips on how to navigate the Mitchell-Lama system for one's utmost individual benefit. Recall the illicit handbag mavens of Luna Park or—to expand the lens—the far more pedestrian fleecing of the public that's an American rite of spring. Come April 15, you can expect a neighbor or two to proudly confide that they got creative with their taxes, just as my grandfather was said to do. Whether for reasons ideological, financial, or a convenient combination of both, tax evasion remains an open secret of American life, often regarded as necessarily strategic or admirably savvy.

The pro-privatization residents of Southbridge expressed a sentiment similar to what many Americans must feel when they hear their neighbors brag about withholding contributions to our public coffers. They looked out their windows onto a changing neighborhood flooded with capital, where those with means—often companies—purchase properties that appreciate in value. That value is then cashed in on a vacation home or rolled over into the next deal. My grandfather's unreported cash income must have looked paltry next to the 20 percent of income that the wealthiest 1 percent shield from taxation—roughly $175 billion stolen from the public every year.[4] Thus the "everybody else is doing it" argument made by teenagers everywhere becomes justification for further privatization. Folks watch as the wealthy distort the tax system to make more money while those of modest means face greater scrutiny than the worst offenders.[5] A "get mine" response kicks in. In New York, the so-called Capital of Capital, these co-ops exist in an environment that can be particularly hostile to the principles that underlie them.

In pushing privatization, Jacob wasn't just holding the door so market forces could slip in, and his beliefs weren't purely a function of growing up in a capitalist society. True, he spent his early years a ten-minute stroll from some of capitalism's icons, the New York Stock Exchange and the World Trade Center, but so did Chris Hresko and many other anti-privatization cooperators. What's more, they were all living in that area in the early 2010s, when those icons found their antipode in a privately-owned park seized by Occupy Wall Street and the 99 percent. Despite the varied nature of their environment, the "spirit of capitalism," an ideology that justifies people's commitment to that economic and political system and encourages profit seeking,[6] surrounds them—us—all.

In a freeze-thaw cycle of many years, this spirit has leaked its way into the cooperatives themselves. The anger that some pro-privatization Mitchell-Lama cooperators carry—born of a sense that a double standard is at play, that they are being held to higher standards than everyone around them—is an open wound through which market logic can spread. Ironically, their frustration is fueled by regret over their own decisions, a nagging sense of having missed out on the riches of New York's great real estate boom.

Back in the 1960s and '70s, when Southbridge and St. James were being built against a backdrop of urban crisis that included widespread property abandonment, the City of New York had assumed a role it didn't want: that of a landlord. When owners stopped paying their property taxes and ceased any semblance of caring for their buildings, those properties were transferred to the City. To lighten its burden and entice middle-income individuals to move into disinvested neighborhoods (in other words, to gentrify poor, often Black and Brown neighborhoods), the City sold these properties to willing buyers for a pittance.[7] In a flyer to her neighbors, one pro-privatizer expressed her consternation at not having taken advantage of the crash: "I could have purchased an entire four-bedroom house in Brooklyn for the same down payment [as her buy-in to the co-op]. I know this because I was looking back then, when houses in Flatbush and Midwood cost about $35,000. Those same houses today are worth nearly a million dollars each!"

The writer didn't elaborate on the reasons she decided not to become a brownstoner. Her appeal was confined to what could have been, a highly relatable strain of what-if thinking that everyone engages in to some degree. But one can assume that, at the time, she reasonably saw the co-op as the better deal. A permanently affordable apartment in a new, modern building seemed to outshine the dilapidated, if once regal, houses in neighborhoods the City had all but abandoned. But once their values appreciated to heights unforeseen, she jumped at the opportunity to profit from her Mitchell-Lama unit. That she was, for now, unable to profit from her home struck her as unfair.

As privatization grew more likely, the Southbridge Rights flyers were joined by a steady stream of literature from real estate firms. "Everybody from Corcoran to Douglas Elliman to Compass . . . were constantly sending mailers. . . . We were probably getting two to three pieces of mail per day," Chris Hresko told me. These intrusions were difficult to keep out and were emblematic of the wider drip of capitalist logic into the co-op. As Jacob implied, this larger build-up could have, perhaps, been arrested by better maintenance from the government agency that oversaw the co-op—a role the State had chosen to abdicate. Jacob and many other pro-privatizers found it convenient to pass on their significant individual responsibility to higher governments, but he knew full well who the co-op's true governors were: the board of directors, of which his cousin was a part. One law governing Mitchell-Lamas is clear that their boards are largely responsible for ensuring that the co-ops serve a middle-income population. Flip to subpart 2 of part 1725 of subchapter C of chapter IV of subtitle S of title 9 of the Codes, Rules, and Regulations of the State of New York, and you'll find this:

> Members of the board of directors of the housing company, whether rental or cooperative, bear a *significant public responsibility*, since they operate under a State-aided program and effectuate public policy by encouraging the building and operating of housing projects for families of moderate income.[8]

Of course, as with the details of privatization in the voluminous Red Herring, most cooperators will never come across that law. The regulations that govern a seventy-year-old housing program aren't a common beach read. These laws, and the archived documents that outline their intentions, must be imparted through political education in order to have power. This is what the Rochdale Principles call for and what had been provided to Mitchell-Lama residents in the 1960s, with pamphlets outlining the ABCs of co-op living. But by the time Daniel Brampton arrived in 2004, such educational materials had ceased to be part of co-op life. Chris Hresko observed this shift across the three generations of his family who lived in Southbridge:

> I think that the change over time really indicates that you have that loss of the transmission of value, and that understanding of value, and the education that comes with running a co-op. If you think about

cooperatives, it's about having this centralizing culture that keeps the co-op solvent and operational. And that once you start losing the principles and what the guiding thoughts of what this co-op meant, then you start to lose the threads. It starts to fray.

A limited-equity cooperator in Washington, DC, echoed this concern: "If people don't have the cooperative education . . . to create a cooperative, a collective owner consciousness—then yeah, something else is gonna happen, and we're gonna lose that housing."[9]

Without maintenance like political education, the prevailing commodification of housing can take root, resulting in a situation where cooperative principles must be reintroduced. Hresko analogized it to the work of extremist deprogrammers: "The only way to deradicalize is to start addressing these points and to start restoring our social responsibility." At Southbridge, though, the only education in action was one of realpolitik and the slog it created.

DEMOCRACY, OR WHO ARE "WE"?

With each revision, the offering plan continued to be beset by deficiencies. "Every time they would correct stuff, there'd be more stuff coming back from the assistant AG. . . . So that delayed things for a very long time. Made me quite happy, and I'm sure drove the board to distraction," Daniel Brampton, the former CORE member, described with a spritely grin. The everyday life of the co-op churned on as well. Then, in October 2012, Hurricane Sandy devastated Lower Manhattan. This put a pause on Southbridge antagonisms, privatization-related and otherwise. "After crises, people come together," Eva Sacks explained. Having lived through both 9/11 and Hurricane Sandy, she had at least two first-person data points from which to generalize. That togetherness was, however, short-lived, and as it waned, the board began to feel more acutely the perils of being in charge. With the privatization process entering its eighth year, Southbridge Rights was wrestling with critiques on two fronts: a barrage of tracked changes in the document they'd been elected to produce and the gripes of cooperators unsatisfied with their wider governance of the co-op.

The pro-Mitchell-Lama crew were especially primed to criticize the sitting board, but they weren't the only ones complaining. Marissa Heine, the real estate believer, wanted to be on the board herself. Some of this desire appeared unabashedly self-serving. Should privatization go through, she'd be well-placed to broker sales. At the same time, Marissa expressed genuine concern for her home: "I'm a single, working mom. I show up at the community board meetings. . . . My heart and soul is in this community. I'm not going anywhere." When Marissa wanted to provide the board with her perspective on co-op matters, she found it difficult to get a hearing. "They closed the board meetings; there were no minutes there. . . . I guess I'll never know [what was discussed] until I get on that board." Southbridge Rights may have been effective in keeping the privatization process running despite stalwart opposition, but that wasn't all that mattered to Marissa. She also wanted transparency and dialogue. The board's new opacity, and what she saw as a kind of dictatorial turn, caused her concern.

Former board member James Szal was quick to seize on this sense of unease among cooperators. He presented to me as a fervent lover of democracy—or at least its questionably representative, nationalistic American version—what with his eagle-plastered T-shirt and the way he waxed poetic about the beauty of the Stars and Stripes waving throughout the US post-9/11. With the board meetings now less accessible to cooperators, he resolved to open up another space for discourse, founding the Southbridge Towers Shareholders Association in 2012. Szal described it as a general-purpose entity created to deal with the consequences of the board's myopic and undemocratic leadership, "to provide a badly needed forum to discuss any and all issues pertaining to our co-op and its governance." The group drew about fifty to sixty residents to its meetings. Szal remembers:

> I helped out a lot of people with issues, because maintenance was tough. One woman had a leak, and they were charging her. It was from her neighbor's apartment, and it came down into her bathroom and ruined the wall. . . . They ripped her wall open to cut off the pipe and to fix the leak but never fixed the wall and told her that she had to pay. . . . Whenever there's someone who's willing to speak up, and just because they were concerned about my voice in the community, they listened; management and the board, as much as they dislike me for doing what I did, would listen and would pay some attention.

The board and their backers made their displeasure with Szal widely known, its intensity increasing in direct proportion to his group's growing criticism of privatization. They did their best to banish the association, barring Szal from holding meetings in the Southbridge community room. He didn't have to go far to find another venue. The association's regular attendees walked a couple of hundred additional yards to St. Margaret's House, a senior affordable-housing development right next to Southbridge. The added steps didn't significantly reduce turnout, but they surely stoked the group's ire. Meanwhile, the board began to explicitly criticize Szal's group, as demonstrated in a *President's Update* that Harvey Marshall sent out to the Southbridge community:

> The "Shareholders Association" is not a truly democratic voting or-
> ganization. In fact, it was invented by its self-appointed president to
> promote his anti-privatization agenda and his desire to be elected to
> the real Board of Directors. This "association" does not hold annual
> meetings to elect directors, and does not elect any officers. As a matter
> of fact, it doesn't even have any officers other than its "president." If
> this were truly a "Shareholders Association," it would hold an annual
> election at which all cooperators would have the chance to elect di-
> rectors and to set it on a course that reflects the values and objectives
> of the majority of Southbridge residents, not just those of a vocal and
> strident minority who oppose privatization. Fortunately, a true share-
> holders association does exist at Southbridge. It's called Southbridge
> Towers, Inc., and all shareholders are members.

The board, not content to simply discredit its opposition, also sought to put down the stirrings of disillusionment with their leadership. "Our opponents say that we are a one-issue board that only cares about privatization," a flyer promoting one of Southbridge Rights' board election slates stated. "Well, for [a] 'one-issue board,' look at what we've accomplished." They touted their non-privatization wins: a new, higher-rent lease with the supermarket tenant on site; the hiring of a full-time director of security and a social worker. The list went on. But those who disagreed continued to speak up. They got the same treatment that Szal's shareholder association had. Southbridge Towers Cooperators for Mitchell-Lama was no longer welcome to meet on their co-op's property. The board, it seemed, would brook no dissent. The exile of the pro-Mitchell-Lama groups "made us pariahs," Leo Aria said, with a hint of respect for the opposition's campaign. However fraught, it was run effectively. "The board was smart," he remarked, a bit dour. "Smarter than I was."

Leo and his fellow pro-Mitchell-Lama cooperators harped on the board's perceived failings, and even those who supported privatization shared a sense that the board was undemocratic. Producing evidence for that charge, however, was complicated. The board was elected. Each shareholder had one vote. Residents with bigger units, who paid more for their share, didn't have a greater say as they do in some speculative co-ops. True, the board may not have been as responsive as the handful of cooperators who came out to their meetings would have liked, but whether this rose to the level of tyranny was a matter of opinion. The Southbridge Rights–endorsed candidates had, after all, been quite explicit about their intentions to realize privatization, and they were ardently faithful to them as they kept winning seats, year after year after year. Adele Niederman, a CU4ML stalwart, told me how DHCR and HPD tended to respond to cooperators who voiced concerns about the board: "They said, 'the board was democratically elected.' We said, 'But they're unfair.' 'Well, life is unfair. You can figure that out.'"

In some circumstances, debate over the direction of the co-op was stifled less by the governors themselves and more by the passivity of the governed. As Harvey Marshall put it, "It's apathy. People come out more when they're angry or they're anxious about something." Tom Goldhaber pointed to residents' satisfaction with the co-op's affordability and noted that "a lot of people don't have that kind of time" to be involved in Southbridge politics. Daniel Brampton agreed that, with the exception of the privatization issue, most people were not active in the cooperative. Folks like Heine and Szal were a vocal minority, with the majority otherwise caught up—often understandably—in the complexities of their own lives. Some were undoubtedly fed up with co-op politics altogether and retreated, caught in a self-fulfilling cycle of ongoing disillusionment and disengagement.

Some residents hardly even knew what Mitchell-Lama was. There were folks who thought privatization had already occurred. There were others who misunderstood how Mitchell-Lama worked. That did not stop them from creating and distributing flyers that implied that if the co-op didn't privatize, Southbridge would be cast out of the program eventually. "Where's the Mitchell-Lama contract?" one read, beneath a clip art evocation of a 1980s Wendy's ad that asked plaintively, "Where's the beef?" Co-op education was lacking and with it the informed decision-making that must underlie any functioning democratic enterprise.

The situation—a mix of misunderstanding, disinterest, and a big potential payday—was ripe for manipulation. Pro-privatizers accused their opponents of fearmongering; pro-Mitchell-Lama residents claimed that Southbridge Rights was deliberately glossing over the risks in its plan. Meanwhile, the Red Herring continued to accrue pages, amendment on amendment, attempting to address deficiencies now numbering in the five hundreds. Pro-Mitchell-Lama folks continued to lose their bids for seats on the board. Eventually, the question arose of whether the elections were being tampered with.

Pro-Mitchell-Lama cooperators discovered that there had been a massive increase in proxy voting during elections. These proxies were similar to an absentee ballot; you could fill one out ahead of time rather than go to the polls on Election Day. Chris Hresko thought there was reason to believe that pro-privatizers were essentially harvesting proxy votes from vulnerable cooperators, getting them to sign a blank ballot and then selecting their candidates for them.

> They would go around and have the elderly or immigrants sign ballots, and they would fill in their names, even though that was really unethical. There was never confirmed proof of it, but there were always questions about it. So much so that the Honest Ballot Association, which handles all the voting procedures for the complex, . . . they had to implement new rules on proxies through time. They had to get to the point where they'd have to send them out later towards the elections than earlier, or they'd have to barcode each proxy, so that they weren't filled out in advance and just assigned to each apartment.

Mistrust was rampant. No longer was Southbridge's relative democraticness in question; now the question was whether it qualified as a democracy at all. What wasn't discussed, however, was whether the co-op's government had defined its constituency correctly. It seemed self-evident to most that the current shareholders were the relevant decisionmakers, the *demos* of this democracy. One shareholder, one vote was, after all, enshrined not just in the bylaws of the cooperative but in the Rochdale Principles that prefigured them.

That interpretation, however, failed to recognize a wider body to whom cooperators also bore a responsibility: not just the interests of the present cooperative and its individual owners but to those of future residents. The waitlist for an apartment was hundreds of families long. These folks could be the cooperators' future neighbors. There was a good argument to be made that the "we" to be considered in the supposedly democratic proceedings of Southbridge should encompass not only current cooperators but potential ones. This sense had prevailed in the co-ops of Denmark in the early 2000s. When those co-ops had decided to raise their prices to facilitate profit-making, they quickly came under fire, indicating to researcher Maja Hojer Bruun that the current cooperators weren't the only owners of the housing. They were instead stewards, temporary caretakers.[10]

The preservation of a Mitchell-Lama co-op, and all public goods like it, is reliant on such stewards: sometimes the state, sometimes a group of individuals like the cooperative. As the Southbridge privatization debate dragged on, this stewardship role had become increasingly obscured. The "we" for whom the co-op existed had shriveled. Harvey Marshall, with the glee of vindication, described this shrinkage in real time.

> There was a family in my building. They're artists and what not, they were some of the last people to get a two-[bedroom] from the outside list, just as the vote was coming up. So I went to speak to them about the vote and so forth, and they said "Oh, we'd love other families to have the same opportunity that we had in the future." So I said "Well, you paid $35,000 for your apartment. Your apartment's worth $1.1 million-something." They go "Yeah? Well I guess it's gonna be hard for us to vote no." It's where you're sitting.

The potential payback was too great for many to ignore. Leo Aria, the pro-Mitchell-Lama cooperator who was nonetheless sympathetic to this profit motive, saw another element at play, one that boiled down to a lack of empathy, something he considered "ideological."

> For the most part, they never internalized the seriousness of homelessness. . . . They were middle-income, working families. And that doesn't necessarily mean that they had empathy with the circumstances with people that had less than them. They were not in touch with them.

Many cooperators' empathy may not have extended to their own neighbors, had the timing of their arrival been different. It may not have even extended to a prior version of themselves. Southbridge's own success in insulating its residents from housing insecurity also had the side effect of eroding their understanding of what contemporary apartment-hunters now face. "If you watch *The Crown*," James Szal told me, evoking the television show about the British monarchy, "it's the way wealthy people grow up, without quite getting what it's like on the other side of town."

The choice put before the cooperators was a complex one, and as a final decision crept closer, they struggled between two minds. Many, contrary to an easy branding of pro- and anti-, held competing impulses, just like the artists who'd just bought into the co-op for a relative pittance, only to then support the instantaneous appreciation that months earlier would have left them on the outside looking in. As Marshall had said, it's where you're sitting. From the outside, the choice of whether to privatize looks freighted with privilege, responsibility, and a sense that some cooperators, despite the risks, have a win-win on their hands. Seated within, under Southbridge's low ceilings or shadowed by the balcony above, the choice carries the angst of a horrible tradeoff.

This begs a rather undemocratic question, or one of democratic scale: Should this decision even be up to cooperators? "No" was the clear answer in the original Mitchell-Lama legislation, "yes" the alluring answer for stalwarts of the self-governance enshrined in the co-ops and for those who believe that ownership should mean total control. Because social housing is a public good, however, the question of whether it will continue to exist should rest with the wider public.

As things stood, though, the choice, with all its ramifications extending far beyond the co-op, remained solely in the hands of the Southbridge residents. To some, it felt like a burden. Choice, however fetishized in American life, is not always a luxury after all. As cooperators endured another year of agony over their collective decision, inching closer to a possible finish line, choice had in many ways poisoned the cooperative well.

HIGH-RISE

Almost eight and a half years since the vote on the feasibility study concluded, a relieved Harvey Marshall sent a one-page memorandum to every apartment: "I am pleased to inform you that on April 10, 2014, the Office of the Attorney General accepted and filed the offering literature to dissolve Southbridge Towers as a Mitchell-Lama cooperative and reconstitute it as a private cooperative." The Red Herring had now morphed into the imposing Black Book, the believed-to-be final version of the red-pen-ridden draft that had been under review for years. The tome would be printed shortly; the back-and-forth with the AG's office was temporarily over, in part due to a change in the office employee handling the matter, a switch that Marshall attributed to complaints made by Southbridge Rights. The final vote on privatization was initially scheduled for June 22–24, just a couple of months away.

The years-long wait gave way to a burst of harried mobilizations that the complex had never before seen. With it came conflict. Southbridge Towers Cooperators for Mitchell-Lama met to discuss their options and strategy. They would have two final chances to kibosh the privatization campaign: if they won enough seats in the May board elections, they could further stall the process; or, come June, if they garnered enough votes against privatization, they could stop it from clearing the two-thirds threshold necessary for implementation. How they should approach these two opportunities was less clear. They'd succeeded in delaying a process that folks like Marissa Heine had thought was inevitable, but now their strategy of critiquing privatization from a financial perspective appeared to be making few inroads. With their last stand approaching and their die-hards—or "the crazies," as Leo Aria called his comrades—weary, the pro-Mitchell-Lama folks could have used some backup.

Cooperators United for Mitchell-Lama made themselves available. "CU4ML offered to help us any way we wanted and said we will not do what you don't want," Daniel Brampton recalled. He took that message back to the leadership of Southbridge Towers Cooperators for Mitchell-Lama, which included Leo Aria and Eva Sacks. Brampton was thrilled to share the news that help was on the way. Some of his allies, however, thought that bringing in CU4ML would backfire. "No," Brampton remembers Aria responding, "You don't understand. You know, I've been at Southbridge for many more years than you. I know the people here and they will simply resent outsiders." Aria, the "general" whom Brampton had recruited, was now calling rank. Debate ensued, and Sacks walked out after a spat with another cooperator. And when the leadership group raised hands to vote on whether or not they would accept further help from CU4ML, Southbridge Towers Cooperators for Mitchell-Lama chose to go it alone.

The moral support, let alone the campaign prowess, would leave a void. As the pro-Mitchell-Lama bloc dealt with their own infighting, marked by unilateral moves and strategic disagreements, they also had to suffer increasing hostility from their pro-privatization neighbors. "People insulted me; people swore at me. I had a death threat from a really crazy guy who lives in that building," Brampton told me, looking wistfully out the glass panes of Squires Diner into the courtyard. He added, with his characteristic levity tinged with exhaustion, "the only thing that really bothered me is a couple of women insulted my wife and that does hurt. It was simply because she had committed the crime of being married to me."

His social circle was one of many at Southbridge forever touched by the co-op conflict. Compared with what had been, Chris Hresko found the new normal baffling: "For the longest time, [Southbridge] . . . operated like a close-knit, family complex. . . . There was really no 'us versus them' mentality. It was very like, 'We just want to make sure that this is a good community that we can live in, that our kids feel good, that it's safe, and that it's a good environment.'" Privatization broke this equilibrium. "It really fomented stratification amongst family, friends, and groups of people," said Hresko. He started to get in arguments with his friends' parents. He began to hesitate before conversing with anyone whose stance he didn't already know. He watched as his grandfather, also an anti-privatization stalwart, fell out with old friends, including the guy that had filed his taxes for years. He witnessed "families who were cut down the line, where sisters did not talk to each other because one was for [privatization] and one was against it."

"It made no sense to me," he said. "It felt very much like dystopian fiction." So much so that he invoked J.G. Ballard's *High-Rise* to describe his home. The 1975 novel's jacket copy describes an apartment complex where "cocktail parties degenerate into marauding attacks on 'enemy' floors" and "society slips into a violent reverse" with the rich tenants "hell-bent on an orgy of destruction."[11] Only through that satire could Hresko express what he felt to be the overall tenor of the privatization debate, one that was destroying the community he'd always known.

Attacks came through all channels. On social media, someone would post about a robot vacuum for sale, only to have it followed by a screed on why a certain neighbor was a liar. Pro-Mitchell-Lama cooperators accused the board and their supporters of spreading "gross information and outright lies." A Southbridge Rights leader called his opponents' flyers "fear-mongering disinformation" from "local propagandists with their own agendas." Jan Naumann claimed that the pro-Mitchell-Lama camp "preyed upon the elderly and the fixed-income people" with "absolute lies" and that they followed James Szal "like a cult leader." Other pro-privatizers characterized their opponents as corrupt communists looking for opportunities to reap profits from the co-op. Some of the pro-Mitchell-Lama folks, no doubt upset by those accusations, hit back with hyperbolic attacks that leaned into the dystopian. One comment on a news article described privatization in Hannibal Lecter–like terms: it was "cannibalism eat your old & eat your young & then eat the one next to you because even cannibals are not safe with other cannibals they are just livestock next meal [*sic*]."[12]

Those residents who had yet to make up their mind on privatization, who were truly trying to make an informed decision, faced a daunting task. They could attempt to wade through the legalese, spreadsheets, and assumptions contained in the then almost one-thousand-page Black Book, or they could rely on the information thrust in their direction on an almost daily basis. Tom Goldhaber, a decided privatizer, described how "when you come home at night, you have like six handouts at your door. . . . You don't know which is right and which is wrong." In a flyer, a pro-Mitchell-Lama board member who had distanced himself from the organized groups counseled cooperators to dismiss both sides:

> PLEASE don't ask someone from the Mitchell-Lama group and at the same time don't ask someone from Southbridge Rights. One will tell you that the sky will fall and there would be chaos and the other will tell you that Southbridge is paved with gold and all your financial concerns will be a thing of the past.

Heeding this advice was difficult. Anyone who had a strong opinion to share was generally aligned with either one side or the other, and there were only two choices available: stay in or get out. At the board level, all sitting members and candidates were either people who called themselves "independents"—in reality, pro-Mitchell-Lama—or were endorsed by Southbridge Rights. With the co-op's final privatization vote approaching rapidly, there also wasn't much more time to reach a final decision.

The voting days for the open board seats arrived quickly. The second day, May 6, started with a cool morning that gave way to the 70-degree weather of spring. Winter had largely been forgotten, the last patches of snow in the co-op's shadowy corners had melted away, and the streets of the Financial District were bustling again after months of commuters rushing straight from subways to lobbies.

In the Southbridge community room, next door to the breakfast crowd at Squires Diner, employees of the Honest Ballot Association—founded by Teddy Roosevelt, they say—booted up touch screen machines behind cardboard barriers. More than eight hundred fingers would tap the names of five neighbors for three-year terms on the co-op board. The mood, tense for months, was now jittery. This board election was one of the most important votes in Southbridge history, second only to the privatization vote expected to take place that summer.

It had been two weeks since hefty copies of the Black Book had arrived at the management office for cooperators to pick up. Since then, Candidate's Night in the community room had devolved into hissing and moaning as opposing neighbors made their pitches: five "independents," with James Szal of the Southbridge Towers Shareholders Association among them, and five candidates endorsed by Southbridge Rights.

As the final day of voting wore on, barcoded yellow proxy ballots in pale green envelopes were dropped into cartons in the community room, adding to those mailed or slotted into a special lockbox the previous week. Rumors of ballot harvesting continued to circulate. The Honest Ballot Association remained on high alert.

Interested residents soon descended to the co-op's ground level in faux-wood elevators and gathered in the community room, lit by a fluorescent glow under a drop-tile ceiling. Official business began at 8 p.m. Robert's Rules prevailed as daylight faded and the plate glass walls turned opaque. All attention swiveled to the podium, behind which *il Tricolore* hung for the annual Italian Heritage Celebration. The Honest Ballot Association rep presented the unofficial results: Southbridge Rights had dominated again, sweeping four out of the five open seats.

Those dissatisfied by recent governance but in favor of privatization had evidently resolved to hold their noses a little longer. James Szal had missed out on a seat by five votes.

FAMILY BUSINESS

With the board vote now settled, the last stand for the Southbridge's pro-Mitchell-Lama contingent would be the vote on the Black Book. Holding fast to their finances-centric strategy, these cooperators redoubled their efforts on exposing the risks of privatization, countering their opponents' overly optimistic projections, and ensuring that the Black Book was as thorough as possible. As before, they bought themselves some more time. They appealed for amendments to the Black Book, which resulted in the privatization vote being moved from June to July. The revised July date soon got pushed as well after the anti-privatizers took issue with a summary of the plan distributed by Southbridge Rights. Its claims required walking back and further caveating in yet another amendment. The offering plan tome kept growing. The staccato delivery of each revision—v1, v2, v3, v4—weighed down cooperators' bookshelves and gave the printers, lawyers, and accountants involved steady business.

The flood of information continued to baffle residents. A cooperator commenting on a post on a pro-Mitchell-Lama blog expressed exasperation: "It is almost impossible to get to the truth here. Both sides exaggerate and put forward their own agenda. . . . God help us if we find out later if we make a mistake and everything falls apart for the middle-class family."[13] This question, of how Southbridge's families would fare, was on many minds. Cooperators *were* willing to consider future beneficiaries of this housing after all—if they were kin.

That's not surprising. The ideology of American homeownership has always been deeply intertwined with a vision of a very particular nuclear family. Real estate is family business—the stuff of memories and inheritances, a perceived birthright for some and the site of familial death for others. The ties that bind us to a place called home can be one in the same, or just as strong, as those that bind us to generations past. I'm reminded of an early scene in Joe Talbot's film *The Last Black Man in San Francisco*, when titular character Jimmie Fails is pegged with a bell pepper while painting the trim on a house he believes his grandfather built by hand. The house has now fallen out of the family's hands, but Jimmie is still maintaining the property on the sly, when the deeded owners aren't home. Occasionally, he is caught in the act.

Jimmie didn't end up with the family house, and under Mitchell-Lama, cooperators' children may not either. Unless they meet certain criteria prior to a share being passed on—living in the apartment for two years, sharing finances with the shareholder of record—the apartment goes to the next name on the waitlist. That, of course, hasn't stopped families from building dynasties in a complex anyway, but the policy remained a sore point. Many cooperators wanted to be able to pass down their place, even though they and their children had already reaped great financial benefit from the low-cost housing over their long tenures in the complex. With Southbridge boasting enough elder residents to earn the guttural acronym NORC—a naturally occurring retirement community—the question of succession upon residents' inevitable, final departure had earned pride of place in the debate.

The pro-privatizers were quick to appeal to this concern. Who doesn't want to leave their children better off than they were? The impulse is deeply relatable and far more socially acceptable than the unabashed pursuit of riches. The argument for familial wealth building graced reams of flyers distributed through the complex. One nonagenarian was so fiercely in favor of privatization that she dictated a statement in Italian for her daughter to inscribe on a flyer with her photo attached:

> I am a long time SBT resident and I am 90 years old. I am voting YES for privatization. I was born in Italy and I moved to NYC to pursue the American dream. When I was left with a young daughter to raise on my own, I figured the dream would never be realized. But now we, as a community, have the chance to make the American dream a reality for us all.
>
> Why am I voting YES? Family! Family is the most important thing in my life. I want to live the rest of my life knowing that even though I had to work hard, harder than most in order to raise a child on my own in NYC, that finally, even if it took 50 years, I will be able to leave my daughter with something that I never thought would be possible. I will be able to rest peacefully knowing that my daughter will have opportunities in her later years that I could never have.
>
> Even if I did not have a daughter, I have nieces and nephews and cousins, and I would still vote YES to leave them, my Family, with some-

thing that they can have for their futures! And isn't that the American dream? To live a fulfilling life and, when the time comes, to leave your family with MORE than you had in your life? By voting YES, by going Private, we can ALL fulfill our American dreams.

It may have been her *nonna* vibe, but this resident's desire to provide for her family struck such a universal chord that accusations of ill-begotten profit seemed to slide right off.

Where that vision for privatization was aspirational, a cherry on top of a fulfilling life, other residents were filled with regret.

After living away from Southbridge for a number of years, I returned to help take care of my mother when she began having significant problems with balance after 9/11 and a series of brain surgeries a few years later. Despite miraculous recoveries and great success in therapies at NYU Medical Center, she had setbacks and was rendered unable to walk. I had neither the physical strength to lift her into her wheelchair nor the money to hire full time help, nor did my sister. That wouldn't have been a problem if she had the ability to get a home equity loan to fund assistance at home. But we were not a full-equity co-op. So she didn't have that option.

So at the end of her life, my mother eventually needed to be in nursing care instead of living at home. The decision was entirely the result of financial limitations, but it greatly impacted her quality of life. It hurt to see how long she often waited for an attendant to shower and dress her, and how after additional hospitalizations, bedsores ultimately led to her demise. Worst of all, although she was not incontinent, she was forced to wear diapers because these facilities didn't have enough staff to take her to the bathroom unless she could get herself to the toilet. Thinking about that still makes me feel both horrified and sad.

Access to money for medical contingencies is just one reason that full equity would have been a great boon for us. It's too late for my mother. But if you are reading this, it's not too late for you! Even if you don't want to sell, by owning your apartment you will be able to tap into the equity as needed and have that peace of mind—whether to paint, refurbish and do repairs; to make those dream travel plans; pay for your grandchildren's education; or just "age in place" gracefully, knowing you can afford the care you require. I wish that had been true for my mother.

The flyer presents a potent argument that will resonate with many folks who own real estate but are strapped for cash. In a country where ever-higher healthcare and eldercare costs fall on families to cover, the owned home represents the key, or only, resource to allow for dignified aging or the chance to get well. Political scientist Herman Schwartz notes that, as risk continues to be shifted from institutions to individuals, housing investment has become the substitute for a proper welfare state.[14] Mitchell-Lamas can provide affordable housing to the middle class, but it can't plug all the holes in our social safety net. As families are forced to turn to GoFundMe and credit card debt just to get by, why wouldn't cooperators look to privatize a public asset for the same reason? Borrowing against your home equity is an imperfect solution, to say the least—you may risk foreclosure should you be unable to pay it all back with interest—but that equity nonetheless is precious money on the proverbial table, to take or leave.

In the American mind, the home is tender for emergency care, for the kids' college fund, for retirement. When the government doesn't provide for such basic social maintenance, people seek myriad ways to put the dimes together to afford what's needed. If doing so means cannibalizing the kind of public resource that they may wish existed to fulfill their other needs, so be it. Of course, that is the individualist approach to personal challenge. One might hope that this pain would instead be channeled into the kind of organizing that could win government-supported eldercare years down the line, but one can hardly fault residents for looking at their options. Public goods will be threatened in a larger system where private needs are unmet, where the short game of survival supplants the long game of justice.

Eva Sacks, however, busy churning out *Just the Facts* newsletters for Southbridge Towers Cooperators for Mitchell-Lama, was quick to point out that the social acceptability of profiting from a public good still cannot fully justify privatization. She readily empathized with her neighbors who wanted to leave something to their families; she counseled them to "leave them something that you've earned. This is not something you've earned." While she did not fault certain cooperators, her friends among them, for supporting privatization as a means to escape trying personal circumstance, she stopped short of extending the benefit of the doubt further: "I don't think there were 1,649 stories of individual need to justify that." Her comrade Daniel Brampton, too, got where such folks were coming from, up to a point: "I don't think you have to be the most empathetic person in the world to say 'well, I kind of understand that.' . . . I was much more sympathetic than somebody who says, 'I don't care. I'm gonna get wealthy. I'm gonna get rich!'"

Brampton and Sacks did not discount the personal and familial concerns that were driving some of their neighbors to support privatization. Rather, they recognized that the folks on the waitlist were also unlikely to be able to avail themselves of similar sources of funds for emergencies or the intergenerational transfer of wealth. Their universe of obligation was much broader; they saw their fellow New Yorkers as the rightful heirs to their social housing. To folks like Eva, one pro-privatizer's exhortation to "vote for privatization for the benefit of those you love" was just a moralized twist on another's blunter statement: "It's very simple. Either you want money or you don't."

OFFICIAL (DIS)INFORMATION

On the spring-like day of July 29, 2014, Southbridge residents made their way north to Pace University, in sight of the stark-white City Hall and the grand Municipal Building, to hear more about the money they did or did not want. It's a short walk, ten minutes max if you're really taking your time. The slab and tower of Pace is after all one of a piece with Southbridge; both were designed to boost the fortunes of the neighborhood when they arose from the Brooklyn Bridge Southwest Urban Renewal Area in the 1960s and '70s. Many residents probably would have preferred to spend that kind of night on their balconies—those with a view of the Brooklyn Bridge possibly continuing New Yorkers' intrigue of the week: wondering who'd swapped out the bridge's usual 10' x 19' Stars and Stripes with white flags of apparent surrender.

But, for some, the intrigue at the meeting that evening in the Michael Schimmel Center for the Arts was just as tempting. The consultants hired by Southbridge's pro-privatization board to put together the Black Book would present its contents in brief, with questions and answers to follow. Management expected a crowd. They instituted a two-person-per-apartment cap. Those left wanting one of the 750 seats occupied earlier in the season by Ravi Shankar enthusiasts would have to settle for a recorded version in the community room at a later date.

The meeting ran on time, but the privatization vote it was meant to precede was once again behind schedule. The attorney general had recently ordered further corrections to the Black Book. The fateful vote was postponed again, now to the end of September, but the meeting to ostensibly explain the legal muddle of the offering plan to a lay audience went on. Stuart Saft, the real estate lawyer in charge, took the stage before the rising half-moon of red seats, beneath the scalloped arches that, when lit just so, evokes a setting sun. In short order, James Szal of the Southbridge Towers Shareholders Association, fed-up with the presentation, left the hall.

His departure did not go unnoticed, and co-op wide flyers would soon allude to it as a knock on Szal's reliability. The remaining seven-hundred-plus cooperators, meanwhile, witnessed Saft's explanation of the offering plan, various points of which contradicted the vetted language of the Black Book. This was spin, as the pro-Mitchell-Lama squad saw it, by the privatizers' paid representative. They took note, gathering fodder for their own flyers that would liken the presentation to a sales pitch for a time share. It was, they would claim, laced with misrepresentations: there's no friable asbestos in the apartments; you'll be able to get a reverse mortgage; the worst-case financial scenario had a 0 percent chance of happening. The risks of privatization brought up were theoretically possible, cooperators remember Saft saying, "but your probability of that occurring is far lower than being hit by a meteor." For Southbridge, however, this metaphor might not have carried much weight: the terrorist attack that covered their home with toxic soot and the hurricane that had flooded their ground floors just two years prior had also seemed improbable. After two and half hours, cooperators headed home.

"YOU CAN'T DEPEND ON CLAIMS MADE FROM THE GUY ON THE STAGE!" James Szal stressed in follow-up missives, countered by privatizers who described him as a "general naysayer about absolutely everything that happens," according to Jan Naumann. She complained that Szal and his peers were distributing incorrect information, were lying for their own benefit. "Whatever your reasons for being against it, if it's ideological, middle-income housing should stay, that's fine. But you don't give people the wrong information when it comes to their finances and their future health and stuff. That's just really wrong," said Jacob Villa. Szal retorted that his information was a necessary counterbalance to the pro-privatizers pushing optimistic future scenarios that were, by definition, speculative.

Everything felt up in the air, including the security of home that Southbridge residents had long counted on. This was especially so for Szal and members of Southbridge Towers Cooperators for Mitchell-Lama. DHCR had at least forced the co-op board to allow them to hold their meetings in the Southbridge community room once more, ending one form of exile. But their status as deplorables was reaffirmed in other ways. Daniel Brampton received threats, shouted across courtyards and anonymously left on his voicemail. Szal was a target as well: "I was out on the campus here in our mall area. And I was approached by a fellow, who doesn't need to be named, who proceeded to tell me that . . . if I managed to stop the privatization, I wouldn't be around to enjoy the victory. I had several people who approached me aggressively, let's say." Jan Naumann remembered those threats too. "I was really afraid that [Szal] was going to get assaulted or worse. I'm just surprised he's still walking and talking," she told me. Her small smirk, however, evinced her sense that such an outcome would have amounted to Szal getting what was coming to him.

Szal was nonplussed. "Now understand something," he began calmly, "I've taught martial arts and combined combatives for 50 years. I know how to handle myself." For added protection, though, Szal made sure that he had "other avenues of coverage": allies who he could call upon "to set them straight as to what might happen if they didn't stop threatening me." Such was the atmosphere in which the final vote on privatization finally arrived.

CHAPTER 5

A Right to Profit

The lead-up to the vote brought more of the same campaigning tactics. The flyers. The complaints. But an edge of finality now gripped Southbridge. The attorney general had determined that the Pace presentation had been peppered with misrepresentations—two dozen, to be precise—and this caused further postponement of the final vote as a second amendment to the Black Book was made to correct the claims. The vote would happen once and for all at the end of September 2014, culminating with a final day of voting on the 30th. While the stalwart campaigners of the various internal advocacy groups held the line on their messages, cooperators who'd stayed out of the fray for the preceding nine years now had to choose sides. If they didn't, they would forego their say in the most consequential decision of the co-op's history. These nonaligned powers, small in number though they may have been according to CU4ML's Adele Niederman, were the key to maintaining Southbridge as social housing or turning it into a valuable commodity.

Some read the CliffsNotes: the summaries of the Black Book circulated by Southbridge Rights and Southbridge Towers Cooperators for Mitchell-Lama. Some went to the real thing, the doorstopper of an offering plan guaranteed to weigh the eyelids of even the most interested, the most savvy. Some felt out their trusted neighbors, their accountants, their children. Many kept their inclinations as close to their chests as possible. As Leo Aria put it, "One way or the other, we have to live together, so be careful how you express yourself and that it's not too personal." The best way to maintain relationships that bridged the partisan divide at Southbridge was to never, ever let slip which side held your allegiance.

The cooperative body's exhaustion was palpable. At least the vote would close this Southbridge chapter, some thought. There was no indication, though, that Southbridge Rights would close up shop should the vote fail. Southbridge Towers Cooperators for Mitchell-Lama touted this as a reason to spurn privatization: "Doubts? Vote NO. Privatization can be raised again but leaving Mitchell-Lama is permanent," their flyers read. Should the "no" vote prevail, pro-privatizers would be able to try again in a year, but they would have to go back to step one: the creation of another feasibility study. The process would start again from scratch. The very thought of another nine-year debate, of hundreds of thousands more dollars spent on lawyer and accountants' fees, may have even swayed some to the side of privatization. At least then the co-op could get back to normal. At least then each and every co-op decision—from dog shit to elevator repair—would no longer be seen through the fun house mirror of privatization. To some, leaving Mitchell-Lama looked like the only path to closure, the only escape from nine of the most annoying, draining years the co-op had ever known—even if the fight for privatization had sparked that slog in the first place. The privatizers' strategy was in some ways reminiscent of national Republicans' approach to shrinking the federal government: defund and discredit it until they could "drown it in a bathtub." Maybe things *would* get better if the Mitchell-Lama era ended, if only by way of taking Southbridge out of its long-standing limbo.

By the time of the final vote, the scope of the "we" to be considered in Southbridge's democratic exercise had long been set: the focus would be on the desires of cooperators only, not future residents or the wider city. But behind the scenes, the board was assessing the voting rights of those cooperators who fell into a gray area. At any given time, there were usually some units in transition: a current occupant had died and a family member was trying to assume shareholdership through succession; someone had moved out, leaving their apartment and share to the next eligible waitlist candidate. There were also those cooperators who had fallen out of the wider co-op's good graces. They were behind on their maintenance fees or involved in a lawsuit over apartment repairs. Should these folks—the delinquent bill payers, the new residents just coming in, the family members whose succession claims were not quite complete—be able to vote? More importantly, should those shares be included in the all-important total from which the two-thirds threshold for a winning tally would be calculated?

The board had requested clarification on these matters from DHCR. Pro-Mitchell-Lama types were wary of how the board and the management company would assess eligibility. It seemed reasonable that no one would receive voting rights from shares in transition. The co-op itself technically owned these shares until a new shareholder was approved. Mitchell-Lama advocates, however, questioned if the board was stalling to keep such shares in limbo—not to try to change the vote's equation, but to pad Southbridge's coffers should privatization pass. The co-op could sell those shares in transition for big money. With no individual shareholder to claim the profit, the co-op would receive 100 percent of the sale price, a significant boost from the 28 percent flip tax. That'd be a tidy sum with which to offset the rising maintenance costs that pro-Mitchell-Lama co-operators had warned about. Such a strategy of warehousing apartments for a post-privatization payday had been tried at other co-ops, but it had to be done delicately to avoid the censure of regulators.

The cooperators in arrears, meanwhile, were seen as more likely to vote against privatization. These shareholders were often lower-income and as such would generally be more secure if Southbridge remained in Mitchell-Lama. Excluding these shareholders from voting could knock a few votes from the pro-Mitchell-Lama side.

The calculus, really arithmetic, of who should be counted was most fraught when it came to determining the two-thirds threshold. This was set not based on how many shareholders had voted, but on the number of total eligible shares. A no-show was counted like a "no" vote. If the shares unattached to eligible voters were included in the overall tally, the pro-Mitchell-Lama faction would have a built-in buffer before voting had even started. Each side had valid points to support including or excluding these shares, but only one side controlled the board and therefore the process. The call was made to exclude forty-four in-limbo shares from the equation, and DHCR expressed no qualms about it. This was the kind of fine-tuning happening in the background, unbeknownst to most Southbridge residents. But if anything was clear from this backstage jockeying, it was the sense that the final tally would be incredibly tight.

While some residents prepared for this eventuality by making threats, others sought to mend fences. A pro-Mitchell-Lama cooperator who'd stayed away from the organized groups struck a tone of relief that the battle was nearly over. "The one good thing is we will finally, one way or another, reach a conclusion," he wrote in a flyer. "Good luck to each and every one of you."

The alchemy of property value is something one gets a crash course in when living in New York City, or in any American city where boom and bust wreak havoc, which is to say most. My first New York lease in 2011, as a stereotypically fresh college grad lured northward from the Carolinas, was for a cramped three-bedroom, shared with two others, in a sixth-floor walk-up on the Lower East Side, the same neighborhood from which many original Southbridge residents had come. Half a block down the street, the Hells Angels marked their headquarters with coned-off parking spaces and tarp-covered motorcycles. Within ten months of my arrival, our building was sold for mega millions, and every resident received a notice that their lease would not be renewed. Capital had flooded the neighborhood long before, rebranding parts of it as the East Village, but the area's gentrification was accelerating, eating its own agents (myself included) in the process.

Back in the 1980s, that block and wider neighborhood had looked starkly different. The City's fiscal crisis was raging, and both city government and property owners had divested from this working-class neighborhood—a seat of Puerto Rican cultural and leftist movements. The results of such neglect included empty buildings taken over by the drug trade. The alphabetic avenues were colloquially rebranded with a mnemonic scale of risk: in one of many iterations, Avenue A was adventurous, B brave, C crazy, D dead. One building, at 539 East Thirteenth Street between Avenues A and B, had been abandoned by the landlord, leaving it with a blown boiler, extensive water damage, and much more to be repaired. The building was then occupied by a drug operation dubbed Outstanding. One night in 1984, gunshots rang out on the property. The NYPD arrived and cleared the building, presenting an opportunity for a different set of enterprising and precariously housed New Yorkers—a loosely organized group of squatters—to move in. They sought to create a community outside of capitalist property relations. Working slowly, they began their renovations.[1]

The residents' new collective, called 539, established the first node in an ecosystem of squats across the Lower East Side, created within buildings that had been abandoned and then acquired by the City. This scene modeled and bred an anti-capitalist approach to living, centered on communal renovation of space. They created the Nuyorican Poet's Cafe and the Fierce Pussy Festival that took over nearby Tompkins Square

Park in 1993. These proto-cooperatives—with names like C-Squat, the Germans, Bullet Space, Umbrella House, and Tenth Door, or like the building at 539 East Thirteenth Street, known by their coordinates— fought to maintain control over the property they occupied as they remade it, turning unlivable structures into homes outside the speculative market. These apartments were considered valuable for their use: an affordable place to live, to organize, to play. Leaders, like Michael Shenker, often married political savvy with construction skills: at once a mentor and strategist, he also served as the master electrician laying and mending the twisted, jerry-rigged wires that powered the squats.[2]

As oral historian Amy Starcheski masterfully documents, the squatters' commitment to such decommodified housing began to fray with time. Financial and legal pressures in the early 2000s necessitated that residents broker a deal with the City to legalize their squats into official housing cooperatives. The process prompted debates about how equity in those new corporations would be determined when a resident wanted to sell. With each circuit breaker installed and each tap into the grid, folks like Shenker had built "sweat equity"—ownership through labor. Shenker had also put his own money into souping up his apartment, earning it the nickname the "bougie squat" among some punk squatters. Many residents in Shenker's building wanted a limited-equity arrangement, like Southbridge, where the price of any apartment sale would be limited in order to maintain affordability. Shenker, facing a series of health crises and concerned about the economic future of the squatters, began to advocate for no cap on resale values, an about-face that stunned many of his collaborators. Others, however, quietly joined him. The prospect of resale, the transition from squatter to owner, and the continued demands of life beyond the home changed the tune. They had earned the potential profit.[3]

To my knowledge, no residents at Southbridge or St. James have been drafted to crawl beneath their buildings to connect it to the electrical grid. But they, too, felt they had earned the value of their homes. Their claim wasn't one based on their physical labor so much as on living in an undesirable part of town that later became coveted. That's not to say that they did not give their time and labor to the neighborhood or that they didn't stick it out in the rough times post-9/11 and post-Sandy. They, like the squatters looking to cash out, felt entitled to the value of their homes because they had put their labor—albeit very different kinds of labor—into them. They may or may not have realized that this argument has its roots in John Locke's 1689 labor theory of value, later enshrined within early capitalist ideology by the likes of phantom-handed Adam Smith in 1776. Locke argued that one comes to own property by exercising labor on a previously unowned thing.[4] Labor, in Locke's view, is the mechanism by which value is produced and ownership acquired. Smith then argued that, upon exchange of that thing, its value is determined by the labor or "energy-like quantity of work" for which it could be swapped.[5]

This conception of value, however, was long ago dropped by even the most ardently neoclassical of economists. Its inability to describe, for example, the recent tremendous increase in New York real estate value readily exposes its shortcomings. The market value of a Southbridge apartment is determined not by the work put into creating that unit, but by someone else's judgment of its worth. Value is not some objective accounting of bricks laid and community events planned; it's a subjective measure unlinked from the actual work that has produced the property being assessed. But as the final vote neared, certain Southbridge cooperators continued to take credit not just for the value of the co-op itself but for all kinds of improvements in the surrounding neighborhood. They were like out-of-touch business owners who attribute the entirety of their companies' successes to their own hard work, with no acknowledgment of all the other private actions and public investment— in infrastructure, education, and technology—that made them possible.

Such a mindset recalls another spate of federal propaganda from a key era in US housing history. Post–World War II, New York and other major cities were hemorrhaging White middle-class residents, who were being lured to the suburbs by the new federally funded interstate highways and cheap Federal Housing Administration–backed mortgages. This new White suburban middle-class and its vibrant housing market could not have existed without federal subsidy. And yet, the feds attributed the boom solely to the hard work of those individual White families.

This may at first seem like poor electoral strategy. What government doesn't take credit for the economic successes created by its programs? This approach, however, meant the federal government could also shirk responsibility for the explicitly discriminatory policies that locked Black families out of those same suburbs. Residential segregation and intransigent racial inequality could instead be attributed to the supposedly value-neutral, nonideological "market."[6] So one of the great American myths was born: that White suburbanites were earning the wealth that they were accumulating as their homes appreciated. It could hardly have been better tinder for the homeownership ideology that the government was keen to foster. The (White) homeowner was a deserving creator of the American Dream, a pioneer in the market. The renter unable to cut it, meanwhile, was a lackluster citizen at best, a leach on the dole at worst.

Jacob Villa, the suave spokesman for the muzzled co-op board and a descendant of the White middle class that had remained in the city, reported that his family had, in 1993, put down $26,000 in exchange for the shares that granted them a three-bedroom apartment in Southbridge Towers. Such an apartment could, in 2014, reasonably be expected to sell for over $1 million post-privatization. After paying the 28 percent flip tax on the sale, the Villas could take home a tidy $720,000. Then, after subtracting the $26,000 that they had originally paid for their share—the equivalent of $54,800 in 2023 dollars—the Villas would reap a profit of $672,000.

Had the Villas done $672,000 worth of labor to build Southbridge and the surrounding neighborhood? How does one separate the value of their labor from the value of the government's investments there— the complex itself, the subway, the water mains? And how much of the neighborhood's increased value should be attributed to the wider financial system of which Lower Manhattan real estate is a piece, in which apartments become a financial investment in and of themselves or a convenient depository for wealth?

Regardless of how you break it down, the main forces driving up Southbridge's value were undeniably public subsidy and market fluctuations—not the labor of the individual cooperators who possessed the property. To argue otherwise is to engage in a kind of selective amnesia of labor and trends much larger than the cooperators. That American homeowners are more often than not the beneficiaries of market appreciation, rather than the creators of value, is a truth broadly accepted today. There was chance involved, or, as the well-wishers to cooperators preparing for the vote called it, luck.

Villa did his exasperated best to convince his neighbors just how lucky they all were. One cooperator, he told me,

> couldn't wrap it around her head that the State would just give her a million dollars like that for doing nothing but voting yes. And you know, there are people who were like "oh, it's not true. Nobody's

going to give you an apartment for nothing." And we would be like "yo, it's kind of like winning the lottery. If you vote yes, you've won the lottery; you've got this apartment that's worth who knows how much money."

They just had to "BE $MART," as one man's flyer said, followed by another exhortation: "Don't throw away your WINNING Lottery Ticket!" All the cooperators had to do was redeem their prize.

As attractive as these lotto analogies were to many cooperators, they also undercut the pro-privatizers' parallel claim that residents deserved to get rich because they had created the winnings. But lotteries have nothing to do with deservingness; that's kind of the point. They are "fair" only in the sense that their outcome is arbitrary. Villa himself acknowledged the state's fundamental role in seeding this jackpot, then driving it up. Government, he implied, was giving money away. The public subsidy that had gone into Southbridge's development, and the ongoing tax abatement that made it affordable, would be theirs if only they voted to go private.

Any lottery, any luck-based game, is founded on happenstance—in this case the fact that certain families ended up in Southbridge rather than others. Luck is also intimately tied with risk: the very real possibility that you will walk away with nothing but a worthless slip of paper. That risk was what pro-Mitchell-Lama cooperators had been harping on all along. Pro-privatizer Jan Naumann knew there was a potential downside, as much as her comrades tried to obscure it. "Do I want to risk not having low monthly maintenance fees?" she asked herself. "Yeah, I'll risk it, because it looked like a good deal."

Jan's family was in a good enough financial place to be able to take that risk, as were many other pro-privatizers. That was thanks to the actual winning lottery ticket: not the opportunity for privatization but the stable, affordable home they'd enjoyed for decades. "We got our benefits right upfront" is an expression common in pro-Mitchell-Lama circles. James Szal fumed: "You were able to save up and put your kids in school. You were able to buy a second home in the country because you saved all the money that you weren't spending while your neighbors were spending it on their regular, market-rate apartments." Daniel Brampton surmised that "you had a lot of people . . . I think a few hundred people at least . . . who had already bought a second place to live in Florida, Arizona, whatever." This didn't sit well with even real estate believer Marissa Heine, who spoke of certain cooperators using their studio apartments as pieds-á-terre while they raised their kids in Florida, flouting the rule that a Mitchell-Lama must be a primary residence. Living in social housing "gave a lot of people the opportunity to buy their Hamptons house or their home in Florida. . . . [At South-bridge] you have the people with the Mercedes and the Jaguars in the garage living side-by-side to the people who are . . . getting Meals on Wheels." Many cooperators had already built their wealth, had already realized their American Dream, then exceeded it. Privatization, in the glint of that gold, looked increasingly to Chris Hresko like "stealing from the government. . . . You come in here, live in this complex, understand the ideas of its affordability . . . then afterward decide you're gonna turn back . . . and make a windfall profit on it." As prior research has shown, wealthier individuals usually lead these efforts to privatize limited-equity co-ops.[7]

The $mart guy's flyer preached the gospel of investment. "New York City Real Estate has and always will outperform every other investment known to man," he claimed. The smart thing to do, he implied, was to act the part of other homeowners who've benefited from market appreciation. Of course, what went unstated was that to "invest" in South-bridge was to dissolve a public good. It is akin to a common practice in contemporary New York in which speculative investors purchase rent-regulated buildings with loans that they can only feasibly repay if the rent regulations are removed or the low-income tenants tossed out.[8] Tenant advocates call this "predatory equity."

The $mart guy's flyer featured a clip art rainbow across the top, a pot of gold at its end. The original Irish fable to which he referred tells of a couple who capture a magical leprechaun and demand that he grant them all manner of worldly goods. The leprechaun instead tells them of the pot of gold at the end of the rainbow and how it overfloweth. They set out searching for it, following a rainbow here and a rainbow there, always seeking its end. But the pot doesn't exist; their search is endless. The leprechaun warns us: greed is not good, especially when fortune is already in your favor.

THE VOTE

The last day of the vote finally arrived: Tuesday, September 30, 2014. The heat of the summer still lingered. Ballot casting had been underway since noon on Sunday, and the unofficial results would be known a little after the polls closed at 8 p.m.

The courtyard outside the voting booths was a picture of common ground divided: blue tape marked a no-campaigning zone inside the plaza. Security personnel lingered nearby, vaguely threatening to enforce its bounds. Just outside the zone, pro-privatization cooperators sported placards and T-shirts with the simple message "Vote Yes." Known pro-Mitchell-Lama cooperators and passersby who voiced their plans to vote otherwise received less affirming messages: the occasional "Fuck You!" or "Assholes!" was heard echoing off the brickwork. It's not surprising that some pro-Mitchell-Lama cooperators chose to avoid such confrontations and vote early. Others, like Daniel Brampton, weren't around to take it in: with all the date shifting on the final vote, he found himself an ocean away, in Italy on vacation with his wife. They voted absentee; the last couple leaflets he'd planned to write went unwritten.

Their pro-privatizer foes displayed confidence. Their celebratory preparations had already begun the Saturday prior at T. J. Byrnes, the Irish pub nestled in one corner of the complex. Concerned Shareholders for Transparency, the Southbridge Rights–front group, had sent out a flyer to publicize an event in support of the upcoming vote. A smiling, sunglasses-wearing sun shone down on the invitation, the pale yellow paper carrying a cursive premonition: "Living the Dream," as if the dream of privatization had already been realized. The admission price of $20, "to cover the cost of appetizers & soft drinks," foretold an expected future of living large. Privatization's supporters would need 1,072 "yes" votes to bring it about.

The sun had long set when the unassuming white tally papers, reminiscent of cut lists for high school sports teams, went up in each building lobby. The numbers, out of 1,458 valid ballots:

YES	1,082 votes
NO	373 votes
ABSTAIN	3 votes

An eleven-vote margin, in favor of the pro-privatization juggernaut.

Screaming, laughing, and crying ricocheted up the towers' canyons. The winners rode their enthusiasm back to the same pub where they'd toasted their vision days before. They evoked the hopes of their forebears—a mother who'd passed on 9/11 whose dream had now been realized, her daughter in tears. The drinks were no longer soft, if they ever had been.

The losers retreated into their homes, the defeat hard to swallow. James Szal had company along the way. Security had been sent to walk him back, for fear that the threats he'd received would be acted upon. He and his allies were now worth money they'd never wanted. A co-operator wrote on her blog the next day: "Now I know how Charlton Heston felt at the end of *Planet of the Apes* when he finds the Statue of Liberty half buried in the ground." In the film, Heston screams: "We finally, really did it. You maniacs! You blew it up! Damn you! God-damn you all to hell!"[9]

The slim eleven-vote margin would birth an inversely voluminous amount of handwringing. What if Szal & Co. had accepted more help from the wider city movement? What if they had fought on more fronts, beyond just the financial? When Daniel Brampton logged into his email on a hotel computer in Venice to check the results, his what-ifs started compounding. "I thought maybe if I had written those two leaflets . . . I'll never know. Maybe I would've convinced eleven people who voted 'Yes' to vote 'No' and we wouldn't have privatized." While Brampton licked his wounds along the canals, his pro-Mitchell-Lama peers back home gazed out at the East River in resigned defeat, anger, and fear.

The blogger who'd turned to the cinematic to describe her melancholic fury summed up her trepidation at the dawning of this new era: "Well neighbors I'm sure the free market is eager to get you back into its clutches. I was going to say God help us all, but I'm afraid that the only true god for many at [Southbridge] is Mammon."

AFTERMATH

The day after the vote saw another pro-Mitchell-Lama cooperator penning communiqués for the masses. Leo Aria, who'd been adopted into Southbridge's pro-Mitchell-Lama fold more than twenty years prior by Eva Sacks's mother, drafted a letter directed in large part to the "crazies" like her who'd been so doctrinaire in their rhetoric. His perspective, he said, had changed overnight: pro-privatizers were not the enemy, and his allies needed to get over it.

"The best letter I ever wrote," Aria told me. "It was meant to bring both sides together and realize that . . . in the end we lost. Losing wasn't an ego thing for me. I knew it would happen eventually. By the way, privatization was always inevitable. It was always a matter of time . . . because people had the choice, and because the choice that they had if they voted for it would result in personal benefit. And so they were motivated by that. It was inevitable." Ensconced in the ruins of social housing, one of its former defenders concluded that as long as more personal benefit could be extracted from a public good, its demise was a foregone conclusion. On the outside, twelve days after the vote, a Southbridge waitlister named Kevin Smith logged onto his WordPress account and commented on a pro-Mitchell-Lama blog post: "I am just wondering what will happen to people who are in [*sic*] the waiting list. Are they totally out of the picture or do they still have a chance to get in?" The blogger broke the news to him that the waitlist no longer existed.

Aria waited until November 28, 2014, to release his letter in the neighborhood newspaper *Downtown Express*. It was Black Friday, the day after Thanksgiving and the preeminent holiday to unfettered capitalism. "We now need to restore harmony to our community," it read. "Under these new circumstances, I pledge my service to my Southbridge community in any way it will be accepted." The vote had been fair, Aria said, and now the work of repair needed to begin.

To his collaborators at Southbridge Towers Cooperators for Mitchell-Lama, though, the letter fractured whatever weak bonds among them remained. "He called me," Daniel Brampton remembered, "and I said—because he hadn't told any of us that he was gonna do this—I said 'Leo, how can you do that? You at least had an obligation to tell us what you were gonna send out.' He was quiet for a few seconds. Then he said, 'Well, if I had it to do all over again, I'd do it again.'"

Aria's letter jabbed a particularly sensitive nerve. For the other leaders of Southbridge Towers Cooperators for Mitchell-Lama, and for James Szal of the Southbridge Towers Shareholders Association, the fight was not over. They lawyered up and went to DHCR to contest the vote itself. After the State reviewed their arguments and concluded in November 2014 that the referendum had been free and fair, the two organizations sought to take their fight to the courts. Kevin Smith, the concerned waitlister, asked around to see if he could contribute. To those still fighting, Aria's evenhanded message read more like a public statement of betrayal. Brampton recalled running into him years later: "We shook hands. I didn't have the courage to say, 'Leo, you son of a. . . .' I'm not always as brave as I wanna be."

While pro-Mitchell-Lama cooperators plotted their next step, the final phase of the privatization process moved along. On December 4, a ninety-day "exclusive period" kicked off during which cooperators would officially decide whether or not to remain owners of their shares. It was a no-brainer for most. They still wanted to own their homes; moreover, only by retaining their ownership would they be able to benefit from their co-op's massive appreciation and sell later on. But the option existed for them to become tenants. They would forfeit the potential to profit from their home, but they would gain certain protections that could insulate them from future expected maintenance increases. For lower-income households, these protections might be the only thing that could prevent them from eventually being priced out of the newly privatized Southbridge. As the "exclusive period" neared its last thirty days, the remains of Southbridge Towers Cooperators for Mitchell-Lama and the Southbridge Towers Shareholders Association began making moves. A flyer went out to raise $10,000 for planned litigation against the co-op and the State.

The move poked a tiger whose confidence had been renewed. Board president Harvey Marshall, triumphant and vindicated, would not let his victory be easily snatched. No longer muzzled by State securities law, Marshall began to use his official pulpit to distribute increasingly direct written attacks on pro-Mitchell-Lama advocates and their "frivolous" lawsuit. Marshall's letters started with subtle shade. "Cooperators who are considering contributing to this [fundraising] effort are advised that they should exercise caution before doing so, as neither of these organizations has provided detailed financial information regarding their income and projected expenses," one read. After his opponents filed their petition on February 23, and with each passing month of privatization delayed, Marshall amped up his smears, targeting James Szal and Eva Sacks in particular.

Their suit centered around the forty-four shares in transition that had been disqualified from voting. Szal and Sacks's coalitions said some of those exclusions had been improper and that DHCR had been "arbitrary and capricious" in approving them. Had those shares been included in the vote, they would have been more than enough to change the required two-thirds threshold and, potentially, the outcome of the vote itself. DHCR and Southbridge Towers, Inc., now firmly aligned on the opposing side of the lawsuit, said everything had been kosher. For a time, the lawsuit and the final touches on privatization ran in parallel.

There was no stay order from the courts to halt privatization's bureaucratic final steps. The opt-ins and opt-outs proceeded through the end of the "exclusive period" in early March. The two sides filed material with the court in April. Come May, however, the attorney general refused to accept Southbridge's filing of its effectiveness amendment—the penultimate step in transforming the co-op—until the lawsuit was resolved.

Marshall's attacks grew with the delay. A June memo ostensibly meant to notify shareholders of an upcoming board meeting quickly devolved into a list of reasons why Szal and Sack's lawsuit would fail. Of Szal, Marshall wrote, "His 'association' is nothing more than a self-serving and self-created forum for Mr. Szal to present misinformation about co-op operations and expound on his negative beliefs regarding the 'risks' of privatization." Pro-privatizers were also quick to skewer Szal and other holdouts for supposed hypocrisy. When the "exclusive period" had come to a close months earlier, only eleven shareholders had opted-out of ownership. None of the pro-Mitchell-Lama leaders were among them. They, too, would profit from privatization. Trolling ensued. A flyer for Szal's most recent unsuccessful bid for the board, still hanging in a hallway, was vandalized in Sharpie. "Hey!!," the message read, framing a photo of Szal and his beloved dog Gucci, "Ask me when U see me what Day I *Opted* in. I Fooled U all!! BIG money for me + Family."

At least three cooperators I spoke with implied that Szal had used the lawsuit to forestall privatization just long enough for his mother-in-law, a wheelchair user after a stroke years prior, to die. His daughter then took ownership of her grandmother's apartment at Southbridge without having to pay the flip tax that would have been required if privatization had already been completed. As one cooperator put it: "He applied for succession for the daughter before the body was even cold." Not only was Szal a purveyor of false information of privatization. Certain pro-privatizers claimed that Szal's entire pro-Mitchell-Lama stance had just been a ruse in order to line his own pockets to the max.

Szal's mother-in-law wasn't the only resident to pass away while privatization was pending. And hers was the rare instance in which there was a surviving relative who already qualified for succession. Others, not so lucky, couldn't pass anything on to their family. Marshall pinned this on Szal and Sacks as well. On June 19, 2015, he reported in a memo to shareholders that "since the opening of the Exclusive Period on December 4, twelve shareholders who signed Participation Agreements [in other words, opted in] have passed away. Six of these shareholders did not have a family member who could claim succession and as a result their heirs have lost the possibility of inheriting a very valuable asset." A double loss for the families but, ironically, a boon to the co-op's bottom line. The co-op took possession of these shares and, if all went as planned, would soon be able to sell them.

Oral arguments for the lawsuit took place in mid-June. July passed without updates, but come August the judge made her decision: she dismissed the suit, noting that "DHCR's determination to exclude those apartments from the privatization vote was consistent with the law, its regulations, the offering plan, [Southbridge Towers'] certification of incorporation and by-laws, and [Southbridge Tower] and DHCR's treatment of those apartments during previous votes. Nor did it fail to properly verify the election results."[10] For privatization junkies, copies of the court's decision were made available in the Southbridge management office.

Only the formalities remained. The AG accepted the effectiveness amendment at the end of the month. The co-op issued a seven-day notice to elected officials in early September, stating that it was leaving Mitchell-Lama. It also filed an amendment to the co-op's Certificate of Incorporation with the New York Department of State. The State accepted the amendment on September 10, 2015. The co-op that had pulled together in the midst of tragedy fourteen years prior remained as divided as ever. The privatization fight was over, and the flow of money beginning. Szal, vanquished, did acknowledge that privatization was benefitting his family handsomely. "They took me kicking and screaming to the bank," he told me, pained by his own good fortune.

Economists use a revealing term of art when describing a market for a place to live: housing consumption. It refers to how many homes are being used out of the total housing stock—the kind of measure that elicits vastly different interpretations based on the assumptions of who's viewing it. What's the ideal outcome? Should there be a Goldilocks-style happy medium: some vacancies to allow people to move from place to place but not too much, since low vacancy often spells some kind of crisis? And what does it mean when there are too many vacancies? Are the homes, or their locations, undesirable? Unaffordable? Do too many people have too many empty homes to their names? Are those homes not really homes at all, just bank vaults parading as domestic life? All fair questions, but they miss a more fundamental one: What does it mean that we apparently like to talk of "consuming" housing? Language and narrative shape our understanding of the world, after all.

Back in 2011, anthropologist David Graeber excavated the origins of the term "consumption" in a vital piece, writing: "The English 'to consume' derives from the Latin verb *consumere*, meaning 'to seize or take over completely' and, hence, by extension, to 'eat up, devour, waste, destroy, or spend.'"[11] To use the term to refer to anything that isn't destroyed by its use—a Matchbox car, for example—is already curious. To use it for a structure that, if properly constructed and maintained, could stand for centuries is deeply strange. In the case of Southbridge Towers, however, consumption is in fact a fitting term, capturing how pro-privatizers seized, then transformed their homes as profoundly as if they'd leveled the brick and steel, the asbestos and tile, the concrete and wood to the ground.

The last step in the privatization process could be viewed as a formality: a simple filing to enshrine the transformation into corporate reality. But conceptually, it was the equivalent of a demolition. Lawyers had to dissolve—or destroy—the existing Mitchell-Lama cooperative and create a new one. Same name, same place, different company, completely different relationship to the outside world. Southbridge Towers was dead. Long live Southbridge Towers!

As of September 2015, Southbridge became a commodity. Yes, people still lived there, and many appreciated that they did, but all anyone could talk about was who was buying and who was selling and what it all was worth. In fact, the very solvency of the co-op was now predicated on the new commodities being traded. Southbridge no longer benefited from the property tax abatement—an annual value in excess of $7 million[12]—that its Mitchell-Lama former self had enjoyed. Now the co-op would need to rely on sales income to offset that massively increased tax burden. If not enough shares were sold, and at sufficiently high prices, the co-op would have to pass that tax bill along to its residents. Privatization had replaced social infrastructure with a teetering stack of million-dollar listings. "The unknown is there now," Chris Hresko intoned. "There is no security here."

Within ninety-three days of official privatization, the first market-rate sale at Southbridge was made: $580,000 for a one-bedroom. The sales prices would only climb from there as the downtown speculative market adjusted to Southbridge's entry, its doors unlocked for capital and its agents. Jan Naumann and Marissa Heine went from collaborators in privatization to competitors for its spoils, seeking to represent buyers and sellers in the complex. The likes of Szal, Sacks, and Brampton retreated from the public eye, weary and downtrodden as they watched Southbridge transform in ways both expected and unforeseen.

The new folks buying in to the cooperative were not coming off a waitlist. Instead, they were sizing Southbridge up against other buildings all across the city, the country, maybe the world. A Southbridge share would be a major investment; would this new asset appreciate in value? Would it remain competitive? Were buyers pouring cash into an apartment that would sell for less when the sea levels rose and Lower Manhattan became laced with next-generation Venetian canals? Southbridge sellers, meanwhile, needed to shell out for improvements to attract these buyers: the hallways needed sprucing, the website modernizing. These contributions were predicated on eventual extraction. These beneficiaries of social housing were now consuming it for private gain and destroying it in the process—societal infrastructure sold for parts.

These pro-privatization perpetrators are also victims. The narrative of the American Dream, driven by capitalism and homeownership, had taught them that they were not true homeowners, and thus were lesser than their neighbors. Social housing is abnormal; it needs correcting, they heard. They may have owned a share and thus for all intents and purposes an apartment, but that ownership was a false one. True ownership means near unfettered control, they were told—no governmental entities checking incomes or reviewing maintenance contracts. Above all, true ownership meant being able to sell their homes for whatever the most profligate buyer would offer. The irony is palpable: whereas being self-made is often a key scene in that dream, it was different with Mitchell-Lamas. Residents had "won the lottery" by getting their apartment, then reaped a profit from a government subsidy that was collectively provided by taxpayers. It just so happens that this is closer to the actual origin story of the White middle-class, fostered by subsidized suburban mortgages, than the prevailing "by-your-bootstraps" myth.

Ownership, in this illusion, defined profit as a constitutive right, a right that transcended any rules. Southbridge Rights, among its many savvy moves, had chosen a name that rang with antecedents, Margaret

Thatcher's policy to decimate social housing in the UK—the "Right to Buy"—among them. A pro-privatizer in a debate with Eva Sacks had even tied this right to the divine, as the British monarchy once did their rule: "You people are keeping us from our God-given right to own our homes." The refrain was clear: any form of ownership that abridges a supposed right to profit isn't ownership at all.

POSTMORTEM

The new Southbridge began to take shape the year following privatization. The true outcomes for the most vulnerable wouldn't be known for years, but a flurry of sales meant more turnover and more new faces than the place had seen since its original opening. Jan Naumann enjoyed hearing from her husband after his meetings on the interviewing committee to vet new buyers:

> He'd come up being really excited about all the different types of new people that were coming in, which brought new life to the community. Each day would be something new. A fellow who's a restaurateur, a fellow who wrote a play . . . 'we should go see this; it's off Broadway.' Every time he interviewed somebody, he would just come in with like, 'So nice. So interesting. So bright.'

To Jan, this meant that Southbridge's slide to the "projects" and a poorer, Blacker populace had been arrested, though she did express consternation "that a lot of Chinese people are moving in."

The security was better, too, Jan told me, "and the guys, frankly, look nicer. They got them blazers, you know what I mean? The guys felt better when they put the blazers on. They were very proud to have the blazers. I mean, it sounds like a little thing. They're not doormen. We're not at doormen stage yet, but we're at somewhere above project-level where they feel that they have a little more respect." Jan felt better when the guys put the blazers on too. She no longer had to feel ashamed of living in affordable housing, no matter that the place looked the same. Southbridge was no longer affordable.

For the winners, privatization did look inevitable in retrospect, and the idea of ownership as defined by a right to profit undeniable. Many sold their shares and skipped town. But they'd struggled, in the decade-long process, to justify privatization to themselves and their neighbors, knowing that it would bring a future contrary to the spirit of what they'd initially bought into. There were those who had resorted to ahistorical takes on the original intention of Mitchell-Lama law, claiming falsely that privatization had always been part of the plan. Others put forward a somewhat self-aggrandizing spin on the role they had played in creating the valuable real estate of Lower Manhattan. Some doubled down on absolutes: profiting was just natural, for one, and an individual couldn't be held responsible for it, no matter the repercussions. Folks like Naumann and Tom Goldhaber advanced the narrative that privatization was actually better for everyone—that there was, in fact, something cooperative in dismantling the central tenet of the co-op. A young monied family could now buy a starter home here, Goldhaber said. This potentiality would have been impossible had Southbridge become the slum that people like Naumann feared. Goldhaber failed to mention that few if any outside indicators had ever signaled that outcome as likely.

Then there were the realities of material needs in a country whose social supports have withered over the years under the influence of the same ideologies that underlie privatization. Many residents felt that privatizing affordable homes was their only path to a desirable life or a dignified death. That's what they'd been taught: that home was the path toward financing not just future success but life's basic needs. Commodifying their home was the only way some could care for their elders in a proper manner or send their kid to the college of their dreams in a country where the cost of both is prohibitive.

So they chose consumption, destruction, rather than stewarding a safety net. They pulled up the ladder behind them. It was no doubt a difficult choice for some, and empathy with their circumstances is warranted. But the end doesn't justify the means here. That end is a mass die-off of safe, stable, and affordable housing—an already endangered species in New York City. Even residents convinced of their right to profit expressed misgivings. They still carried a lesson so fundamental as to fit in *The Children's Book of Virtues*: the ability to exercise a proclaimed right doesn't make doing so an unqualified good—no matter how many times the annoying kid on the playground utters "It's a free country." As Daniel Brampton put it, "Their legacy is that they destroyed 1,649 apartments for moderate-income people. Our legacy is that we tried to stop that from happening."

Brampton's pro-Mitchell-Lama faction could be proud of this legacy, but the eleven-vote loss at the final stage made their postmortem all the more fraught. By spurning the support of CU4ML, they'd chosen insularity over solidarity. "That, I think, doomed us," Brampton assessed. They'd also allowed their opponents to set the terms of the debate, as young cooperator Chris Hresko acknowledged, focusing purely on financial arguments against privatization for fear of being branded "ideological." As it turned out, Southbridge Rights continued to accuse the pro-Mitchell-Lama folks of being ideological anyway, when not calling them fearmongers. For little benefit, they ceded the moral ground in their campaign. They lost control of the narrative. The moral weight given to an individualistic conception of ownership by decades of federal public policy and private industry propaganda—an edifice accepted by many as "nonideological"—rushed in to fill it.

After the final vote, Leo Aria's quick pivot to reconciliation was unique among the anti-privatizers. The process of privatizing a public good for profit had gotten quite personal. Szal told me years later that "there are people who still don't speak to me, who walk by me like I'm the anti-Christ, because I opposed this." With DHCR no longer overseeing Southbridge, the Southbridge Rights–controlled board wasted little time in retaliating against its former opponents. Eva Sacks reported that "after privatization, they would not allow us to use the community room. We weren't arguing privatization anymore. We were just being kind of a forum for people to, in a sense, vent, in another sense to say these are specific problems. We could not bring them as specific problems as a committee because [the board] didn't recognize us as a community, so we're not allowed to use the community room. We basically disbanded." Between her dejection at being marginalized and her sporadic grimaces brought on by chronic arthritis, Sacks strikes a picture of defeat.

Some on the winning side were willing to at least recognize the commitment shown by Sacks & Co. Pro-privatizer Goldhaber summed it up, in language befitting his role as part-time tour guide of the World War II–era USS *Intrepid* aircraft carrier docked on Manhattan's West Side: "It was a tough fight. . . . They were very good politically. Legal wise, they fought us every way. They had some people from the State on their side. They fought us hard, but we fought harder."

The pro-Mitchell-Lama folks, however, didn't feel the people from the State had been much help. They felt abandoned. Yes, the attorney general's office had played a role in slowing the process down through its reviews of the offering plan, but that wasn't out of opposition to privatization. The office was just fulfilling its commitment to ensuring comprehensive, accurate information for investors. DHCR had stepped in when the pro-Mitchell-Lama organizations had originally been exiled from the community room, but after the Southbridge board rebuffed the agency's offer of its one, sweeter incentive for remaining in Mitchell-Lama—more subsidized debt—its role became procedural. They dispensed with their role as stewards of a public good and adopted the view that only current residents' takes on privatization mattered. And so the State's largest contribution to the process was to unintentionally affirm the privatizers' view of housing as an individual financial asset. It's illustrative that DHCR and the Southbridge Rights–controlled board ended up on the same side of the pro-Mitchell-Lama faction's last-gasp lawsuit. Both levels of government had bought in to a narrow view of what their role was, the State as referee and the board as bringers of privatization, both operating from a financialized mindset.

Politicians occasionally made supportive gestures to the pro-Mitchell-Lama camp, but as shown by Scott Stringer's instantaneous waffling amid pro-privatizer pressure, most regarded the politics as too hot. The benefit of coming out in support of social housing wasn't worth the wrath of a powerful voting bloc and the potent retaliatory message that pro-Mitchell-Lama politicians were keeping homeowners from rightfully profiting off their homes. They sat it out. As we finished one conversation, Eva Sacks pointed vigorously west from her apartment past a crowded CD tower and through a wall lined with concert posters, toward City Hall. She said, "We were not under City supervision, but it always struck me . . . I wanted to just go right up to [Mayor] Bill de Blasio and say, 'Do you realize that three blocks away from your office, there are 1,649 apartments that are going to go private?'" Sitting back in her chair, voice lowered in resignation and bathed in sarcasm, she added, "But there's nothing he could have done about that though."

So the residents of Southbridge were left alone with a terrible decision that many relished, others avoided, and still others fought tooth and nail. A group of Americans most insulated from a viral conception of ownership, in which a right to profit, a right to consume, trumps all responsibility, was ultimately not immune to the infection that brought on the death of Southbridge's stable, affordable, decommodified housing.

Southbridge, though, is just one front in a larger battle over what housing is for and how public goods can be better maintained. Some of Southbridge's players moved on to other fights. Jacob Villa would attempt to implement the Southbridge privatization playbook at his new Mitchell-Lama community in Midtown Manhattan. Daniel Brampton would join forces with CU4ML. And Harvey Marshall, stepping away from the Southbridge board after reaching his holy grail, would meet to swap notes with another retired educator turned Mitchell-Lama board president, Deborah Norton, keen on replicating Southbridge's "success" elsewhere.

Norton's is a much smaller co-op, St. James Towers, in a very different kind of neighborhood, Bed-Stuy. The two co-ops have, however, faced the same pressures across their histories, and the same allure of profit. Lester Goodyear—the FDR-quoting, cowboy-hat-wearing privatization booster at St. James—thinks it's only fair that he get to cash in after centuries of discrimination against Black Americans like him. His neighbor Wenna Redfern thinks differently, grounded in empathy for her neighbors, both inside the co-op and out. As the privatization movement reared its head at St. James, and with it the specter of becoming another locus of displacement, she asked, "Where are we going to go? Where is anybody going to go?"

PART III

St. James Towers

CHAPTER 6

A Piece of the Rock

If any year in New York City can lay claim to being dull, 2011 is not one of them. In August, a rare earthquake emanating from Virginia shook the five boroughs, the tremors disrupting workdays and flooding sidewalks with residents and their tales of mild distortion. Less than a week later, Hurricane Irene made landfall, wreaking significantly more havoc. In September, Occupy Wall Street took over Zuccotti Park, just a few blocks from Southbridge Towers, speaking out against inequality and its capitalist roots through its people's microphone. Across the East River in Brooklyn, the new Barclays Center—a prime example of the kind of rapacious real estate development that Occupy opposed—was emerging from its scaffolds. When completed, it would be home to the NBA's Nets, lured from Jersey, with luxury developments to guard its flanks. The causes and consequences of their arrival—among them, Brooklyn's ascendancy in global cool—rippled throughout the borough. Its neighborhoods, Prospect Heights and Red Hook, Crown Heights and Bed-Stuy, were savored on lips that may have previously spat them. And yet, at St. James Towers, not at all that much was going on.

Yes, the Black mecca of Bed-Stuy had changed in ways that residents couldn't help but notice with a mix of curiosity and fear. More White folks. Bigger money. An old townhouse kitty-corner from St. James's defunct playground had sold for $1.45 million in September 2009.[1] Residents recalled how, decades ago, such homes had been regarded as worthless, abandoned and then sold off by the City for a pittance. The gentry were arriving. But inside St. James, things were mostly quiet. The co-op board had entered a period of stability, helmed by former middle school principal Deborah Norton and peopled with long-standing residents like the cowboy-hat wearing and FDR-quoting Lester Goodyear. The 326-unit building, pushing fifty years old, was in better shape than it had been in a decade. A few years of handwringing on how to raise the necessary funds to pay for some large capital needs had finally yielded a plan that paired shareholder assessments with limited borrowing. New brick now patched old wounds, the repairs evident in subtle differences of shade. Perhaps one of the more consequential occurrences at the co-op that year was the absence of something. In 2011, the board paid off the last of the co-op's non-mortgage debt and resolved to avoid similar financing for the foreseeable future. Killing off this debt meant the co-op could focus on paying down its mortgage from the City, which would remove one hurdle toward privatization. Lester Goodyear claimed that privatizing had been "a goal formulated at the very beginning" of St. James, "a vision born in 1963 from the aspirations of the original, first-time Mitchell-Lama homeowners." Like the similarly inclined cooperators at Southbridge, Goodyear and his compatriots were rewriting history to claim privatization as the intended outcome of the Mitchell-Lama program.

No matter its ahistorical nature, the story wielded power that only grew as the years passed, as the narrative was repeated, as a right to eventually sell and profit was proclaimed, and as cooperators became more and more removed from the founding ideals and intentions of their social housing. This promise guided successive boards: they spurned government loans available to fund capital improvement projects, instead raising funds directly from cooperators, the occasional grant, or bank loans, even when the latter carried higher interest rates than the public option. They took every precaution to stay on track for Goodyear's version of "eventual 'Private Home Ownership' in a private cooperative apartment building."

St. James's boards had done a solid job stewarding the complex. The co-op was "recognized by its peers and city officials as one of the "*BEST COOPERATIVES IN THE* [MITCHELL-LAMA] *PROGRAM*," as one board memo said. It got high marks from its supervisory agency, the City's Department of Housing Preservation and Development (HPD)—what DHCR had been to Southbridge. Maintenance charges were affordable. The cooperators were happy. The community was solid, the kind of place where kids like Graham Hales grew into adults who looked after elders like Wenna Redfern, no longer the twenty-something she'd been when her parents had moved into the co-op almost fifty years prior, though still spry enough to aspire to ass kicking.

Questions began to stir, however, about whether this success story of safe, stable, affordable social housing for middle-income folks would be sustained into the co-op's next half century. Once its mortgage was satisfied, St. James could start its own privatization process, the one Southbridge was then still muddling through, with a feasibility study. "It had been sort of talked about quite a few years before we reached the point where we were debt free," Hales, then a privatization skeptic, told me. "We knew there was sort of this impetus kind of brewing under the surface. . . . So because of that, and as the communication started increasing about the study and everything, that's when I became more concerned."

In June 2014, with internal fanfare, St. James received notice that its mortgage had been paid. Now the only questions were how heated things would get as the co-op explored privatization. In September, across the East River, Southbridge made its final, irrevocable vote for privatization, setting a model for other aspiring privatizers. Fifty years from St. James's birth, Deborah Norton and her board of privatization dreamers sought the same irreversible transformation as their Manhattan cousins.

BAD DEBT

While leaving Mitchell-Lama was the clear end goal for the pro-privatizers, for other cooperators the release from their mortgage was nearly as significant. Escaping indebtedness—even the collectivized kind the co-op held—was not only a means but an end in itself. Resident Simon Doran made his views on debt, especially debt from government, abundantly clear when we met at a Thai restaurant for dinner. I'd already been seated when he—a thin, tall man clad in all black, his tawny beige face split by a nervous grin—arrived. We changed tables at his insistence. He'd come through the restaurant a half hour earlier to scope out the setting. His back was now safely guarded by an exposed brick wall.

Doran is admittedly prone to seeing the nefarious in the mundane. "I think of everything as a conspiracy," he stated plainly. This sense of suspicion, however irrational at times, is baked into Doran's personality. His slight drawl gives away his childhood in small-town South

Carolina. Growing up during the Jim Crow era, with a clear sense that the system was both racist and rigged, Doran had come to believe strongly in self-reliance. He relocated to Brooklyn, built a long career as a building inspector for the fire department—a job he mischaracterized as akin to welfare because of how he received a check for minimal work. He eventually parlayed his earnings into a series of real estate investments, all within a block of the still resonating boundary of the Pratt Institute Urban Renewal Area. His first purchase was a building at the intersection of Myrtle and Classon Avenues. He then sold that building to buy a share in a speculative co-op called Willoughby Walk, a product of the urban renewal scheme that had created St. James. He also joined the waitlist for St. James itself, and when his name came up, he bought in. This was not to secure a safe, stable, affordable place to live. He was already a homeowner. Rather, he regarded a share in the Mitchell-Lama cooperative—in a capitalist real estate market, a scarce commodity[2]—as "the best investment in the world."

That is, should St. James go private and if HPD would stop meddling in co-op affairs. The agency was known to be much more involved than DHCR had been at Southbridge. To some residents, like Graham Hales, that was appropriate: "They do have their problems, just like any bureaucracy, but . . . I think having that oversight is a good thing, because it keeps people honest." To others, like Lester Goodyear, HPD's oversight was paternalistic and would, as privatization began its march, overstep a line of control. Doran thought that line had been crossed long before and with such severity as to warrant a reference to one of the US' foundational sins in a word plucked from the Southern fields he'd grown among. HPD, he said, were "overseers."

This sense that HPD was out to control, even to dominate, the predominately Black cooperators of St. James was why Doran cared so fervently about debt. The loans the City and State had made to Mitchell-Lama co-ops were the exclusive mechanism that the government used to try to maintain the complexes as social housing. From the government's perspective, this arrangement simply replicated the structure of most other affordable-housing investments: the City and State give the co-op subsidized financing so that it can take care of its maintenance needs and keep costs low. In return, the co-op agrees to forego privatization for the ensuing fifteen to thirty years. To Doran though, trickery was afoot. This deal was hardly benign, he claimed, but rather a scheme to convince cooperators to pawn what they already owned and to act against their own interests. Or, in Doran's words, to "re-enslave" them. St. James was "like a raisin." Under Mitchell-Lama, that "raisin can get just so dry, it cracks up." Privatization, though, offered a rejuvenating possibility: "You reconstitute it by adding water; it becomes a grape again."

Even HPD had "no hope at all" that St. James would take on new debt. One official told me that the co-op's board had "been very clear for ten years that they want to buy-out"—that is, to privatize. Much to Doran's dismay, two other Mitchell-Lama complexes down the avenue from St. James, Ryerson Towers and Pratt Towers, had already fallen for the City's supposed ruse. Both complexes, from their boards right down to their loan terms, were firmly entrenched in the Mitchell-Lama program for the coming decades—duped, Doran said, by "lies" in a set-up that's "almost like indentured servancy." "They fool them to say that they'll get them a loan, when they could just pay for a capital expenditure from a maintenance increase. Instead [the co-ops] get debt service and are locked into the program." His argument echoed the initial reaction of a Black cooperator in Washington, DC, in the late aughts before he became a limited-equity proponent: that "it sounded like something a bunch of White people thought up to keep Black people poor."[3]

The lack of unanimous interest in privatization at St. James led Doran to the curious conclusion that "people don't want money, especially my people. . . . We're so easily manipulated. People act like zombies. They think they should stay on the reservation." Doran was connecting a government's attempt to maintain social housing with settler colonialism and genocide of Indigenous people, adding a splash of contempt for the victims in the process. He then felt the need to go international. "Have you ever read the book [*Confessions of an*] *Economic Hit Man*? Same thing here, same way the US is doing around the world, the City is doing here. It's empire."

I had indeed read John Perkins's largely undocumented and thus questionable account of his time as a consultant tasked with loading foreign countries with unpayable debts as a way to exert American power abroad. There's no doubt that debt, whether between sovereigns or individuals, has long been used as a tool of authority and control. Doran would likely have been familiar with sharecropping in the American South, where farmers working the land of another often became indebted to its owners in a cycle of debt bondage that mimicked slavery. His distrust of government debt wasn't in itself unfounded. At

Southbridge, the State's use of financing to incentivize social housing preservation had unintentionally served to further commodify and financialize that very housing. The same dynamic was in play at St. James, but with a twist. In this majority-Black community, a deeply negative association with debt, rooted in a torrid history of discrimination by government and other lenders, meant that some cooperators like Doran feared that the City, too, was now trying to exploit them.

This fear is reasonable. It is historically unassailable that debt has been used as a form of social control in the housing sector. René Moya, a tenant power organizer with the national debtors' union the Debt Collective, is well-versed in this history and the role that debt continues to play in people's lives. When I ask Moya what he sees in arguments like Doran's, he's quick to point out that the American obsession with homeownership is itself about social control. You'll recall the Little House, dropped in Midtown Manhattan in 1934 to spout the ideology of homeownership and its role in the fight against socialism. Mass homeownership, Moya says, keeps people "focused on trying to pay off that mortgage" rather than trying to improve social conditions, while also "building a society of small capitals—people who themselves are able to build enough equity that they can then put it into other types of investments." As sociologist Brian McCabe notes, support for widespread homeownership in the 1910s and '20s tracked directly with the rise of labor unrest in American cities. "Owner-occupied housing, business leaders hoped, would contribute to the creation of a docile, stable workforce, ending unrest in American factories."[4] With skin in the capitalist game and a mortgage to pay, the radical potential of workers could be neutralized.

Then there's a much more recent history of debt and housing that leaves folks, especially Black ones, rightfully wary. Moya notes: "The question of debt is intimately tied to the question of housing, right? It was very clearly tied to it in 2008, where the inability of people to pay their mortgages as they got reset with higher interest rates was foundational to the housing crisis." Not only did this poor-quality debt bring the financial system down and wipe out over *half* of all wealth held by Black families; many lost their homes in the process.[5] Analysis after the crisis showed that these subprime mortgages were disproportionately given to Black families.[6] Experiences like these contribute to what Moya describes as cooperators' "rightful mistrust of the state, because the state itself obviously, has failed people routinely in the past when it comes to the provision of housing. . . . I think there's a real understanding in their bones that the state has had a role to play in the perpetuation of the dispossession of people of color."

For cooperators like Doran, it's beside the point that, in the case of St. James, the government loans on offer sought to maintain social housing. For that is just one face of the governmental coin. The flip side is minted with complicity in a system of dispossession for the purpose of moneymaking. Doran's suspicions suggest a need for social housing programs to move beyond debt as the only means for preserving complexes like St. James. To him, this decommodified housing appeared not as the opposite of the commodification of real estate, but the enticing toy in a junk-food Happy Meal—the whole deal, for Doran, rather raw.

In October 2014, mere weeks after Southbridge voted to privatize and four months after St. James had made its last mortgage payment, a survey from St. James's nine-member board went out to all St. James shareholders. It was now open season for the future of the co-op. The survey was far from being a consequential vote, but it marked the opening salvo in the privatization process. The answers could build a constituency for the official first step: the feasibility study. Who needed more information to decide whether to remain in Mitchell-Lama or privatize? Who wanted to be able to bequeath their apartment to any relative they desired? Who wanted the board to be able to reject co-op applicants for nonfinancial reasons? Unlike Southbridge, St. James residents hadn't gone through previous privatization attempts, hadn't honed their debating and voting strategies through such experiences. The pro-privatization board at St. James thus believed it important to get a pulse on cooperators' general leanings toward Mitchell-Lama preservation. Who thought that St. James remaining as a development accessible to low- and middle-income New Yorkers was important?

Sixty-five percent of survey respondents were keen to keep St. James a middle-income bastion, for themselves and their heirs or future possible residents, depending on how the question was interpreted. Other results of the survey, however, gave the board confidence to move ahead. Almost 50 percent of the survey respondents said they needed additional information. That—plus the people whose minds, like Doran's and Goodyear's, had long been made up—would be enough to get the majority vote to allocate $65,000 for a feasibility study. Seventy-one percent of folks wanted to be able to leave their apartments to a family member of their choice, not just one who was living with them. Sixty-one percent wanted board veto over new residents. These were openings through which to pitch privatization to skeptical cooperators. So with an expectation of easy passage, the board put the process in motion, scheduling a vote for a feasibility study in November.

As Graham Hales remembered, "It was really kind of a benign way of presenting it," he told me. "It wasn't really presented in a way that it was definitely going private. Because we were in this financial position to make a decision as to which way we wanted to go, it was presented as . . . let's see where things stand and how we can move one way or the other." Most cooperators bought that argument. Skeptics like Hales took a wait-and-see approach. They, like all cooperators, had other life matters to deal with: Hales had a demanding job; Tia Ward was co-ordinating full-time care for her mother, then in her nineties; Wenna Redfern was settling into her well-earned retirement after caring for approximately 365,000 newborns across almost five decades at Einstein Medical Center. With little rebuttal, then, a narrative in favor of privatization began to circulate throughout the complex.

OWNING WHILE BLACK

The prime vector of this narrative was Lester Goodyear. He was a "leftover" like Wenna Redfern, an old-timer who'd perched atop St. James for over five decades. He'd made decisions on the board and gazed out on a changing Bed-Stuy from his twenty-first-floor balcony near the building's rooftop, one visible beyond the neighborhood and occasionally marked by utility exhaust with the bearing of a papal conclave just resolved. His tenure and community work had given him a pulpit. And he was keen to use it to set the terms of the privatization debate to come.

Many of Goodyear's go-to arguments had also circulated at Southbridge. Ownership in a limited-equity co-op was not "true ownership." Privatization was a built-in "promise" of the Mitchell-Lama program. Residents had earned the value offered by privatization of a public good through their "diligent management" of the co-op. It was a "Financial Reward for our constant vision of private 'Home Ownership,'" a "benefit from your contribution over the years," the earned "fruits of our labor." Or, in the same contradiction seen at Southbridge, Goodyear claimed he'd taken "a chance on a [New York State] Lottery. Not by the purchase of a ticket, but by investing my meager resources, in 21 Saint James Place." Now he wanted to "collect on my winning ticket." Like the pro-privatizers at Southbridge, Goodyear also appealed to the American Dream:

> Private ownership of Real Property is the bedrock of the American system of free enterprise. . . . In America, Home Ownership is the first step in the creation of personal wealth that can be transferred to other family members, such as Life Mates, Children, and Siblings. Home ownership is also the first step in acquiring status as a First Class Citizen in America (Owning a piece of the Rock). Ownership of Real Property gives the owner the essential first step in becoming a person of economic substance in American Society.

If Goodyear was intentionally quoting the 1970s funk groups 100 Proof (Aged in Soul) and Dynasty, or the old Prudential Insurance jingle of the same era—"Get a Piece of the Rock," that is, the Rock of Gibraltar—he could have stood to update his references. Another—in which he framed homeownership "as the first step in acquiring status as a First Class Citizen in America"—dated back not just decades but centuries to a time when only property-owning men could vote and when Black men like Goodyear were considered the property of others. Scholar and activist Keeanga-Yamahtta Taylor knows this association between property ownership and citizenship well. As she describes in her essential book *Race for Profit*, the tie between homeownership and belonging was particularly strong for Black Americans:

> Indeed, the very first civil rights bill to be enacted in 1866 tethered the right to purchase property to freedom and citizenship: "All persons born in the United States without regard to any previous condition of slavery or involuntary servitude . . . shall have the same right, in every State and Territory in the United States, to make and enforce contracts, to sue, be parties, and give evidence, to inherit, purchase, lease, sell, hold, and convey real and personal property, as is enjoyed by white citizens."

The American connection between citizenship and property was further identified, Taylor points out, "In the 1948 landmark Shelley v. Kraemer decision that affirmed, 'Equality in the enjoyment of property rights was regarded . . . as an essential pre-condition to the realization of other basic civil rights and liberties.'"[7] Native Americans, meanwhile, were offered US citizenship under the 1887 Dawes Act only if they privatized their collectively held, sovereign lands.[8]

Recall: government-subsidized property ownership had built the White middle class. Federal, state, and local policies systematically denied Americans of color the same opportunities. Those policies instead enforced segregated neighborhoods and locked non-White Americans out of the government-backed mortgages that made widespread White homeownership possible. Racial discrimination and real estate are such intimate partners that contemporary municipal programs meant to provide reparations to Black families—such as those in Evanston, Illinois, and Asheville, North Carolina—focus on promoting homeownership. It remains the strategy most commonly pitched to decrease the nation's yawning racial wealth gap. Whether this is the right approach is, however, hotly disputed.[9]

In America, owning while Black has never been a straightforward success story. (To be fair, neither has owning while White, though it has been vastly more lucrative.) Black Americans have long owned homes, but, as Taylor writes, "racism and exclusion made the costs higher while the quality was lower. . . . Black housing was valued differently from white housing, thus stripping its supposed asset-like quality away."[10] Take, for instance, contract lending or rent-to-own, whereby a Black family unable to get a mortgage would pay the owner of a house (who held onto the deed) in monthly installments. If they missed even one payment, the owner would consider the contract broken and all the equity already accrued to be forfeited. The owner would often then rinse and repeat, starting over with the same family or a different one. There was no mechanism for getting out of arrears or even a foreclosure process. They did not own the home until they paid for it in cash, in full, without any missteps—a predatory approach common in the 1950s and '60s that's making its way back today, branded as a new form of access to homeownership in an impossible housing market.[11] Taylor writes that in the 1970s Black folks, after decades of being excluded from mortgage access, were "welcomed into the housing market on terms most favorable to the [real estate] industry. . . . The housing was not viewed as an asset but valued for the capacity to extract profit out of it."[12] Poor Black women were sold decrepit properties with mortgages backed by the Federal Housing Administration. Saddled with unpayable debt and unlivable structures in still-segregated neighborhoods, this new "access" not only failed to help Black families build equity; it in many cases plunged families underwater on their mortgages. Their homes were foreclosed, even condemned. "For the poor, it exacerbated and deepened one's descent into the ranks of the poor," writes Taylor.[13]

The mortgage-expansion policy failed in its stated purpose as an anti-poverty program. Its slightly more veiled goal—to calm the urban rebellions erupting in divested neighborhoods across the country—also went unmet. "For some, the promotion of homeownership and access to credit in neighborhoods and communities that previously had been ignored was appealing as a new means of social control. Desperate federal and local officials believed that greater investment and inclusion in mainstream society would stem the tide of rebellion and property destruction," Taylor notes.[14]

Mortgage debt as a form of social control: Sound familiar? This new mortgage access also provided cover for waning government investment on other housing fronts: funding for public housing and the likes of Mitchell-Lamas was replaced with support for a racist real estate industry hell-bent on extracting profit. It was neoliberalism writ on the housing sphere—a "political, social, and economic rejection of the social welfare state and the social contract more generally" with the subtext that the individual was the locus of either success or failure.[15]

In this way, the Goodyear's supposed ticket to becoming a "First Class Citizen" morphed into the opposite of reparative. It became, in fact, a new form of predation. "Predatory inclusion" is the term Taylor puts to it. It's become a useful one not just in the housing sphere but across society, from access to student debt to the crypto bonanza.

CROSSTOWN TRAFFIC

In the 1970s and '80s, before Bed-Stuy became a byword for gentrification, it was filled with precisely the kind of decrepit properties that government and realtors colluded to sell off to Black buyers. Buildings were shells of their former, rather stately selves, needful of care and maintenance. This was the era when the City took ownership of properties by way of tax foreclosures—properties stripped of grandeur and wiring, riddled with structural failures—and quickly sought to offload them to willing buyers for a song.

Simon Doran chose not to take advantage of those deals. It is the first in a string of his real estate regrets, followed by selling his pre–St. James apartments at nowhere near the properties' peak values, and now the possibility that his privatization ploy at St. James might not work out. "Those were dumb things I did," Doran lamented. Homeownership on the cheap, however tainted, presents an alluring opportunity to those socialized to believe it is the be-all and end-all of civic and economic life. As we drank coffee together in a diner across from the co-op one day, he jabbed his finger south, past the kitchen and down the street, toward the formerly rundown homes next to Emmanuel Baptist Church. He was incensed that his profiteering attempt should garner a side-eye from his neighbors when the City has supported it in so many other forms. "What about the people who bought brownstones for $1 and back taxes? What about them?" Doran said.

This is one of many problems with our current housing system: it positions home as a commodity, then attempts to mitigate the deeply negative consequences of doing so with one-off programs. Contradictions like this are inherent in what author Samuel Stein terms the real estate state.[16] It is true that the City and the feds had subsidized those "brownstoners" while simultaneously discouraging people like Doran from profiting from their subsidized housing. It didn't matter to him that the brownstoner gamble often ended in loss, especially for Black families without the deep pockets to turn a house in shambles into something livable. He still sensed a double standard that could only be explained with the unsatisfying point that the deals between government and individuals in those situations were different.

The clearest benefit that folks like him saw in the Mitchell-Lama program was the break on property taxes. But here, too, Doran sensed hypocrisy: "They tell you that there's reduced real estate taxes. That's the biggest jive there is. All of these places are abated. Million-dollar places on Pacific [Street] and Atlantic [Avenue]."

Doran was referring to the massive Atlantic Yards project that will, in theory, one day erect apartment buildings over rail yards to join the aforementioned Barclays Center atop Brooklyn's prime transit hub. The project, now rebranded Pacific Park, is only partially realized at the time of writing—the portion over the rail yards has yet to commence—but not for lack of public funding. The City has granted it cheap land and huge tax abatements, meaning that the mostly luxury apartments it will produce are underwritten by the same public mechanisms used to create

St. James Towers. What was Doran supposed to think when high-end apartments got the same treatment that his co-op did—but without the same kinds of restrictions?[17]

That the government did not require Atlantic Yards to include deeply affordable social housing and other public goods in proportion to its massive investment is a major sore point. As Doran sees it, why prevent some middle-income Black folks from making cash off their housing when developers are routinely handed giveaways in the course of their designed profiteering? It's a question, an inconsistency, that's hard to brush off, no matter that a deal is a deal and, in the case of Mitchell-Lamas, actually a good one for the public.

That was understandably unsatisfying to some cooperators, and folks like Doran and Goodyear directed their resentment to HPD—the City agency that both residents referred to as "overseers." Goodyear claimed that the cooperators were in fact victims of public theft: the maintenance of the sales restrictions at the heart of his co-op's afford-ability was akin to a loss of ownership, and HPD's advocacy of the same amounted to the agency robbing them of it. "Do We Really Want to Give Our Homes to HPD for Public Housing? We Should Be Very Alarmed by This Latist Atempt [*sic*] to Steal 21 St. James Pl.," Goodyear titled one of his screeds against the City. Among Southbridge pro-privatizers, comparisons to public housing were evoked as a racist dog whistle to stoke fear of an influx of poor, non-White residents. At St. James, pub-lic housing became the watchword for alleged government overreach. To Doran, the simple presence of City supervision was enough to make the complex "public housing."

It was difficult to breach this impasse, this crosstown traffic. When presented with the key distinctions between St. James and Lafayette Gardens, the seven-building New York City Housing Authority devel-opment down the street, Goodyear doubled down on his original point:

> Why should I want to be under their supervision? Is the average home-owner under supervision? Why shouldn't I want to be like any other homeowners? Why should I want to be a stepchild of the government? I might as well move into public housing if I want them to handle ev-erything and tell me everything and be the owner of my home.

As much as I disagree with Goodyear's conflation of government over-sight and government ownership, I do get it. For Goodyear, privatization was ultimately about "the pursuit of self-determination." He believed that, as a Black man, he was once again being screwed in the real estate market, being kept from what others have been allowed, encouraged, and even subsidized to attain. The Mitchell-Lama provisions thwarting a sale for profit were just another entry in the annals of procedural disenfranchisement—another poll tax or voter ID law. He may have once felt that St. James offered something similar to what a cooperator saw in Co-op City when he joined it in 1970: "For a Black man like myself, this was a chance to get in on the ground floor, instead of settling for some place that the white man had used and left."[18] But Goodyear was also a contemporary fabulist of the American myth that casts a particular kind of ownership of property as tantamount to freedom. Privatization seemed his only pathway to liberation.

Goodyear didn't explicitly argue that privatizing would be a form of reparations. But Eva Sacks, a White woman and the self-anointed "most progressive of all of them, the most leftist of all" pro-Mitchell-Lama cooperators at Southbridge, did articulate that argument and found it compelling, though not ultimately satisfactory. Because there weren't many Black families at Southbridge, this argument wasn't prominent in its privatization debate. But, as Sacks said:

> One of the arguments that was raised by one of the African-American shareholders was our community, our people, have not gotten the wealth, and this will give us wealth. I can't argue with that. I still say you should get your wealth some way that you earned it. However, it's not even a debate that the reason why there is a wealth gap goes back to slavery. There's not even a debate except among the most rabid white nationalists. . . . That one I could understand. I could understand it in my head; I could understand it intellectually; I could understand it emotionally.

If privatization can be seen as liberation or reparations for Black cooperators, its impact would still be severely limited. The benefit would accrue only to a small number of Black families while systematically excluding others. Privatization would eliminate one of the few havens for Black folks in an otherwise hostile real estate market. That, all while also driving up the surrounding housing market and threatening to displace some of their most vulnerable neighbors. The wealth that privatization would generate would be of the same exclusionary variety created by the Federal Housing Administration–financed White suburbs.

This is, in part, the issue with many of the "affordable" homeownership programs that aim to build wealth for Black and Brown folks. Many of these programs work by using public funding to subsidize the construction or renovation of a home. This makes the purchase price accessible to a wider range of buyers, who then take out a (sometimes subsidized) mortgage to buy said home. In exchange for public subsidy, buyers agree to a deed restriction on the property, limiting the resale value for fifteen to thirty years. These subsidies, however, are still not enough for low-income families who have very little savings to begin with—families for whom taking on debt could lead to an eventual foreclosure. For families who can buy in, they're likely to end up asset-rich but cash-poor, limiting their ability to invest in other areas of their lives.

Perhaps most crucially, this model is predicated on public investment eventually being pocketed by the private owner in an unfettered sale. Market appreciation, rather than savings accumulated through a steady, low-cost housing payment, is the preferred mechanism for building wealth. The affordability is temporary. Once the fifteen-to-thirty-year period is up, the home becomes just another inaccessible asset that the next family who needs housing can't afford. This model may work out for some families, but it fails to reform a larger speculative system predicated on unaffordability. As René Moya said: "If we think that we're going to be able to game the system that is premised on our dispossession, then I think we're talking past each other."

It doesn't help that these kinds of programs usually come with a dose of indoctrination in the church of homeownership. First-time homebuyer classes are a standby of community development corporations that advertise these programs as a way to close the racial wealth gap. Taking the classes can lead to better lending terms or may even be required to enter a lottery to purchase that alluring "affordable" home. I attended one in the Boston area in 2021 and found the presentations littered with the myths of homeownership and capitalism: that homeowners are more invested in their communities; that "the pride of owning a home" is benefit enough; that if only you stopped buying coffee at Starbucks, you, too, could afford a down payment. Perhaps most pernicious and inaccurate, though, was the framing around control, one that stokes resentment for any kind of regulation that touches on supposedly sacrosanct private property. In her introduction to the homebuying class, the instructor stated: "I own my own house, and no one can tell me what to do with it." True, in a sense. A slide followed on the advantages of homeownership. Number 1 on the list: "You can do whatever you want." Not true, in the least, for any homeowner.

Lester Goodyear was clearly goaded by the fact that he couldn't do whatever he wanted with his home at St. James. However, the truth was that, even with his co-op under the Mitchell-Lama program, he already had a significant amount of control, if not unfettered power. The cooperators, not the City, would choose whether to privatize, and the argument that the supposedly paternalistic HPD was to blame for cooperators' attraction to privatization was akin to blaming your dad for the CD you shoplifted because he hadn't stopped you. The privatization process was, in itself, an affirmation of the self-governance Goodyear and his neighbors did have, for better or worse. Through it, the co-op would exercise agency over its future. With the first vote in the privatization process approaching, Goodyear, Doran, and the rest of the pro-privatization set would soon learn where their ardently negative portrayals of Mitchell-Lama and the City had got them.

FEASY, PEASY

With the mortgage paid and the feasibility study vote scheduled, co-operators at St. James rolled into the end of 2014 with a sense of transition. That was the word in the air, not just for the co-op but for the surrounding neighborhood. The *New York Times* Real Estate section would, a year later, run one of its rather skewed neighborhood profiles with that word right in the title: "Clinton Hill, Brooklyn, a Neighborhood in Transition." Following some choice quotes from realtors and new arrivals who'd purchased or sold million-dollar condos in the area and one token snippet from a longtime resident, the author sketched a "history" of this section of Bed-Stuy. First, the rise: a working-class neighborhood got the Gilded Age treatment with mansions for the likes of oil baron Charles Pratt, after whom the university was named. Then, the fall: "Low-cost high-rises were developed in the area." Specific buildings aren't mentioned, but the stretch of Lafayette Avenue that hosts three Mitchell-Lamas and one public-housing development are assuredly part of this reference. The rest of the history focuses on the fact that Patti Smith and Robert Mapplethorpe—two very cool and very White artists—lived there in the '60s in an apartment whose walls, according to Smith's alluring memoir, "'were smeared with blood and psychotic scribbling.'" End of history.[19]

"Transition," in real estate, usually means that a neighborhood is becoming Whiter and richer or the supposedly negative inverse—becoming Blacker and less moneyed. This is how the American real estate sector has always been structured, with good neighborhoods tied to Whiteness and less desirable ones to a darker Other. St. James's neighborhood was now fully in the sights of that real estate industry and its clients. The possible transition within its own walls would be determined by whether its residents chose to hop on the bandwagon of real estate appreciation or to instead maintain some of the vast history, culture, and people that the *Times* would so easily discard as unimportant.

The feasibility study vote arrived on November 17, 2014. It was a low-key affair. No allegations of vote rigging like at Southbridge; no confrontations in the lobby, where a large print of a zebra hangs. The surrounding neighborhood and city were braced for a grand jury's decision on whether to indict Michael Brown's killer, not a decision on how a co-op will take stock of its boiler and run the numbers on hypothetical sales. For Graham Hales, the results would signal whether an all-out mobilization against privatization would be necessary. Tia Ward, despite being a privatization skeptic, had yet to fully reject it as an option, summarizing her curiosity as "Wow, condo, like, *cool*."

As Goodyear, Doran, and Deborah Norton expected, privatization—or at least its exploration—had legs: the majority ruled in favor of the study, 158 yeas to 73 nays. St. James cooperators would receive projections of their potential windfall in the coming months. For Hales, the alarm bells went off.

CHAPTER 7

Keeping the Faith

As is Hales's nature, he navigated the successful first vote on privatization with aplomb. The guy is nothing but calm, considerate, content. His close-cropped, gray-flecked hair is often crowned with sunglasses, his shirt usually a short-sleeved collared polo. With the exception of the publicly known board members, he was too proper to name the pro-privatization cooperators with whom he'd butted heads. A generalized, rather neutral summation was about as close as he got to gossip or blame: "There are always, as in any community or neighborhood, some philosophical differences in how things should be run, but, you know, we fight it out and wind up living together without any major consequences." He had faith that it would all work out, and he wouldn't let my queries implying the contrary disturb him from the blueberry pancakes he was attending to when we met one afternoon. He was so polite and nonconfrontational, he tried to protect me from my own embarrassment at having smeared the contents of my chocolate croissant across my cheek by simply not mentioning it. Nonplussed, he offered me some of his pancakes.

This bearing made Hales a valuable leader for the nascent opposition that began to organize after the feasibility study passed. The vote was a wake-up call: privatization was a real possibility, and the future of St. James—so predictable for so many years—was now in play. Hales knew that he couldn't go it alone. Wenna Redfern, already like family to Hales, quickly joined the discussions about possible next steps. So did Tia Ward, who had evolved from privatization-curious to privatization-opposed since first hearing about it. A gang of eight anti-privatizers started to coalesce in early 2015, first meeting in Ward's apartment before moving to her office thirteen blocks east and a couple of avenues north due to the thin walls at the co-op. "I didn't want to do it in the building because this was cloak and dagger. . . . People stand to make a lot of money, and I said, 'It's not us. We will not be the ones to make the money.'"

Ward explained to me, over appetizers at the Southern restaurant down the street where we met one evening, her change of heart and why she'd decided to fight for Mitchell-Lama: "Looking at [privatization] just for me, I said it could be a good idea," but then "I sat down, really thought about it, and saw the concern of the seniors in the building—that's why I took up the cause." The mussels in front of her had gone cold, on account of her unbroken talking and open flirting with the wait staff. She struck a commanding pose, her triangular face framed by gold hoop earrings, her lithe figure in a blue jumpsuit. She perched her three phones on our high-top table, taking one from the stack periodically to answer a call or show me video of the *Great Gatsby*–themed bash she'd hosted to celebrate her mom's hundredth birthday.

Ward could hardly be less like Hales. Where Hales refused to traffic in personal attacks, Ward minced no words in branding board president Deborah Norton "evil" or declaring that another board member "can go back to Cuba." Whereas Hales can easily fade into the background, Ward defines the fore—she knew everyone in the restaurant and felt no shame taking calls that everyone could overhear. One can imagine Hales enjoying a nice seltzer; Ward proclaimed herself a "party girl" and reminisced about "drinking down corn liquor in a juke joint" during family reunions in Cordele, Georgia. Hales might dance but probably not the way Ward did that night: wiggling her knees while putting on her coat and sunglasses, as Michael Jackson piped through the restaurant. No doubt Hales did not, at one of his mother's milestone birthdays, shout, as Ward did in her video, "That's my diva! THAT'S MY DIVA!"

Differences aside, the new alliance was less wracked by internal strife than the pro-Mitchell-Lama wing had been at Southbridge. Redfern and Ward have differed on how to run a board campaign, but there was no fundamental disagreement on questions of "ideology," no one calling their supposed ally a "crazy." Crucially, the St. James group also had no squabbles over whether or not to involve "outsiders" in their fight. It seemed a no-brainer. Why not bring in organizations explicitly dedicated to thwarting privatization? Why not call on local politicians to stand in solidarity, to appeal to their neighbors' civic sides? Sure, some may not like it, but they knew they needed firepower that couldn't be found within the co-op itself.

Some of the willingness to call on folks beyond St. James was due in part to Tia Ward's three phones. The lady had connections, and she was clearly not shy about using them. Ward described herself as a "community advocate" who was "connected politically." That "100th Birthday Blowout" for her mom was a case in point. Among those in attendance had been New York City councilmember Laurie Cumbo, who'd presented Ward's mother with a proclamation honoring her history with Congresswomen Shirley Chisholm and Bella Abzug and New York City Mayor John Lindsay. Ward had then invited Congressman Hakeem Jeffries, her "friend for years," to present the centenarian with a letter of congratulations from Barack and Michelle Obama. Power buzzed in those ties, and Ward would call on them for support.

The group soon sought out the leaders of Cooperators United for Mitchell-Lama. "I had to go study up on [privatization], do some research, and get some help. That's when I joined CU4ML. . . . They helped educate me on the topic," Ward told me. Her crew also reached out to the Mitchell-Lama Residents Coalition, an organization primarily focused on the program's rental buildings, as well as the Brooklyn Mitchell-Lama Task Force. In short, Ward, Hales, and Redfern made sure to connect with anyone working to maintain Mitchell-Lamas as social housing. The insularity of Southbridge's Mitchell-Lama advocates, and their unwillingness to frame their work in the context of a larger struggle in solidarity with others, had arguably worked against them. St. James's pro-Mitchell-Lama cooperators would not make the same mistake.

ALL THAT RIGAMAROLE

By summer, the pro-Mitchell-Lama group, which had taken on the name Concerned Shareholders of St. James, were ready to bring their campaign into a public meeting. The feasibility study was still being crafted by the lawyers and accountants hired by the board, but that hadn't stopped the board members from distributing memos about privatization—material that the Concerned Shareholders regarded as biased. "They weren't being forthcoming and honest with the shareholders," Tia Ward told me. "They were making it seem like a cake walk, and it was gonna be all wonderful. . . . They weren't giving them enough information."

As skewed as Ward considered the board's circulars to be, however, they were neutral compared to what Southbridge Rights had churned out. The board at St. James repeatedly stressed that nothing would change without a vote. It also laid out a third option beyond Mitchell-Lama and privatization—converting the complex to a Housing Development Fund Corporation—a kind of middle ground that advocates have dubbed privatization-lite. They encouraged people to attend meetings and ask questions. Maybe the St. James board was just more committed to transparency and the ultimate will of the cooperative. Or maybe they needed to be more subtle than Southbridge's privateers had been. The co-op-wide survey the prior October had shown that staunch pro-Mitchell-Lama co-operators—those who'd "strongly agreed" with the statement "I think St. James should remain in the Mitchell-Lama program and stay exactly as it is"—outnumbered their pro-privatization peers, 29 to 22 percent. With that 51 percent of cooperators already decided, the fight would therefore center on swaying the remaining 49 percent who said they needed more information. If the undecideds didn't trust the board's information, they were unlikely to be won over to their side.

So the board provided factual information and put its creativity into downplaying certain issues, accentuating others, and eliding key distinctions. A three-page comparison table that it circulated in late 2014 reads like an ad comparing the free version of an app to its paid, professional upgrade: an X in the "free" column next to each feature, checkmarks all the way down for "pro." The table set up a dichotomy that, while accurate on its face, obscured the relative scale of certain costs and also flattened the relative importance of all the programmatic differences. The comparison was presented in part like this:

REGULATORY AGENCY: HPD	NO REGULATORY AGENCY
Inheritance is not permitted	Inheritance is permitted
Sales prices remain limited	Sales prices are unrestricted

The most egregious obfuscation came around the question of maintenance increases and the subsidies available to the co-op. This was forever the rub: Would it cost a lot more for cooperators to live in a privatized St. James? Would rising charges ultimately leave longtime residents with no choice but to sell because they could no longer cover the maintenance costs?

The board did its best to skirt those questions, burying them at the bottom of the second page:

MITCHELL-LAMA:	PRIVATE OPTION:
Maintenance increases are authorized by the Board and approved by HPD. HPD can require larger increases than the Board recommends.	Maintenance increases are authorized by the board.

Excluded from this comparison was the relative scale of likely maintenance increases, which were likely to be higher over time under privatization. A comparison on subsidies followed, saying only that the shelter rent break under Mitchell-Lama would be replaced by a different cooperative real estate tax abatement. Again, there was no mention of the relative scale of these subsidies—namely that shelter rent was massively more generous than its supposed replacement. Most cooperators wouldn't have had enough knowledge of the Mitchell-Lama program or privatization to draw the distinctions that exposed these false equivalencies for what they were. They might have just selected the professional version that was so apparently superior, unaware that the true cost wouldn't be presented until the very last screen. Tia Ward saw through it: "[The board president's] telling them, 'Oh, your maintenance is not gonna go up.' I said, 'If you believe that, I have three bridges to sell you, the Brooklyn, the Manhattan, and the Williamsburg.'" She branded privatization "a crap shoot."

This was the context in which Ward, Hales, and Redfern distributed their first flyer to every apartment door across St. James's twenty-four floors early in July 2015. The flyer encouraged all cooperators to attend "an informational presentation on the benefits of remaining a Mitchell-Lama cooperative" on the evening of Wednesday the 15th. They would be joined by Richard Heitler from CU4ML—the same man who'd been dubbed "Powerhouse Dick" by Eva Sacks at Southbridge.

The Concerned Shareholders expected to use the St. James community room for Heitler's talk. That's what the flyer read. But when Hales started the usually pro forma process for booking the room, he found new roadblocks put in his path:

I had just said I wanted to book the meeting for a specific date as an open meeting for all the shareholders. A couple of days later, [the board member in charge of the process] called me back and asked me to submit a letter to the board specifying what I wanted the room for. So I did, and mentioned that it was for CU4ML, and they wanted to give a presentation on the benefits of the Mitchell-Lama program. . . . I was called to the management office by the property manager, and she said that the type of meeting that I wanted was considered a special meeting, or something along that line, because it was involving business for the building. . . . It was something in the by-laws. . . . Having a special meeting you need a petition with a certain number of people to sign and all that.

The St. James board had taken another page from the Southbridge playbook. With only a few days to go before the fifteenth, Hales & Co. decided to forego "all that rigamarole" and book the community room in the neighboring Mitchell-Lama, Ryerson Towers.

Hales remembered being "a little nervous" leading up to the gathering "because I wasn't sure how it was gonna go." Come 7:30 p.m., though, the community room was standing room only, with an estimated sixty to seventy cooperators in attendance, including some board members. Hales and his fellow organizers made some brief introductory remarks before handing the mic over to Dick Heitler and CU4ML. As Hales recalled, they led with a slide presentation "on the Mitchell-Lama program, the whole history of it, the background of cooperative living." They then shared a cost-benefit analysis using basic financials from St. James to preview what the feasibility study might show—that privatization would bring profits, yes, but also eventual maintenance increases. "There wasn't really that much tension," Hales remembered. "People wanted more information. . . . They asked some good . . . intelligent questions."

One of the board members who'd attended the meeting approached Hales a few days later. She "was trying to discredit the whole thing," Hales told me. "I remember she asked, 'was there a lot of fall-out following the meeting?' And I very happily said, 'no, not at all.'" The exchange carried a whiff of backhanded, Southern "Bless your heart" vibes. On July 28, the board circulated a letter to all cooperators. It subtly rebuked the CU4ML presentation, stressing that the board's "priority goal" was to maintain "'affordability' for all shareholders" and that the feasibility study would soon provide answers. The quotes around the term affordability were doing some heavy lifting, acknowledging that the term was relative but also accelerating the erosion of what meaning it had left. "'Affordability' is a common goal shared by all St. James Towers, Inc. shareholders; however, the definition of affordability is based upon individual philosophy and a multitude of contributing factors." It could mean whatever one wants it to mean.

The letter went on to say that, until the feasibility study had been completed and "documented facts for shareholders to analyze and discuss in follow-up focus group sessions" were provided, it was premature to draw any conclusions on privatization. The board had made clear that they welcomed outside opinions from the accounting firm they had contracted to conduct the feasibility study but not from anyone else. "We, the shareholders of St. James Towers, are able to have these discussions ourselves. *We are educated and experienced in interpreting, analyzing data and reports and developing effective plans to address the specific needs of St. James Towers, Inc., our corporation.*[1] For the past 50+ years, St. James has successfully handled our own affairs without taking direction from any outside cooperatives or entity other than HPD." The message to CU4ML and cooperators like Hales who'd welcomed them into the local debate was clear: stay out of our business.

I found it revealing that the St. James board always seemed to append the "Inc." to the co-op's name, that they called the community a "corporation" just as often as they called it a "cooperative." The co-op is indeed a corporation, but the board's word choices suggested that they thought of St. James as a profit-making ploy just as much as a place to call home. I remembered how Simon Doran had closed one of our conversations with one of his characteristic, riddle-like assertions: "You know, it's truly in the best interest of people to wanna be for themselves, their family, and their corporation. Now, their corporation is their game. Everybody is in games. They love games. America loves games. . . . They give them names, but they are still games."

If anyone was living by the adage "Don't hate the player, hate the game," it was Hales. At this stage, he just wanted people to have the full picture, all the information, a range of perspectives, not just the narrative controlled by the board and presented only in fora it approved. But he had reason to be frustrated with some of the players. The board had exiled the Concerned Shareholders of St. James to the co-op across the parking lot. Tia Ward had come to regard Deborah Norton as a "dictator." Hales, in his considered manner, limited his concern to the rules of play. "Abusing the bylaws as a way to manipulate me from not using our own community room . . . I thought that was really underhanded."

THE EMPATHY OF TRUE COOPERATION

In the aftermath of the CU4ML presentation, Wenna Redfern grew in her resolve against privatization. "A lot of people walked out of there, same as I did, [saying] that this could not happen—would not happen." It seemed like folks at St. James were far better primed to see the value of Mitchell-Lama than their peers at Southbridge had been. True, there were folks like Doran and Goodyear who saw privatization as their ticket to full citizenship and as a kind of reparations. But more of the cooperators seemed to regard privatization with a certain wariness, a sense that it was far too good to be true. The lure of profit could ultimately draft cooperators into participating in their own displacement. Redfern had never forgotten Mrs. Wheeler, the woman who had refused to sell a Bronx lot to Redfern's father once she'd found out he was Black. Mitchell-Lama had insulated Wenna from such debasements for the fifty-two years since. As scholar Kavita Kulkarni found when researching Fort Greene, a neighborhood adjacent to Bed-Stuy, "By eliminating the obstacle of mortgage financing for developments in nonwhite neighborhoods, and by preventing lower incomes and racial bias from hindering opportunities for nonwhite homeseekers, the Mitchell-Lama program gave African Americans and Puerto Rican Americans in postwar New York City access to the ideal of homeownership, offering stability, independence, and a sense of prolonged investment in their community."[2]

In recent years, Wenna had been sitting on her friend's porch and watching the demographics of Bed-Stuy change. "I think that minorities are being displaced," Wenna expressed with great heaviness. She had no interest in being complicit in the change. "I'm a hard person to get along with, because I tell the truth, and I know what's going on," Redfern, feeling wise to a scheme, remarked. "I wouldn't do a sell-out. I can't put my people out on the street."

For folks like Redfern, keeping St. James in Mitchell-Lama appeared to be both good for them *and* good for others—in a word, cooperative. Redfern's opposition to privatization was not a matter of foregoing her self-interest entirely, but rather making a decision that benefited her and her neighbors. Some of her allies, like Graham Hales, did believe that privatization would be in his own financial best interest. But he didn't see it as aligned with the interests of St. James as a whole, and he understood he benefited from staying in the program as well. Hales edged closer to the altruistic end of the pro-Mitchell-Lama spectrum.

How Hales and Redfern had each reached their reasoning is complex, and their conclusions hadn't come from some cost-benefit analysis, as some economists would have you believe. Privatization debates in general are highly relational, often splitting families and prompting threats of assault—or, on the other extreme, spurring memories of neighborly casseroles delivered in times of need.[3] The social ties among the community inflect individual decisions. The line between cooperation and altruism gets muddy. A tendency toward altruism appeared much more prevalent among the pro-Mitchell-Lama movement at Southbridge, while cooperation appeared to predominate at St. James.

Why the difference, given the same fundamental benefits and risks? St. James cooperators' experiences with the larger real estate market— and their fears of what would await them should they reenter it— was everything. Their conclusions were deeply intertwined with race. Redfern talked through a privatization scenario in which she sold her apartment: After the flip tax to the co-op, "you take your $300,000 and where are you going to go? Yeah, you can go buy a house, you could put that $300,000 or $200,000 down, and guess what, have a mortgage. You have taxes, you have electric, you have water. So where are you going?" Not anywhere in this neighborhood or New York City, Wenna implied. Plus, she stated, "Blacks can't get mortgages. . . . Where are we going to go?"

Even if she may have slightly overstated her case, Redfern's overall assessment was spot on: she and her fellow Black cooperators would face a stiff challenge in getting a fair shake. The pervasive racial bias in real estate is well documented in everything from mortgage terms to appraisals.[4] Add this onto the concerns about rising maintenance costs under privatization, and the argument for sticking with Mitchell-Lama proved rather stout.

Tia Ward was more focused on the other piece of "cooperation"— not that of benefit to self but benefit to others. She held particular concern for both the seniors in the development and the broader Black community for whom Bed-Stuy real estate was no longer an accessible option. A subsidized complex like St. James, she said, was "the only place where Black people will be able to live in a decent area and be able to afford it." While a higher maintenance cost in a privatized co-op was something she thought she could handle personally by working another job or supplementing her income some other way,

> a retired person on a fixed income, they don't have those options. The building is majority seniors. . . . I thought about what if my mom didn't have me. Well, surely she can't go back to work, 90-something-years-old. Where she's gonna work? So, how would she supplement her income? [Her children] would've had to take care of her, but a lot of people don't have children and grandchildren, a lot of them, or they can't afford to help them. People, everyone is struggling just to pay bills from month to month. People can't afford to take care of someone else, and it's just not fair. I just feel like the intention of Mitchell-Lama was for middle-income individuals, lower-middle-income people to live in a decent building and don't have to spend two-thirds of your income on living expenses.

Ward wanted the co-op to remain an option for families like hers. Empathy drove her, born of her years growing up "around here with crack barrels and dope fiends and drug addicts" and then seeing the neighborhood become unaffordable for those who'd stayed, stuck it out, and had given to the wider community. Though she herself was removed from the vagaries of the market by St. James's limited-equity structure, she'd internalized what it meant to be vulnerable to the whims of a hot, racist housing market. When she heard that her elderly neighbor in the co-op, Harriet Brighton, just wanted to live out her days in stability, Ward empathized. Brighton told me: "I don't ever plan on leaving . . . I decided to stay here as long as I can manage to. I get up in the morning, and I go out like I'm going to work, and I come back in late in the evening. I'm a member of the senior center. I go there every day. I try to help in anything that I can help." As for privatization, Brighton said simply, "I don't have time for that."

The pro- and anti-privatization sides did share certain concerns. They both believed that existing residents should benefit from their years of dedication to their neighborhood. They both wanted future generations to benefit from the co-ops. What those benefits should look like was the key point of disagreement. For Ward, the cooperators' investment entitled them to staying in the stable community that they'd built. She and the other Concerned Shareholders of Mitchell-Lama thus saw it as their responsibility to uphold the infrastructure that had, up until now, allowed these families to enjoy their neighborhood.

The pro-privatizers, meanwhile, believed that such a return was insufficient and that their investment entitled them to profit from their homes and to pass that profit along to their nuclear families. This perceived right to profit from their homes was predicated on extraction, on removing Mitchell-Lama's benefit from the neighborhood and quite literally displacing it. Pro-Mitchell-Lama cooperators held a wider view of inheritance: a broader idea of family, of community, of whose good was worth considering.

Acting on this kind of empathy came easier to the folks at St. James. If they hadn't directly experienced the racism or dog-eat-dog nature of the commodified real estate market themselves, they'd watched their Bed-Stuy neighbors struggle with both. They internalized this. It wasn't like at Southbridge, where Leo Aria had remarked that "for the most part, [residents] never internalized the seriousness of homelessness. . . . They were middle-income working families . . . and that doesn't necessarily mean that they had empathy with people who had less than them. They were not in touch with them." Ward and Wenna were, and they would draw on those experiences as they framed the debate at St. James, intentionally summoning a particular meta-narrative, what one PolicyLink report describes as the kind of overriding story "we tell ourselves about the world, rooted in our values, that influence how we process information and make decisions."[5]

How St. James and Southbridge sat in their respective communities and contributed to the makeup of the neighborhoods themselves likely played a role in the differing tenors of their debates. Southbridge had been designed as a self-contained community, surrounded by centers of commerce and government. It was insular by design, and when Lower Manhattan started its full-on luxury turn post-9/11, Southbridge cooperators were less concerned with how that gentrification would affect their neighbors in the wider district and far more focused on how expensive their nearby shopping options had become. Southbridge was big; there were enough people within it such that people could live out their entire social lives within its bounds. St. James, though, is significantly smaller, and stands exposed in Bed-Stuy: a watchtower with an expansive view on neighborhood change and its discontents.

Tia Ward and I had shared food family style, splitting chicken sand-wiches, fries, that plate of mussels. I'd noticed that she'd avoided the mussels whose shells were still closed and assumed it was on account of her rather impressive red acrylic nails, unsuited for prying them open. But then she counseled me, as she later did her fellow cooperators, to avoid extracting and consuming all. "You know, when they're not open, you're not supposed to eat them." This may not be the case in reality, but Ward's caution was instructive. St. James was closed to market sales for a reason, and she didn't want to see anyone who was seated at her expansive table potentially poisoned by the alluring promise of more.

The pro-privatizers at St. James had hoped the process would be a rela-tively quick affair. As at Southbridge, however, it began to drag almost as soon as it started. The feasibility study was taking longer than expected. The blips of action—a vote, a survey, a cooperative-wide meeting—were punctuated by long stretches of business as usual. That monotony could breed a sense that nothing was really happening, that the campaign had ground to a halt or never truly taken flight. But those intimately involved in the debates—the Goodyears and Wards, the Redferns and Dorans—knew this was not the case. They were keeping an eye out for potential plays that could give their side an advantage.

The main target was, as at Southbridge, the co-op's board of di-rectors. The annual vote for three seats at the end of their three-year term on the nine-member body would arrive in early December, and the Concerned Shareholders were eager to loosen the pro-privatization faction's firm hold over the co-op's governing body. There had been no candidate slates or proto-political parties at work à la Southbridge, but many of the incumbent board members had been motivated to run in part to help bring privatization to fruition. In Lester Goodyear's soar-ing rhetoric, they had "kept the faith."

Graham Hales, after years of mostly staying out of co-op politics, was now ready to dive in to try to flip the board. He'd be following in his father's footsteps if he won the vote. Gaining board control was the only foolproof way to stop privatization, both in the short and long term. The barrier to doing so was not necessarily the strength of pro-privatization candidates but, in Hales's opinion, the fact that there was "quite a bit of apathy in the building." Among anti-privatizers, there was simply limited interest in being on the board. Even Tia Ward, despite her political sensibilities, dismissed the possibility out of hand when she was encouraged to run. "You think I got time? I don't wanna," she replied.

Hales made his stump speech at the Candidate's Night. On December 9, 2015, he went to the polls to mark his name on the ballot. Voter turnout was mediocre—that apathy at work, perhaps, or distraction by other matters, not the least a different, much larger campaign in which Donald Trump had just announced his intention to ban all Muslims from entering the United States upon his election. The night ended with a glimmer of success for the Concerned Shareholders: Hales won and became one of three pro-Mitchell-Lama board members, effective immediately. It wasn't control by any stretch, but he'd be in the room where things happened, attempting to moderate the headlong push toward commodification.

Ward was pleased with the outcome but skeptical of its replicability. Working her phones and helming other campaigns weren't the only reasons she wouldn't give time to running for a board seat. She was also skeptical of the integrity of the elections, no doubt connected to her distrust in board president Deborah Norton. "Let me tell you how crooked I knew the building was," Ward explained. "One day [the property manager] told me . . . 'run for the board, I'll make sure you win.' I didn't say anything but I never forgot what she told me. How you gonna make sure I win? How? . . . Everything has a price tag on it." Once again, allegations of ballot fixing were in the air at a Mitchell-Lama.

Wenna Redfern's efforts would seem to confirm Ward's suspicions. She would run for the board twice over the next two years, and each time she would lose, garnering the exact same number of votes—eighty-nine. "Now how is that possible?" she asked, incredulous. "People are saying to me 'Why aren't you on the board? We voted. What is going on? The votes were mixed, and this is terrible. What happened? They did something to the vote.' And we know that they did something to the first one." Redfern never disclosed how she knew this. It may well have been pure supposition. But despite Hales's prediction that co-op conflict would eventually all come out in the wash, both the pro-privatization and pro-Mitchell-Lama sides now regarded each other's campaigns as underhanded and unfair. The Concerned Shareholders' next steps would only strengthen their opponents' conviction that the playing field was tilted against them.

O COME, O COME EMMANUEL

Two years of the privatization process had passed by the time copies of the feasibility study were made available to shareholders in October 2016. The debate heated up just as the building's boiler turned on for the winter season. The board took steps to tamp down organizing and conversing outside its scheduled meetings. The community room, denied once for the CU4ML meeting, was now seen as off-limits entirely for the Concerned Shareholders. The board also "instituted this policy that anyone who wanted to distribute flyers, they had to be shown to the board first for their approval," Hales told me. The stated rationale behind the change was to prevent the spread of misinformation on privatization.

This concern wasn't entirely unfounded. Southbridge had been awash in fake news. However, with the board majority openly in favor of privatization and opposed to any outside advice that they didn't already agree with, the Concerned Shareholders naturally questioned the true intent behind the new regulation. So as they organized their next CU4ML presentation, this one to review the newly released feasibility study, "we just went ahead and put flyers on the doors anyway," Hales stated matter-of-factly.

The papers caused a stir, not for the quasi-illicit posting but for the event speakers that they announced. "Our local elected officials are very concerned about our future and will be attending: Public Advocate Letitia James, New York State Senator Velmanette Montgomery, Assembly Member Walter T. Mosley, City Council Member Laurie Cumbo." Each name was accompanied by a head shot; Dick Heitler of CU4ML was relegated to the end of the flyer. Local politicians were now involved, and the hackles of Lester Goodyear and Simon Doran—those so concerned about a conniving government stealing their homes out from under them—raised.

The meeting was scheduled for December 8, 2016. St. James was still reeling from the results of the presidential election the month before. For Wenna Redfern, President-elect Trump was just one more reason to be wary of privatization: "Where you going? So long as that man sits in the White House, where you going? It's called good luck!"

The event would be held across the street at Emmanuel Baptist Church. Its opulent, sandstone Gothic architecture struck quite the contrast with the utilitarian, straight-and-narrow lines of St. James. This wouldn't be the first or last contentious gathering held at the self-described mega-church. It prides itself on its social justice orientation; in 2019, it would become the first church in the US to host a summit on the nascent legal cannabis industry and its opportunities for Black entrepreneurs.[6] The church was quite familiar to both the cooperators and the politicians. Many were Emmanuel congregants, including Letitia "Tish" James. She'd risen from public defender to the neighborhood's city council member; in 2013, she was elected citywide public advocate. (As of the time of writing, she's the state attorney general, the first female and Black holder of the office.)

So on the evening of the eighth, interested residents left their apartments, bypassed the turn to their community room, and exited the building through the back door that's kept locked at night for security. Some may have taken the long way to the church to make use of a crosswalk, but others made a diagonal across the asphalt of St. James Place, skirting between bumper-touching parked cars. As they went in the church's side entrance that's crowned by a turret, the believers among them may have carried the spirit of Advent, which called upon them to look beyond themselves to the needs of others. In the conversation to follow, however, this theological directive was likely to disrupt another seasonal prerogative: peace on earth and goodwill toward men.

An estimated seventy-five to one hundred folks gathered in the church's auxiliary hall, with far more of the pro-privatization bloc present than had been at the prior CU4ML meeting. Deborah Norton was not among them—"she never, ever, ever came" to their meetings, Tia Ward said—but the other board members were. Hales observed, "Because it was so close to the time that we were going to vote on [funding the] offering plan, I think more of them wanted to come out, whereas with the Ryerson meeting, they just didn't think it was that important." The inclusion of politicians had piqued the privatization camp as well.

Although the politicians had been headliners on the flyer, once the meeting started they assumed a role on the sidelines in solidarity with the pro-Mitchell-Lama cooperators. They did make some remarks, laying out the two-part formula of cooperation: (1) it was good for you, the individual, in that privatization would eventually mean rising maintenance costs and the possibility that you would no longer be able to remain in the home you currently owned, and (2) it was good for others, in that voting to preserve this social housing in a sea of gentrification was a vote to give other middle- and low-income folks the chance to take advantage of it. Then the mic went over to Heitler from CU4ML to present his barebones but heartfelt PowerPoint: "Thoughts About the St. James Feasibility Study."

He started his talk on a positive note: "This is one of the better feasibility studies that I have seen." The study's appraisal, engineer's report on capital needs, and outline of the legal steps needed to effectuate privatization were all useful, in his opinion. He applauded the accountants' decision to allocate the flip tax revenue to fund capital repairs rather than fill gaps in the operating budget. The positive comments, however, largely stopped there. In Heitler's estimation, the study was still skewed toward privatization, presenting an inaccurately negative portrayal of staying under Mitchell-Lama while exaggerating the benefits of life in the unfettered market. He jumped into the numbers, showing side-by-side comparisons of the co-op's budget under different scenarios, teasing out gaps and inconsistencies, and presenting his own recommended budget for a continued future under Mitchell-Lama, one that would result in no new maintenance increases. His analysis showed, on the other hand, that a privatization budget would require a spike of 20 percent.

Heitler then came with the what-ifs, questioning the assumptions underlying the feasibility study. What if there were fewer sales than expected? What if the shares sold for lower prices than projected? What if the market collapsed? He drew on his years of knowledge on other co-ops, pulled from their numbers. Trump IV in Coney Island (privatized in 2009) had fallen short in its sales and flip tax revenues, driving maintenance costs up. The same thing had happened at Rivercross (privatized in 2014) on quirky Roosevelt Island in the middle of the East River. Maintenance costs there had climbed like one of the island's elevated tramways to Manhattan, and some cooperators were now stuck, as tram riders occasionally are, with a decision that no longer looked so good. Or, what if the process to pursue privatization dragged out, as already seemed likely, and the costs for all the high-price lawyers and accountants ballooned like they had at Cadman Towers in Brooklyn Heights or at East Midtown Plaza in Manhattan?

These arguments were, of course, largely appeals to residents' own interests. Yes, the Concerned Shareholders would overall be considered "ideological" from the perspective of Southbridge Rights. They openly discussed the ethics of dissolving social housing, privatizing public subsidy, and eliminating opportunities for future families. But they also cared about current residents, their interests, and their perspectives.

"It was intended to be just another informational session," Hales described, "but it was more pointed towards not going for the offering plan." That angle was especially clear as Heitler reprised his arguments about what privatization would mean and what Mitchell-Lama housing was supposed to achieve. As things stood, a two-bedroom apartment at St. James could be had for a total of $44,000—quite affordable for a middle-income family. Under privatization, the cost would rise to $768,000 according to the feasibility study—accessible, in Heitler's estimation, to only those with an annual income above $176,000. Who then could buy into St. James? Not you or your families, Heitler reminded cooperators.

Heitler closed by echoing a phrase that Lester Goodyear had used in one of his pro-privatization rants: keeping the faith. He invoked the original vision behind Mitchell-Lama, the ideals enshrined in the program and the cooperative movement that birthed it. He called forth the Rochdale Principles—democratic control, nondiscrimination, advancing the common good, and the kind of education in which he was now engaged—that had spread from quaint Toad Lane outside of Manchester to the entire world. He quoted Abraham Kazan, titan of the United Housing Federation: "Where all personal gain and benefit is eliminated, greater good can be accomplished for the benefit of all." And he reprised the stellar deal that Mitchell-Lama presented—the affordable, stable, accessible housing for middle-income folks. Heitler noted, too, that the greater good wasn't inconsistent with individual benefit. The cooperators' low housing costs had allowed them to "save money every single month," as evidenced by the second homes some, like Wenna, had been able to purchase, by the college tuitions paid, and by a comfortable journey into eventual senescence for elders like Tia Ward's mother.

It was an uplifting end to a presentation otherwise mired in the confusing yet consequential minutiae of cost projections. Questions and clarifications followed. Hales was unsurprised by the sporadic interjections, by the back-and-forth jabs that erupted between pro-privatizers and pro-Mitchell-Lama cooperators. He remembered one particularly vocal board member bringing up "the point about outsiders coming in to tell us what to do. . . . Those who are pro-privatization felt that politicians . . . had no business being there."

But Hales and his collaborators hardly saw CU4ML and those elected as outsiders. "We felt having elected officials there was important because of what was at stake," Hales said. Although they were not from the same building, they were nonetheless neighbors. They were co-creators of the city they all called home. As everyone filed out of the church, the pro-Mitchell-Lama set hung back. Hales was approached by a resident who wanted to go private but, in this instance, "was being conciliatory. She gave me a hug because . . . we grew up together, basically. . . . She just wanted to express her feeling of having unity and working together." He chatted with his CU4ML collaborators, "just kind of sharing our feelings kind of thing . . . and they just gave us words of encouragement to keep fighting, if we needed anything else to know that they were there to support us." Together, in solidarity, they kept the faith.

CHAPTER 8

A Responsibility
to Steward

The new year, 2017, came quickly after the meeting at Emmanuel Baptist. The second privatization vote, on whether to fund an offering plan, would follow soon after. The CU4ML presentation had mostly solidified cooperators' existing stances—there'd been no come-to-Jesus moment for the pro-privatizers. And those who distrusted any outside influence, especially from representatives of the City and State, felt more than ever that the government aimed to keep them from profit that was rightfully theirs.

Despite this increasing polarization, St. James had managed to avoid the kind of hostility that at Southbridge had led to defaced flyers and death threats. That, however, did not mean St. James was completely free of ad hominem attacks or silent treatments. Some cooperators no longer spoke to Wenna Redfern. To them she said, "Y'all went from low-class to no-class. What do you want me to do?" Tia Ward kept up her beef with board president Deborah Norton, who she called a "habitual, pathological, chronic liar." Say what you will about Ward's confrontational style, but she owned it. "If I do something, I'm going to tell you 'yes, I did it' or 'yes, I said it.' [Norton] asked me not too long ago . . . 'did you call me a bitch?' And I said, 'yes, I did.' . . . And I did. I'm not going to turn around and say, 'I didn't say it.' That's not who I am. . . . She's funny, you know? She's funny. I pray for her."

All this still looked like child's play compared to the national context, where the early days of Trump's fascist presidency saw the Muslim ban implemented and unprecedented protests against the new administration erupt in airport terminals and city streets. At St. James, too, certain co-operators were turning their ire toward their government, though the pitch of their outcry was different. The entry of local politicians into the fray had made "the City" an enemy of the pro-privatizers. They may have been able to politely disagree with their fellow shareholders, but a paternalistic government sticking its nose into their affairs: that was unconscionable.

Lester Goodyear's full-throated rejection of any City involvement was particularly ironic. He was a member of that government himself, whether he liked to think of it that way or not. His post on the local community board—what the City calls "the most local, grassroots form of City government"[1]—had given him a bully pulpit on all sorts of neighborhood matters, from the granting of liquor licenses to all manner of housing issues. Community boards participate in the City's Uniform Land Use Review Process (or ULURP, as the unsettling acronym goes), weighing in on proposed zoning changes and developments in their district. Their purview includes the number of affordable homes in new residential construction and the depth of that affordability. Goodyear could argue for more subsidized housing out of one side of his mouth while damning City officials for trying to preserve it out the other. He seemed comfortable with the government advocating for certain housing policies but only if they didn't touch his own.

Goodyear believed that HPD and other entities "should be 'neutral,' not adversarial in the decisions M/L Coops make" and that "HPD has not been an 'Honest Broker' with regard to maintaining a true neutral position in the choice of the 21 Saint James Place Board of Directors to pursue 'Privatization' of the Co-op." In Goodyear's opinion, "HPD appears to feel it has the 'right' to determine our future possibility as 'Private Co-op Homeowners,' based not on the M/L Law, but on overall housing needs of NYC at any given time." He regarded HPD as an arm of the state meddling in the supposedly autonomous market. But his framing failed to acknowledge that almost all housing is dependent on government—as St. James was on HPD—because government creates and sustains the housing market. It does so through infrastructure provision and contract law, enforcement of property rights and building codes, funding, and health and safety reviews. You can't be an outside force on something that you are also continuously bringing into being.

The second privatization vote was scheduled for February 23, 2017. As per the co-op's bylaws, only shareholders of St. James Towers—not

HPD officials or local politicians—would decide whether to move forward with the privatization process, despite Goodyear's attempt to
frame their involvement as determinative. Some public officials were,
however, likely feeling a sense of responsibility as another social housing option came under threat in their ever-more-expensive city. Their
counterparts with a connection to Southbridge had largely shirked this
responsibility under the guise of respecting the co-op's self-governance.
The Brooklyn delegation wasn't willing to do so, resolving to continue
their direct lobbying of St. James residents. Goodyear himself touched
on this in another public letter bemoaning the exercise of public policy:

> Unfortunately, St. James' self-governance goal has been overshad-
> owed by the focus on the New York City housing development boom
> and increasing real estate prices. "Affordable housing" has become
> the mantra of state and city politicians seeking to strengthen their
> constituency base for their next re-election. In recent years, the NYC
> real estate boom has reached Clinton Hill. The politicians have not
> been successful in stopping the private developers from building all
> around St. James. However, they are congratulating one another that
> they . . . interfered with St. James' efforts to achieve its goal of SELF-
> GOVERNANCE, specifically, to opt out of the Mitchell-Lama program.

Goodyear wasn't wrong to question public officials' success in countering the housing crisis or to point out that elected officials likely
wanted to be able to tout a social housing win in their next campaign.
But this was less an instance of pandering or scheming than it was a
response to the genuine needs of their constituents. Perhaps the public
officials coming out against privatization were simply doing their jobs.

St. James Towers' 326 units may not have appeared significant compared to the city's overall need for affordable housing. But every unit is
crucial if New York is to remain accessible to individuals at all incomes.
The rental arm of Mitchell-Lama demonstrates this point. While only
10 percent of co-op units have left the program, the rental stock has
been raided: over 50 percent of those units, some thirty-six thousand,
are now market-rate, in part because the decision to privatize a rental
Mitchell-Lama is made by landlords, not residents. Over sixty-nine
thousand of these rental units were built in New York City at the same
time another sixty-nine thousand co-op units went up in places like
Southbridge and St. James. For comparison, under the housing plan im-

plemented by Mayor de Blasio's administration starting in 2017—then considered the most ambitious in New York history—the City hoped to spur the construction of 120,000 new units by 2026. Without the preservation of existing affordable units like those remaining Mitchell-Lamas, any new construction completed by the City is just catch-up.

Indeed, preservation makes up a much larger part of New York City's affordable-housing strategy than new construction. The longer the term of affordability you can get out of an initial investment in affordable housing means less money needs to be allocated toward locking units into additional periods of affordability. Maintaining buildings is generally cheaper than building new ones—especially in a place like New York City, where land and construction costs are particularly high and where preservation can be achieved by offering loans that are eventually repaid. Simon Doran felt he had scored a gotcha when he told me that the City "gets money from the feds for affordable housing, and if they can keep us in the program, they can use [that money] for something else." He was implying that saving money that can be put toward other programs was somehow nefarious. Instead, he put forth a compelling argument for why HPD and politicians were right to try to maintain St. James as social housing.

Preserving older units also means preserving affordable housing in some of the city's most expensive neighborhoods. When the Mitchell-Lama buildings were constructed in the mid-twentieth century, they were largely placed in areas that needed investment. Now, many of those areas have few affordable market-rate options. This makes complexes like St. James even more valuable, especially if neighborhood safety, health, and schools have improved alongside the rise in prices. These districts are now areas of displacement risk for lower-income residents just as they have become (arguably) more opportunity-rich.

Given all this, the politicians using their public voice to call for the preservation of St. James was a no-brainer. They had all been elected with a mandate, a responsibility, to address housing affordability. Goodyear and Doran, however, saw only duplicity. Doran, his gravelly voice giving his words the air of a fireside tale of horror, described Mitchell-Lama as a program transformed: "the greatest idea, the greatest concept," in which co-ops were meant to be privatized according to his erroneous interpretation, that "became a monster" when people fought to preserve them as social housing. Goodyear, intent on isolating his actions and their consequences from the larger ecosystem of the city, said simply, "If they need more housing, build more housing, but don't come and renege on me. That's not my fault."

CALL IT A CONFERENCE, CALL IT A RALLY

In the days leading up to the vote on funding the creation of the draft offering plan, or Red Herring, a fight that Graham Hales termed the Battle of the Flyers was underway. His side issued one that emphasized the $120,000 price tag of the Red Herring, the possibility of it all being a waste, and the other expenses that money could otherwise cover at the complex. It appealed to residents' sense of stability: "You will have the security and peace of mind of remaining in affordable housing in a desirable neighborhood by continuing in the Mitchell-Lama program; there is no risk of low turnover of apartment sales, uncertainty of flip tax revenues, and fluctuations in the real estate market, all of which are possible with reconstitution."

The pro-privatization group, meanwhile, borrowed a headline from the Southbridge debate: "KEEP OUR OPTIONS OPEN." "If we vote no now, we will never know the possibilities of what life at St. James would be like IF we left Mitchell-Lama and controlled our building ourselves," one of their flyers read. That enticing lure of what could be was hard at work. At the same time, pro-privatizers also clearly felt the need to reassure their neighbors that they did not yet have to commit to this future, however lucrative it might be. They spent the first half of the flyer stressing the lack of finality in this particular vote: "Just having an offering plan does NOT mean the building will go private. That decision can only be made with a shareholder vote. *No one else can make that final decision for us.*" On the back foot, they sensed they still had more convincing to do before a possible final vote later that year or, more likely, in 2018.

The flyers from the pro-Mitchell-Lama crew were curiously devoid of appeals to altruism or empathy. They had another tactic up their sleeves, one that would speak as much to the larger neighborhood as their fellow cooperators. On the morning of February 22, 2017—the day before the second vote—Tia Ward held a press conference in the defunct theater in the round at St. James's playground. The co-op's tower rose behind her, its siblings aligned like dominoes down the avenue.

The journalists who'd gathered in the asphalt circle were soon joined by two groups of supposedly unexpected participants. The first were the same politicians who had appeared at the meeting at Emmanuel Baptist Church months prior. Ward insisted that she had not invited them, that they had shown up out of the blue, an assertion that the second uninvited group—the pro-privatizers—regarded as bullshit. They'd found out about the press conference, or what they termed a rally, only the night before, through the grapevine. Those who were able threw together the necessary cardboard signs to make their presence known.

Ward gave brief comments in support of remaining in Mitchell-Lama, urging cooperators to halt the privatization process with a "no" vote the next day. Then, as so often happens, the politicians took over.

"Why do we not want to leave the same opportunities that were available to us to someone else?" Public Advocate Tish James asked, sparking a call-and-response worthy of Emmanuel Baptist across the way. "Should living in Clinton Hill only be an option for the rich? Should Clinton Hill only be an option for the powerful?"

Ward, ever forceful, led the responding chorus of "No!"

James continued: "If that's the case then why not be concerned about the next generation as opposed to your own pocketbooks?" Privatization, James said, would not only make those pocketbooks a lot lighter as maintenance bills inevitably rose; it would also "erode the character" of their beloved neighborhood, a "last bastion of integrity and diversity" in Brooklyn.[2]

Lester Goodyear then made his way before the microphone, clad in his signature cowboy hat, tinted glasses, and dark leather jacket. This was not his first rodeo, and he used his ride at the mic to tell the politicians to stay out of the co-op's business.

The next day, a St. James resident, writing under the pseudonym Brooklyn Girl, commented on a *Brooklyn Paper* article about the gathering:

> The fact that a rally was being held in our own building's playground was only known to a select few shareholders who have been discussing the building status with local politicians for a while now. That is their right to do so, I respect that, and that is why we have a Public Advocate—to address ALL of our concerns. But when a public event about a building is not made known to ALL building residents, regardless of their position on privatizing or not, it becomes clear that the Public in Public Advocate is missing. The rally was organized in a way that people who do not agree with Letitia James would not

know about it, thus not show up, making the public event a perfect photo-op. . . .

And here is the REAL kicker! Letitia James is so concerned with our seniors, yet she did not even let all the seniors in the building know that she was coming to their rescue! Some seniors walked past the rally in our playground and asked, "What's going on here?" So I guess some seniors are worth more than others to our Public Advocate. Let's change that to Selective Public Advocate. This move was a shoddy one, lacking transparency and genuine care for seniors— or other constituents who live in the building! Shame on Ms. James for her lack of transparency, and for the way in which she made (or tried) to make sure that those in attendance were only members of the "choir" that she could preach to.[3]

Brooklyn Girl was posting anonymously, she said, because of hostile people in the building and the possible repercussions of her post. Then Tia Ward entered the chat, engaging in a tit-for-tat comments battle. Brooklyn Girl then unveiled herself as Miranda Lynch and called out Ward as one of the hostiles. She accused Ward of threatening to kick her cat and throw acid in her face over an assortment of neighborly disputes unrelated to privatization, accusations that Ward denied. The tea was spilling out on the sidewalk for all to see.

The ire toward the local officials, Public Advocate James in particular, grew. Simon Doran mused on the nature of power in one of our conversations: "Politicians are so easily corrupted. I've got enough dirt on Ms. James that she could never be mayor." Lester Goodyear drafted another missive, this one to push back on the claim that a privatized St. James would contribute to gentrification. "There is a notion, fostered by Government Officials, from the 35th Council District, that privatization of 21 St. James Place would represent the falling of the first 'domino' in the beginning of a radical change in Clinton Hill available, affordable, subsidized housing, which would alter the 'complexion' and 'political persuasion' of the area." But look at the buildings next door, he said: Ryerson Towers and Pratt Towers had both recently re-upped on financing from the City and would remain in Mitchell-Lama for the foreseeable future, providing a bulwark against that change. Plus, gentrification was already in full swing.

It was true that St. James's privatization wouldn't start anything— but it would expand it. Most cooperators had seen enough dominos fall by then to understand that, even if they wouldn't admit it openly. That gave the narrative that St. James residents could help interrupt a destructive cascade even more power.

THE VOTE

With cases made and passions burned off in rhetorical flares at the press conference, the vote the following day was rather tame. Tia Ward watched vigilantly for any incidents, but there wasn't much to see. The vote was administered entirely via absentee ballots, handled by the same Honest Ballot Association that had run Southbridge's elections. It was dull in the way that one might hope governance matters at a limited-equity cooperative to be.

The pro-privatizers needed a two-thirds majority—218 votes—to trigger the drafting of the Red Herring. When the ballots were tallied and the results posted to the bulletin board next to the elevators a couple days later, only 132 cooperators had voted in favor of this second stage. An almost equal number, 129, had voted "no," while 65 shareholders had abstained. The pro-privatizers hadn't even come close to getting the support they needed.

Ward wanted to make sure that the message got through to privatization ringleader Deborah Norton. "She thought [the vote] was almost even and it wasn't," Ward told me. "I said, 'silly rabbit, don't you know if a person didn't vote, that meant "Hell No."' That didn't mean 'No'; it meant 'Hell No.'"

All of a sudden, that was that. Celebrations by the winning side were understated. No bar trips or lobby whooping for this crowd. Graham Hales said that the Concerned Shareholders "really didn't do anything special" to mark the occasion. "We just kind of congratulated one another, either by email . . . or if we bumped into one another. We were kind of high-fiving, stuff like that." The relief of these pro-Mitchell-Lama cooperators was humble. St. James Towers would remain social housing, a public good, for now.

They would be secure in their victory for only a short while, which was perhaps why Hales and friends thought only high fives rather than highballs were in order. The majority of the co-op board was still staunchly pro-privatization, and in another year they could try again.

Granted, they'd also have to start from the top, like an unforgiving video game. They would have to hold a new vote on a new feasibility study and go from there. Some of the most fervent pro-privatizers seemed undeterred, attempting to rally residents with a sense of aggrievement and a reminder that they did not have to give up yet. Lester Goodyear wrote to his allies: "Although we did not obtain the required number of shareholder 'yes' votes to take the second step towards 'Homeownership,' We should not abandon Our original goal." He did, however, acknowledge that the defeat had changed him, from a "winning ticket" holder in the lottery of New York's real estate market to the author of yet another public letter, this one titled "21 Saint James Place, Brooklyn, 11205: A Story of the Betrayal of the Public Trust by Brooklyn Political Officials in the 35th Council District of Brooklyn."

Simon Doran, for his part, soon felt the fight fading from his fellow pro-privatizers. "I've seen a few of the older guys, Mr. Goodyear, . . . become weary, overwhelmed by our stupidity." He was less than optimistic about their ability to regroup and go again: "I don't see it because . . . [the pro-Mitchell-Lama side] know that they can win mainly because they got nothing but time. . . . I was sort of weary. They know this. They know that we are growing older, and we will die out, and they'll bring in new people, and like I said it's a part of the whole scheme. It's the scheme, and they're gonna win." The scheme, apparently, was just letting the program work as intended: as a reliable, affordable, stable form of social housing that would remain for the next generation. Those who'd organized to keep St. James Towers from going the way of Southbridge were guilty as charged.

HOUSING, DEFENDED

Right around the time that St. James cooperators voted down privatization, two scholars of urban studies and sociology, David Madden and Peter Marcuse, published the book *In Defense of Housing*, which lay bare the contemporary politics of the places we call home. The authors take issue with the dominant narrative of "a system in crisis" that took hold after the crash of 2008. "We need to be careful with this usage of the concept of crisis. The idea of crisis implies that inadequate or unaffordable housing is abnormal, a temporary departure from a well-functioning standard." That isn't what is happening, say Madden and Marcuse. They add: "Housing crisis is a predictable, consistent outcome of a basic characteristic of capitalist spatial development: housing is not produced and distributed for the purposes of dwelling for all; it is produced and distributed as a commodity to enrich the few. Housing crisis is not a result of the system breaking down but of the system working as it is intended."[4]

In short, the very causes of the crisis are one and the same with the central ideology of homeownership. When that ownership carries a perceived right to profit from housing, without any responsibility for the collateral damage, crisis will be perpetual. Housing becomes a commodity, but one that has no rivals in its importance for organizing our lives and our politics. That is distinct from the role of housing that needs defending: housing as home.[5]

Structuring housing as a limited-equity co-op, as the Mitchell-Lama program did, is a defense of home. The program sought a path to sheltering middle-income folks that was different from the exclusive suburbs supercharged by government-backed mortgages—subsidies immediately privatized and transmogrified into morally deserved earnings. The permanence of this defense can, however, never be guaranteed. At the program's outset, co-op privatization wasn't a possibility, but then laws and politics changed. The bulwarks against commodification need to be continually maintained, rebuilt, occupied, and augmented.

A total of 194 St. James cooperators, with their votes on February 23, 2017, managed to preserve their collectively owned social housing. Southbridge's defenders were unable to do the same. That fortress against commodification in Lower Manhattan was transformed into a pillar of the housing system it had once stood against. How, exactly, did the Concerned Shareholders of St. James, with so many prevailing winds blowing against them, achieve their victory?

There is no exact formula or single answer. But we can learn lessons from how the battles at St. James and Southbridge diverged and in their different qualities as places and communities. These are applicable to how we might preserve other social housing in the future. As Madden and Marcuse point out, housing can be "a vehicle for imagining alternative social orders. Every emancipatory movement must deal with the housing question in one form or another. This capacity to spur the political imagination is part of housing's social value as well."[6] The lessons of Mitchell-Lama extend beyond the housing sphere. Any attempt at realizing a truer, deeper form of our commonwealth must heed them.

Where Southbridge's defenders spoke solely of the financial side of privatization—countering its alluring rewards with the specter of its risks—St. James's Concerned Shareholders broadened the frame. They stressed that privatization wasn't just a financial decision but a moral one: a statement about who the city was for, what recipients of public support owed to future generations, and how their own lives and choices intersected with those around them. They coupled this altruistic message with information that showed how privatization presented a financial risk—not only to the wider community but to the cooperators themselves. They activated three different forms of unselfishness: empathic unselfishness through identification with future beneficiaries, communitarian unselfishness through identification with their neighbors who feared maintenance increases, and moralistic unselfishness through arguing that privatization was, in a sense, theft.[7] In doing so, they triggered a key causal mechanism of collective action: a shared narrative, with which defection (privatization) was incompatible.[8]

St. James's predominately Black cooperative body, situated in a neighborhood where gentrification and displacement had transformed the streets for all to see, was particularly well primed to hear these messages. Many of the cooperators had themselves experienced discrimination in the housing market. Even among those who hadn't, most knew the history of Bed-Stuy and could see where its future seemed to be heading if action wasn't taken. Moreover, that future was not abstract but proximate, already right outside their doors. The prospect of big money through privatization came with an asterisk: they would still be Black in a real estate system that had racism baked into its core. They'd internalized the need for social housing. At Southbridge, Lower Manhattan's luxury turn didn't have the same effect on the residents. The already-insular community remained at a remove from the rest of the neighborhood. As the prices on everything from groceries to movie tickets shot up with the glossy skyscrapers catering to capital, they felt under siege. Privatization beckoned as a bulwark against those high prices. If you can't beat them, the pro-privatizers seemed to say, join them. This call simply did not appeal to the residents of St. James in the same way. Because they had connections to their wider neighborhood, joining "them"—the monied companies and individuals snapping up buildings for passive profits—would have meant selling out their very sense of community.

Just as St. James's Concerned Shareholders didn't see their privatization decision as only about their individual well-being, they also didn't go it alone in the debates. Where Southbridge's pro-Mitchell-Lama residents considered it too risky to bring in outsiders, their counterparts at St. James heard those critiques and pushed through anyway, calling on the solidarity of CU4ML and local officials. In doing so, they gained access to crucial resources while also broadening the debate. CU4ML brought tactics, expertise, and the kind of political education that both Southbridge and St. James were internally starved of. Public Advocate Tish James and her coterie of other officials packed up their bully pulpits and stationed them onsite, driving home the need for cooperators to consider a "we" beyond their own building. They connected the struggle at St. James to other struggles, and the strugglers to one another, activating another causal mechanism for collective action—what sociologist Charles Tilly calls "straightforward coercion by outsiders."[9] Southbridge's privateers had been able to keep most politicians out of their debates by wielding the sheer heft of their voting bloc. That complex is roughly 4.5 times as populous as St. James. It was thus much more difficult, and ultimately impossible, for the St. James privatizers to drown out the local politicians speaking to the clear public interest of preserving social housing amid a housing crisis that they had been elected to address. Southbridge board president Harvey Marshall, looking on from his now-privatized home across the East River, considered the politicians' involvement at St. James to have been instrumental in defeating privatization there.

One can't say what the outcome of the final Southbridge vote would have been if the anti-privatizers there had recruited nonresidents to their fight or if they had added moral, normative arguments to their rhetoric. But if Daniel Brampton can wring his hands over the additional flyers that his Venice vacation left unwritten, it's also valid to speculate that those approaches may have closed the paltry eleven-vote difference. Then again, it's worth recalling that Southbridge had thwarted an earlier attempt at privatizing their co-op years before. At any Mitchell-Lama co-op, voting down privatization is never a permanent solution. Within a year, the whole process could start again. St. James remains an island of social housing, destined to be eroded if its floodwalls aren't maintained.

For that reason, Madden and Marcuse endorse some skepticism around housing models like Mitchell-Lama that both oppose and exist within a larger system of commodification. "Human relationships cannot be confined to the boundaries of a housing estate. It is not possible to insulate a small group from what goes on in society as a whole; any such group is likely to be shaped by broader patterns of oppressive relationships. And islands of residential liberation will have limited impact in a sea of housing oppression and commodification," they write. Islands are good locations for lighthouses, though. They continue: "But experimental dwellings and emancipatory movements have wider significance as living demonstrations of housing's potential. They should be seen as beacons pointing towards a broader possibility: that housing might support non-oppressive social relations, not in some utopian realm but in everyday life."[10]

That is one of the beauties of social housing: the models exist, and they work, even here in the capitalist United States. Activists like Graham Hales, Tia Ward, and Wenna Redfern have managed to keep the light on at St. James. And across the country, interest has grown in establishing new limited-equity co-ops, community land trusts, rent control, and public housing at a level that, less than a decade ago, seemed politically untenable. But as with all infrastructure, just building these refuges in a sea of commodification is not enough. Our public goods need to be maintained, and central to the maintenance of social housing is a wholesale transformation of the prevailing American conception of homeownership. We must abolish the notion that ownership includes a right to profit. The defenders of St. James and Southbridge point the way toward an ethic to install in its place.

Those who claim that ownership endows one with absolute control over some definable thing—a piece of land, a house, an instrument, a toy—are preachers of isolation. As I took in the stories of Southbridge and St. James, I was struck by how pro-privatizers willingly curtailed their perception of the spheres of their influence and concern. They didn't consider their neighbors or even friends with whom they'd built a community over decades. They denied any ties between their own decisions and the well-being of their fellow New Yorkers, save for the hypothetical rich family who would now have another housing option at their disposal, possibly at a slightly lower price. Their sense of entitlement to profit overpowered any sense of connection to a public program that had provided them a most fundamental need: a safe, stable, affordable home. They were under the sway of what Rebecca Solnit calls the ideology of isolation. "If you forget what you derive from the collective, you can imagine that you owe it nothing and can go it alone," she writes, but "we are nodes on intricate systems, synapses snapping on a great collective brain; we are in it together, for better or worse."[11]

Those who fought the privatizers largely bought into an ethos of connection. Their definition of ownership, of course, was still not entirely devoid of rights and entitlements. Just as James Szal could decide to paint his walls a screaming shade of red to complement his shoe-shaped furnishings, he could also tell you to get the hell out should you find his aesthetic, or the barking of his senior shih tzu, to be too much. But he and his allies also saw the layers of responsibility that came with owning something. As residents of social housing, they knew this entailed more than just paying their share of collective costs or ensuring that their leaking toilet was fixed before the apartment below suffered a collapsed ceiling. They recognized their responsibility to steward the public good they'd been given control of, even if that meant declining a major influx of personal wealth. They operated on a different spatial and temporal scale.[12] In doing so, they fulfilled their responsibility as stewards of not just a building but a neighborhood, a city, and, crucially, the future inheritors of their homes, be they a family member or a stranger pulled from a list.

For the pro-privatizers, their right to profit came first, and their responsibility to care for their asset—to "conduct your business well," as Lester Goodyear put it—came in service of realizing that right. For those who believed in social housing, ownership was bundled up with a responsibility to steward. This understanding is similar to the idea of reciprocity in gift economies that predominate in Indigenous societies. As Potawatomi writer and scientist Robin Wall Kimmerer describes it, "Responsibilities and gifts are understood as two sides of the same coin. The possession of a gift is coupled with a duty to use it for the benefit of all."[13] A safe, stable, affordable home is a gift, just as land and life are, and residents' fulfillment of their responsibility to steward that gift is what made their ownership real. When pro-Mitchell-Lama cooperators stood up for their co-op as a public good, they affirmed their ownership of their homes, their communities. "True ownership," to borrow a phrase from an exasperated Goodyear, isn't achieved when the possession can be sold off at any price. True ownership is consummated with care, maintenance, and preservation—with faithful stewardship.

After privatization was voted down, life at St. James returned to a relative dullness, a state befitting its ongoing role as key infrastructure. The aftermath brought no lawsuits or major character assassinations, as had occurred at Southbridge. The wounds of the debate were still raw, of course. Lester Goodyear managed to all but ghostwrite a take-down of the politicians who had played a role in thwarting his dreams, signed by the editors of *Crain's New York Business*.[14] Tia Ward and Deborah Norton continued their feud. Ward recalled arriving at a co-op-wide meeting partway through, her hands full of groceries: "Do you know she stopped the whole meeting to have a stare down with me? For like, six, seven minutes, just staring at me and I'm just staring back. . . . I hadn't opened my mouth."

No doubt Ward didn't take many steps to stitch up the gap between them, and the fact that privatization could be raised again within a year didn't help either. The future was still open. Privatization had been deferred for the time being. The co-op had no ironclad commitment to Mitchell-Lama; no new City funds had yet been accepted. The board majority was still firmly pro-privatization. Each side remained ready to go again, to tussle in the proxy wars of board votes.

Across the parking lot at Ryerson Towers, where the Concerned Shareholders of St. James had launched their first salvo against privatization alongside CU4ML, reinforcements in the citywide campaign to preserve Mitchell-Lamas were mustered. There, in October 2017, eight months after St. James's decisive second vote, Mayor Bill de Blasio stepped to the mic in the community room, accompanied by a drummer. "Mitchell-Lama housing: for years it was great until suddenly the bill came due, if you will. And these buildings started to be threatened and their future, and your futures, your ability to live in your own building, your own apartment—like so many tens of thousands of New Yorkers—was threatened," he intoned.[15]

The mayor had returned to his home borough of Brooklyn to announce $250 million aimed at preserving fifteen thousand Mitchell-Lama homes, mostly on the co-op side of the program. This would add to the debt with strings attached that Simon Doran so despised, the debt that had played its own role in financializing the privatization debates at Southbridge and St. James. As de Blasio made his announcement, he was flanked by many of the same elected officials—Public Advocate Tish James and local councilwoman Laurie Cumbo—who'd defended St. James months prior. The mood was celebratory. There was hope in that room. Perhaps they could turn the tide against the wider threat of privatization; perhaps stewardship could outweigh profit. As de Blasio closed out the event, he pointed to his backup: "I want my brother the drummer ready—get ready, okay? Because as we conclude . . . the credit goes to the people who stood up for years and years and made Brooklyn great." Brooklyn's stewards, that is.

Those stewards are not exclusively pro-Mitchell-Lama cooperators. Folks like Lester Goodyear had also done their part, serving on community boards and advocating for what they thought was right. Goodyear and other pro-privatizers had served on the St. James board over the years, worked to keep it a great place to live despite the tumult outside its doors. This was its own kind of stewardship, even if these residents eventually wanted to transform it into undue profits. Casting a narrative of heroes vs. villains is easy. Less so is highlighting the gray areas—all the folks who struggled with this decision and all the reasons why supporting privatization is understandable though unjustified.

Geographer Amanda Huron, who studied the commons of limited-equity co-ops in Washington, DC, puts it well: "In being caught in this tension between maintaining the collectivity of the commons and being coopted into capitalist markets, [limited-equity co-op] members are hardly alone; commoners from the English peasantry to the native peoples of New England have succumbed to pressures of enclosure, to individualize and monetize resources previously managed in common. This does not make these co-op members unethical individuals, but rather it points to the difficulty of maintaining commons in highly commodified landscapes."[16] These decisions aren't easy. Scholar-activist Matt Hern notes that "people are forced to make searing choices, to instrumentalize their homes, reimagine them as property, and then navigate that commodification based on incomplete market information and limited options." This is because of the "structural conditions that leave all of us maneuvering to protect our own interests, constantly edging us into contention with our neighbors and undermining the best possibilities of urban life."[17]

This difficulty isn't born only of the prevailing commodification of place and home across the US. It's also born of narrative, held up by ideology, supported in policy, and fueled with the scraps of a collapsing safety net. Buying and selling a home for profit is held up as the American Dream. It's positioned as the way to attain full citizenship and a voice. Home equity is the only tool many Americans have to attain economic, educational, and aspirational family goals at a time when wages aren't what they should be, work security is nonexistent beyond unions, and higher education is dependent on increasingly large sums of cash in its own commodified hellscape. Equity in a place one calls home is the backstop for disaster, for the unexpected or inevitable.

Americans have been breathing in the spores carrying these messages for generations. That, of course, doesn't absolve individuals of their attempts to privatize public goods for personal profit. They must own that as well. But just as empathy for others is crucial in defeating these attempts, empathy for the would-be privatizers is also called for. So too is a wider view of how to maintain social housing that includes political education, narrative construction, incentive reform, and an attention to the moral questions at hand.

Southbridge and St. James are but two outposts in a much larger contest against commodification and in favor of building and maintaining public goods. There are many others worth visiting—arenas beyond the realm of apartments and split-levels. The dispatches in the next chapter demonstrate that prioritizing stewardship over profit isn't as foreign as we're told it is. This ethic too has roots in American soil, roots in fact deeper, wider, and more connected than the isolating tendrils of commodification—and far more life-giving.

PART IV

Commonwealth

CHAPTER 9

Land and Trust

Soil and roots were, in a sense, what took my attention from the asphalt of Brooklyn to a gravel drive in New Hampshire one October afternoon in 2021. The interstate gave way to country roads lined with white colonial architecture and telephone poles sprouting American flags. The crunch of gravel began at a sign for grass-fed beef beyond the Litchfield town commons. Having grown up outside Athens, Georgia, with a barn at my high school and pasture across the street, I felt something familiar in this drive. I trundled past the odd pig and chicken. If I hadn't been exhilarated by the exchange of my usual city sights for these country tableaus, the area might have seemed dull. The farm I'd come to visit looked like a farm, the land a bit waterlogged after days of rain but otherwise appeared to be regular land. On the contrary, however, it was about to be transformed into something special. I soon spied a couple of dozen folks celebrating on the lower field alongside the Merrimack River. They were the only indication that something was different about this place—that it was being cultivated not for profit but for the common good.

The party to which Ian McSweeney, the executive director of the national nonprofit Agrarian Trust, had invited me was modest: a small tent sheltering some tables and a beer cooler, a porta potty, and a trailer-hitched smoker packed full of barbecue chicken, tended to by a barefoot White dude with dreads named Jeremiah. Thirty or so additional folks milled about until a group of six gathered in a crescent around a vase of wildflowers to share remarks on the occasion. On this day, the sixty-three acres of Normanton Farms were being passed from the local Monadnock Community Land Trust to the just-launched New Hampshire Agrarian Commons. Their stewardship would hold those acres and more in up to eleven farms in the surrounding area, outside the speculative market in perpetuity.

Steve Normanton, the ample-bellied White South African tenant farmer, had already been practicing his version of regenerative agriculture across these fields for twelve years. Now, the new Agrarian Commons would ensure that he'd be able to continue to do so for as long as he desired, having granted him a ninety-nine-year lease on the land. Some of the same folks who'd looked after the plot as part of the land trust would continue to play a role in its governance as members of this new commons. Among them was the party's emcee, Deb, a Waldorf School enthusiast with the bearing of an outdoorsy Bette Midler.

The gift of this land from one commons to another would better secure the land outside the market, foster a more sustainable model for its farmers, and create new opportunities for community oversight and access to resources. This transfer also marked a new milestone for Agrarian Trust. The land being transferred on the day of my visit marked the creation of the twelfth Agrarian Commons the organization had seeded in just a year and half. By sheltering land within these new ownership structures, Agrarian Trust was piloting a new model for a very old thing: holding land in common for the benefit of the community, preserving a public good, and ensuring proper governance and stewardship. The model aims to maintain that most fundamental of infrastructures: the land itself.

Before we tucked into the chicken wings beckoning from the smoker nearby, Normanton, still sporting the look from his previous career as a safari guide—outback hat, cargo shorts, leather Chelsea boots— consecrated the new commons with a reading of "Law of the Land" by Oswin Ramsay, a poem that has long guided him in his work. "We don't really own the land, son / We hold it and pass away," he read. He was followed by another in the group, Whitney Carpenter, who rose to say a few words. He'd been savoring this moment with his eyes closed, blissed-out on a dream come true, a fitting capstone to his lifelong efforts in cooperation: organizing tea picker co-ops in Sri Lanka and supporting the formation of a cooperative grocery in Fiji before settling in the land trust nearby. Carpenter now paid homage to the area's Indigenous Pennacook people, who would traditionally pull fish from the river nearby and dry them on the banks. "It's the same land," Carpenter affirmed. Within the same economic and political system that had forced the Pennacook's dispossession in the late 1600s, a new commons to reconceive our relationship with land was now in formation.

THE COMMONS

To speak of the commons is to evoke references both expansive and narrow, technical and rhetorical. Some associate it with the time before the British enclosure of once-shared lands by elite owners who, most intensely from the seventeenth century through the end of the nineteenth, passed laws and planted hedge barriers around fields that had previously supported communities of commoners. Author Eula Biss writes, "In addition to common pasture, commoners were granted rights of pannage, of turbary, of estovers, and of piscary—rights to run their pigs in the woods, to cut peat for fuel, to gather wood from the forests, and to fish. These were rights to subsistence, rights to live on what they could glean from the land. In the course of enclosure, as written law superseded customary law, commoners lost those rights."[1]

The term also recalls economist Garrett Hardin's unduly influential 1968 thought experiment, "The Tragedy of the Commons," which posits that any shared resource will inevitably be overused and destroyed by partakers' individual self-interests. As Biss points out, "Hardin was writing long after the commons had been lost to enclosure, and his commons was purely hypothetical. Actual, historical commons weren't the free-for-all he imagined." Instead, rules and customs protected the commonly managed land from over-exploitation: there were limits to the number of animals a single shepherd could graze on the land and rules for how that volume could change seasonally so lean times didn't follow abundant ones. "What Hardin considers the 'inherent logic of the commons' is actually the logic of capitalism," Biss reminds us.

The term can also refer colloquially to arrangements that manage what are known as common-pool resources—a good that benefits a group but can be degraded if participants act only in their individual self-interest. Contemporary economist and Nobel laureate Elinor Ostrom, along with her colleagues and mentees, have done much to catalog and analyze such systems, from communal land management in a small Swiss village to irrigation systems in southeastern Spain. Their work has both set out principles for successful commons governance and also refuted Hardin's dystopian claims about shared ownership.

Then there are the commons that are big-picture visions. Scholar Amanda Huron articulates how philosophers Michael Hardt and Antonio Negri imagine the commons as "that which is collectively generated by humanity and is necessary for life."[2] In the context of our cities, she pulls from scholars Martin Kornberger and Christian Borch to tell us that "the urban commons should be understood as that which all urban dwellers collectively generate,"[3] vibing with political scientist Margaret Kohn's take that the city itself is "a form of common-wealth, a concentration of value created by past generations and current residents."[4]

If these descriptions bring to mind infrastructure and public goods, you're not alone. Kohn, in further theorizing the urban commons, regards it as "more like a pair of glasses than a set of parameters. It helps us see the value in the interstices of the city, the 'in-between' sites that nourish the lifeworld: streets that facilitate encounters and imagination, visual delights that can astound or comfort, institutional safety nets that can provide for the needy, and the libraries and parks that educate and entertain."[5] Kohn goes on to argue in *The Death and Life of the Urban Commonwealth* that social housing, too, is part of this commons. Huron, who follows the lifecycle of limited equity co-ops in Washington, DC, in her book *Carving Out the Commons*, rightfully considers co-ops like Southbridge and St. James to be commons as well, "because this form of housing fits the main traits of the commons: collective self-organization and decommodification."

All these broad and narrow definitions make clear that commons are found everywhere, whether as the natural outgrowths of our collective endeavors (e.g., the city) or constructions pushing back against the prevailing societal winds of commodification, like Normanton Farms and its peers in New Hampshire. Huron writes that commons are far from utopian—that they are in fact "totally everyday, and almost unremarkable." The mundane quality of commons implies "that to live and work in non-capitalist ways does not necessarily require a huge sea change in how we see and experience the world." Examples of such practices already exist, among them the anti-privatization movements at St. James and Southbridge, which mobilized against a contemporary form of enclosure of their commons. The challenge is how to scale them to a point where they are no longer the exception but the rule.

The current system of maintaining our public goods is fraying. Yet many people—among them the co-op residents in New York, some of whom felt pulled by both sides of the privatization debates—do aspire to care for place over mere individual consumption. The collectives visited in the pages that follow—beacons shining from New Hampshire, Massachusetts, and Missouri—can show us how. Each is maintaining pieces of the public infrastructure needed to address not only housing affordability but also historical injustice, community disruption, and possessive individualism. A renewed ethic of ownership, spread through savvy and strategy, can forge a more just way forward for the vital work of commoning.

OPERATING WITHIN CAPITALISM

As executive director of Agrarian Trust, Ian McSweeney did his best to limit his involvement as Normanton Farms became part of the New Hampshire Agrarian Commons. Local governance was of the utmost importance, he emphasized. As a veteran of the agriculture and conservation nonprofit sector, he's seen how entities ostensibly created to address social problems are in fact often "set up to operate in perpetuity and serve themselves." He therefore emphasized that Agrarian Trust was acting "to support, not extract" from the network of local Agrarian Commons: collections of decommodified, locally managed farmlands. The Trust is meant to be the infrastructure and resource provider to each.

The Agrarian Commons model was developed to address three intertwined challenges: land that had become unaffordable for farmers, the ecological and social damage wrought by industrialized agriculture, and the histories of injustice embedded in American land. It draws inspiration from precedents like New Communities, Inc., that community land trust formed in 1970s Georgia to support dispossessed Black farmers. However, Agrarian Trust also stresses certain distinctions from the land trusts that have come before it. The most important appears to be its melding of external oversight with local control. An Agrarian Commons cannot form without significant interest and drive from a community living on or near the lands in question. Once those exist, the Trust brings resources.

One of those resources is, of course, money: McSweeney and his colleagues are skilled at obtaining the philanthropic and grant funding required for the expensive task of buying land off the speculative market. They also provide legal guidance: How to navigate the 501(c) nonprofit section of the tax code to create structures antithetical to the private-property system in which it exists. How to structure the rules of each Commons to ensure the land will be decommodified while also giving farmers access to financing and equity building. And how to help each Commons cultivate a culture of commoning in collaboration with local communities and farmers. Like the Mitchell-Lama model that created St. James and Southbridge in New York, the Agrarian Commons approach must find ways to decommodify land while still operating within capitalist systems built on its commodification.

McSweeney and Agrarian Trust are quick to acknowledge the contradictions inherent in this—the fact that their work "creating alternative models for land ownership is a radical solution that operates within the constraints of existing, and harmful, legal frameworks."[6] For St. James and Southbridge, this set-up was always rather tenuous: You can take the housing out of the market, but could you keep the market out of the housing? In both co-ops the answer was no, even though St. James was able to banish the prospect of privatization, at least for the moment. Agrarian Commons does not yet have the decades-long track record of the Mitchell-Lama program, but its approach to decommodifying land in perpetuity already shows promise.

The most obvious distinction between the two models is that privatization is legally possible for Mitchell-Lamas, while selling land out of the Agrarian Commons is not. (Of course, it's worth remembering that privatization was not always possible for Mitchell-Lamas and that the legislation that opened that door was likely never intended to apply to co-ops.) However, the bigger difference between the two programs is found in the layers of governance that each Agrarian Commons puts in place to preserve its vision. That starts by including not only direct beneficiaries in the governance of the commons but also the wider community around it. The farmers who hold leases on Agrarian Commons farms all sit on its governing board. They are the equivalent of the cooperators at St. James and Southbridge. But whereas within Mitchell-Lamas only current shareholders are able to make the key decisions regarding their co-op, Agrarian Commons boards also include community members and representatives from Agrarian Trust. Each of these three groups composes one-third of the board. This governance structure ensures that those closest to the operations—the farmer, the residents—are a driving voice at the table while embedding an understanding that decommodification has import for folks beyond those who work on or live near the land.

Both Mitchell-Lamas and the Agrarian Commons have a level of governance that sits above local beneficiaries: housing agencies in the former case and Agrarian Trust in the latter. Those entities attempt to walk the fine line between respecting local decision-making and ensuring that those decisions fulfill the intention of the whole endeavor. Their methods for doing so, however, diverge dramatically. Because privatization is not possible in the Agrarian Commons, Agrarian Trust's support and oversight does not need to be predicated on preventing it. The appearance of coercion that poisoned Lester Goodyear and Simon Doran's perception of government oversight at St. James is thus avoided altogether. Rather than Agrarian Trust's involvement being viewed as a kind of paternalistic refereeing, it can play the role of partner. The City and State don't have that luxury in the case of the cooperative commons, but they often also neglect or misuse their oversight to the point that their value is easily questioned. Presence and engagement crucially justify the role the government or Agrarian Trust have in their respective models. Their involvement reinforces the collectivity of these endeavors—that there is more at stake than the narrow prosperity of direct beneficiaries.

This speaks to the narrative that such guiding institutions must instill and maintain if the vision of these commons is to be sustained. Agrarian Trust broadcasts its vision constantly, from its website's illustrated FAQs to its well-produced podcasts. Its staff are, necessarily, evangelists for this vision. They must convince others to fund it, but, more importantly, they also need to maintain support for the model among its participants. McSweeney told me that:

> We're struck by that as being maybe the most sustainable aspect of this model. There's the legal framework and structures and documentation and such that help to hold land in this way. But all of that is just legal documentation that requires people to follow it and align with it and support it. Building culture between these Commons and building awareness of a shared value system and a diversity of people in places is something where we're doing a fair amount to really try to build that kind of Commons community of people, both internally within our work in Commons but also externally: others who are creating their own commons structure to share resources, make connections, build networks around that, to build that human alliance to one another around these values.

This work can seem ancillary to the operational nuts and bolts that keep things running, but the perils of demoting this kind of cultural maintenance are clear at Southbridge and St. James. The purpose of the Mitchell-Lama co-ops often gets lost over the years, creating a cultural vacuum that may then be filled with the dominant cultural narrative of for-profit ownership. Sustaining a cooperative culture has to be an everyday endeavor.

Agrarian Trust knows their model doesn't fit every farm or farmer, just as a limited-equity co-op may not be the best option for all households. McSweeney said their model best addresses the needs of farmers looking to acquire land and those eager to sell it. But for those with an existing farm business, the transition into a commons can be difficult because of how they have used their land as collateral to access the credit needed to grow their business. Jeremiah Vernon—he of the dreads and the delectable barbecue chicken—was considering whether to follow in the footsteps of Normanton Farms and add his family's farm to the New Hampshire Agrarian Commons, but he had yet to pull the trigger, despite serving on the organization's board. The model is still a work in progress, and the organization is open to experimentation on new legal and ownership structures. At the same time, all parties agree that there are certain lines that the Agrarian Commons simply won't cross. For one, the bylaws prohibit land from ever being removed from the Commons.

The comparison of Mitchell-Lamas and Agrarian Commons has its limitations, but looking at them side by side reminds us of some of the fundamental cooperative values that simply eroded with time at Southbridge and St. James. Another area in which Agrarian Trust provides a model for commons operations is how it has confronted the histories of oppression embedded in the land it seeks to decommodify.

A STEP IN THE RIGHT DIRECTION

When Whitney Carpenter invoked the Pennacook people at the celebration of Normanton Farms, he inadvertently touched on an uncomfortable truth for initiatives like these. In the United States, even decommodified land remains stolen land, dispossessed from Indigenous peoples through genocidal settler colonialism. Agrarian Trust readily admits this in its FAQs: "Land ownership in the U.S. is the embodiment of gross injustice. 98 percent of farmland is owned by white Americans of European descent, and land ownership by white-led nonprofit organizations in many cases simply further perpetuates this gross reality. Agrarian Trust is a white-led nonprofit organization."[7] The Agrarian Commons model may "honor (though it cannot replicate) pre-colonial systems of relationship, and encourage deeper connections with land," but it remains embedded in "the colonialist construct of private property" on which Indigenous dispossession was founded.[8]

Agrarian Trust is, of course, not the only body charged with acknowledging and redressing the unredressable. Any American movement that conceives of ownership as stewardship is drawing from Indigenous thought, and that fact must be honored with more than words. Author Matt Hern draws from scholars Eve Tuck and K. Wayne Yang to write that "claiming commonality all too often acts as a sleight of hand, a deceptive stalling tactic, a 'move to innocence' that bathes the speaker in a soft glow of righteousness while demanding little. While commoning is a start, it 'neither reconciles present grievances nor forecloses future conflict' and is only as good as its ongoing commitments."[9] Building an ethic of stewardship into contemporary commons requires dealing with the theft of Indigenous land, the legacy of slavery, and the ongoing racism central to our property systems today.

Doing so is not only good in itself; it is also key to maintaining these commons. History shows why the commons are necessary and allows us to understand attempts to dismantle them. At St. James, for example, countering Lester Goodyear's arguments for privatization required his neighbors' recognition that his desire for "true homeownership" was rooted in a history of Black Americans like him having long been denied full citizenship. Cooperators like Tia Ward and Wenna Redfern drew from their own experiences of racism to encourage their fellow residents to preserve the public good of social housing. Similarly, the association that some cooperators had with debt as a form of social control, based on prior histories of dispossession, did much to undermine the City's sole mechanism for keeping St. James in Mitchell-Lama. Had the City acknowledged that history, it might have changed its approach, offering different incentives and dealing with this association in a more productive way. Historical reckoning is not just lip service: it's a way of realizing a fuller vision of what a commons can be. It helps legitimize an alternative model of ownership and acts as a form of political education that builds ongoing support for that model.

Agrarian Trust has taken this work more seriously than most. "All of our leases are set up with the intention for some solidarity with

Indigenous communities," McSweeney told me. In some cases, the Agrarian Commons may make monthly land tax payments directly to communities with ancestral ties to the land. They may also arrange for "some type of shared used easements or rights conveyed to Indigenous communities so that they have rights to collaborate and be part of that land along with the lease holder." Agrarian Trust also seeks to lease land to BIPOC farmers, who have historically had difficulty accessing this resource. As of 2022, 75 percent of long-term leases within the Agrarian Commons had been conveyed to Black, Indigenous, and other farmers of color.[10]

McSweeney didn't claim to have all the answers. He considers his work to be "a slow process: relationship building and trust building and connecting with the land." It is a step in the right direction, but McSweeney was accustomed to hearing that the Agrarian Commons model "might sound better, or might accomplish some things, but it's really just a new version of . . . the problem as far as how land is held." "That's true and important and great to hear," he acknowledged, but "given the enormity of the land acres and the issue at stake, we can't think that one solution is going to be adopted by all and taken forward." He and his colleagues continue to test many approaches, to learn as they go, gleaning as much from the commoners at the local level as they provide at the national.

"It's really sobering to think about how we're doing such small work, and we're so inspired and humbled by the ripple effects it is having," McSweeney told me after I'd sat in on a New Hampshire Agrarian Commons board meeting. The agenda had covered a debrief of the Normanton Farms celebration, as well as plans to integrate the farm with its larger community: allowing walking trails to run through it, placing a garden for a local school near the entrance. They wrestled with the delicate balance between ensuring an Agrarian Commons farmer could sell their ninety-nine-year-lease, thus allowing for them to pass their business and land improvements on to a future farmer while also ensuring that this option wouldn't become a back door for commodification. Small this organization's ripples may be, but they have recently traveled to the freshwaters of central Massachusetts. There, in the town of Millis, lies the Black Swamp Commons, where no acknowledgment of the land's displaced original stewards need be made. The land has gone back into the care of the Nipmuc people, who have known it as home for centuries.

CHAPTER 10

Abundance and Return

On a cold, clear January afternoon in 2023, I sat with two of those Nipmuc people, Kristen Wyman and Pam Ellis, in a screened breakfast nook in a farmhouse on Black Swamp. The windows looked out onto pasture ringed by a low stone wall. I asked them what they saw around them. "I can tell you what's here," Ellis said in her forthright manner behind her tortoiseshell glasses. "Firstly, and fore-mostly, the water, the freshwater, the *nippy* is here. . . . And the people are here: the fish people, the bird people, the plant people, all the people are here, and human beings, too. For me, it's the possibility of the world the way that it should be." Ellis and Wyman are freshwater people; that's what Nipmuc means. Neither of them now lives on this land. Ellis practices law on Cape Cod, and Wyman is raising a daughter in Hull and working for a hunger-eradication nonprofit. They drive hours to do their re-commoning at Black Swamp. But the travel time is more than worth the chance to come home.

"To actually have space within your ancestral homelands, I think it's in the soil. There's a physical connection. I have certain kinds of physical sensations in my body when I step onto Nipmuc land," Ellis told me, saltwater welling in her eyes. "My spirit lives, and I start feeling happy because I know I'm getting closer to a place that I belong to. And I think that sense of belonging to place is something that's been . . . missing for a long time." That she and her people fundamentally belong to this land has never been in question. What has changed is that the land, legally speaking, now belongs to them again. It is an instance of landback—the return of stolen lands to Indigenous stewardship. Wyman, comfortable in her green Carhartt sweatshirt and red beanie, sees this reunion of people and land as reciprocal. "I think the land was calling us back." Ellis notes that not only are her people returning, but so are the fish, as dams are removed from the surrounding watershed: "There's no mistake here that if they would come back, we would come back, because they are some of our closest relatives. . . . As they return to their ancestral places, we would too."

Wyman had been working toward this return for years. She'd engaged in ongoing discussions about landback with fellow Indigenous folks in the region, had scrolled through land sale listings that fell within her ancestral territory. Eventually she was introduced to Ian McSweeney. Both sides made "a huge leap of trust" when a sixty-four-acre property on Nipmuc land went up for sale at an asking price of $1.5 million. The grassroots Nipmuc collective that Wyman and Ellis are a part of didn't have that kind of money, and they knew the land wouldn't be available on the market forever. So they teamed up with Agrarian Trust. The rematriation of the land "would not have happened in the timeframe that it did if Ian wasn't willing to be like, 'we trust you; whatever we need to do' . . . Keep in mind: they were willing to take a mortgage on for us . . . Being in touch with donors, even the acquisition process with the real estate: we did not have capacity for that. . . . Agrarian Trust was willing to step into that place of unknown, and risk, frankly, its 501(c)3 status, its relationships, all of it to just be like, 'I trust you; we're gonna move forward with this.'" Agrarian Trust was able to buy the land on the Nipmuc collective's behalf in November 2021. Agrarian Trust will hold title for an estimated couple of years until the Nipmuc collective builds its processes, establishes its infrastructure, and settles on the legal framework they will use to own and govern the land.

For all their joy at this return, the process itself leaves much to be desired. There's "pain in putting $1.5 million towards getting our land back," Wyman said, not the least because, for the Nipmuc, land is kin, and putting a number to its value is anathema. Ellis was more direct: "The whole thing is really loathsome and, for me, truly disgusting that we're having to buy this land . . . but I can hold my nose because I feel that having the land is really the most important thing." Beyond the pasture, a brook wound through wetlands to a pond. "There's a nice circle path that walks a wooded area . . . that's so perfect for elders or people who are coming that want that opportunity to hike or walk but can't commit to going too far." Members of the Nipmuc collective have planted fields of blueberry and white flint corn, and they have established a sacred camp honoring Wyman's departed aunt. There are also plans for a future orchard site, a spot to practice bow skills.

"It's just such an important place. . . . There's just been so much loss in the history of our tribe . . . so to actually have something, a gain, to have something that's added . . . it's a big, big thing," Ellis told me. Among those losses was the denial of federal recognition for the tribe during the George W. Bush years, despite positive initial signs and official recognition from the Commonwealth of Massachusetts. Without that recognition, getting access to Indigenous lands held by the federal government is less feasible. "For federally unacknowledged people like us, this . . . is the only way we're going to have a land base, . . . and that land base is primary to everything," Ellis explained. Intertwined threads of language, culture, and food all tie back to the land. Ownership of it is in some ways a means to an end. It was a treasured goal, of course, but largely because it could facilitate "the connection to land and place" that ultimately had much to do with identity. Land in hand was just the beginning of a return. What came next was the arguably more difficult process of relearning how to be on it, how to common.

THE BANALITY AND TRANSCENDENCE OF REMATRIATION

Both Wyman and Ellis have maintained Indigenous practices in different ways. Wyman harvests quahog clams from the same coastal waters as her ancestors, passing the meat onto folks in need and fashioning the shells into wampum jewelry and art. Deep purple and creamy white shell earrings dangle from her ears. Ellis, too, takes to the saltwater to harvest shellfish and maintain Indigenous foodways. But as Wyman insisted, "We're all colonized," and over time she "realized the impact the displacement of native peoples from our traditional lifeways and our foodways over generations had on our ability to actually know what to do around management." When she began to look for ways to return to her land, she "knew it was going to take a lot of time, in season-to-season learning, to really know how to live into our ways of holding land," a realization that at first led her to believe "we don't need land right now. We need to reintroduce our folks to this way of life."

Wyman has pursued this relearning as a leader of Eastern Woodland Rematriation, a network of "Indigenous womxn restoring spiritual foundations through sustainable food and economic systems."[1] She spent "time in all of these different tribal communities really grounding myself literally and being like, what is the need here?" That is the question from which stewardship starts, in Wyman's estimation: "What does the land need? It's extremely hard to have a vision of what we're going to do without knowing it. . . . I think we're so disconnected from natural cycles that no matter what, I think we can find answers in really observing. What is nature trying to tell us? . . . Because nature is really the one in charge." She gave the example of the blueberry patch. After the land purchase, they invited the tenant who'd previously farmed the land to assist them in management. On her recommendation, they pruned the plants in March. "We had a good couple of weeks of delicious blueberries, and then we lost [part of] the crop during the drought. We didn't foresee that was going to be an issue and had we not known to prune, we probably would have had a complete loss. . . . I kind of see myself as an informal apprentice right now. How much knowledge can we glean from somebody who has worked this land and discern in a way, this will fit for us and this probably won't."

For Wyman, knowing the land is also about knowing the "names to these places" and the names of "people who have suffered. We're still alive, we're around, and we're living in the vicinity of these places that we've been displaced from in our own homeland. . . . Those names need to be surfaced and understood and acknowledged." Ellis described some of this process of refamiliarization:

> One of the things we found when we were looking at this land is that the name that people gave this place makes no sense in our language. . . . This is what the English people heard. The word they call it is Bogastow, and the word is more like *Bôgwasso*,[2] which means 'the shallow place.' And it's perfect for the tributary here that runs off of the Charles River because, for Nipmuc people, a lot of the descriptions that we give to places are descriptions of the condition of the water in that place.

The beauty, pain, and spiritual significance of becoming reacquainted with this land is paired with the mundanity of managing it. Ellis and Wyman reminisced about the minor yet significant acts of maintenance: getting Wi-Fi hooked up in the house, registering the farm truck, forming the LLC they needed to legally shoehorn the commons into an antagonistic structure, sorting out how their commons will operate and how it will be governed. Some of their group feel discomfort with Agrarian

Trust temporarily holding title to the land, but Wyman saw that "them holding the land for a couple of years created actual space and opportunity for us to continue figuring out what this looks like. . . . We're slow at it, but the idea is that [commons governance] would be through committees, and that there is some level of sharing of that power between the LLC and the community structure that forms so that everybody has a vested say." We talked consensus decision-making techniques, the fist-to-five method of gauging a group's opinion by show of fingers. We considered their collaboration with Agrarian Trust on the creation of a nonprofit structure that will eventually remove that entity from the picture so that the land is fully under community control.

Time, patience, and constant relearning are key ingredients to commoning and stewarding. It's a "build-the-road-as-we-travel ongoing act of emergence,"[3] to use Matt Hern's description of how commons can grow in our current moment. As Amanda Huron reminds us,

for people raised in an environment saturated with capitalist practices, commoning may not come naturally. It takes practice. . . . Learning commoning might involve learning about the history of commoning in relation to capitalism, and also the ways commoning happens all around us in the present. . . . Learning commoning might also mean learning how to work collectively, through such seemingly mundane practices as learning how to run meetings well, and learning how to argue with a thoughtful mind and open heart. . . . The commons is a pragmatic practice, and teaching and learning the skills of commoning can be a decidedly pragmatic affair.[4]

Many of the folks at St. James and Southbridge were out of practice. Their governance structures had been distorted over the years for other purposes, the mission of the co-ops lost as political education dried up. Each co-op may have been exemplary in managing its physical and financial maintenance, but the social maintenance was left wanting. When they faced a threat to their commons, they had to revive the basics of political education in order to defend themselves. The Concerned Shareholders of St. James were able to do this, with outside support. The anti-privatizers at Southbridge, in contrast, stuck largely to financial arguments that reinforced capitalist practices and drew a thick boundary between themselves and the wider ecosystem around them.

Disregarding that ecosystem seems hardly possible among the Nipmuc collective. When you regard the land, the fish people, and the plant people as your relations, it's difficult to separate yourself from a larger "we." The Nipmuc language reflects this. Ellis told me that "in the first person plural, we have an inclusive form of 'we' and an exclusive form of 'we.' So if we think of the commons as being the inclusive 'we,' then we really need to think about and figure out how we live together, how we work together on the land in this new [way]—well, not new, . . . but it feels new in some ways because most of us haven't had to live that way." Wyman and Ellis, having just returned to their homelands, were already thinking of how to broaden that "we" even further.

MONATASH

Had the Nipmuc collective chosen to insulate themselves entirely from outsiders, one could easily forgive them. Historically, the generosity of most Indigenous groups to newcomers has rarely been reciprocated and has often led to their dispossession. But that kind of isolation would not be the Nipmuc way, Wyman pointed out: "There's this cultural aspect . . . a tradition of diplomacy and welcoming and connection that has been interrupted by colonialism." To close themselves off—that is, to enclose—would be to give into the very logics that underlay their people's oppression. "I've just been very sensitive to not wanting to repeat colonialism," Wyman said. So while most of the people involved in operations at Black Swamp Commons have ancestral connections to the land, the space is open to others, too. Wyman told me:

> We want this to be a cooperative: held in common where we really rely on multiple people coming here and feeling invested in this place and calling it their own, which is happening through a kind of informal volunteerism. Many of the folks that come out are displaced, kind of landless urban folks, some of them indigenous. We connected with a woman who's from Peru, and living up here with her family for the last couple of years . . . and just feels really isolated, like she can't make connections here. . . . She loves coming out here and feeling like she's connecting with other indigenous women, and that she has some sort of place of privacy. . . . So continuing to have it be a place where people feel connected, where they feel like they can raise their kids and have their kids come here and where families can come and

just have the respite and the time away and where people can relearn these agricultural traditions.

Rather than operate from a perspective of scarcity, where this land and its fruits are reserved only for a small group, Ellis's approach to the commons stems from a vision of benefit to many:

I think about this being full of food for our folks. And that none of our people ever have to not have food, not have good, healthy food that they know where it comes from. . . . I want this to be a place of bounty for our Nipmuc people, and then for our intertribal kin, for all of the relatives from all the other communities, and then for all of the people who need food . . . regardless of who they are, where they're from. . . . The word in our language for abundance is *mon-atash*. I hope that this becomes that kind of place, that it's really a place of abundance with that openness and willingness to share and that we'll be able to do that.

The commitment to sharing abundance is so strong that Wyman and Ellis began chatting about whether Monatash should be the permanent name for the commons.* Exclusion plays no part in their definition of ownership or their ethic of stewardship. The trick is figuring out what that sharing ultimately looks like. As Wyman put it, "I don't think landback is predicated on people having to leave or be landless. But it calls into question what our values are when you're saying inclusive and exclusive. What does that mean in this context?"

The connection between landback and urban social housing was particularly evident when we discussed the Nipmuc collective's desire to help curtail the current housing crisis in nearby metro Boston. Wyman has held informal conversations with outside advocates who wish to welcome "new arrivals" to the region. This grew out of what she calls the "contradiction of creating space for us to return to the land" while the collective also has "vacant housing, and . . . we have folks that really need homes." We are not talking apartment buildings' worth of units, but between the colonial-era farmhouse that carries a marker from the town's historical commission and the name of an early European

---

*Like many things there, Black Swamp Commons is a working title that can be revisited as things evolve.

settler's son, a couple of cottages, and the possibility of constructing more housing on a small portion of the land, the Nipmuc collective was keen to explore their responsibilities to others in need. Ellis is interested in sharing this shelter in part because "the immigration policy in the United States has become the new federal Indian policy, because the application is mainly to people who are coming from Central and South America, who are our Indigenous kinfolk. There's a certain justice in a really interesting, sort of complicated, way that we would be able to connect with folks who are coming, with these relatives who are coming, and many of whom still carry with them a lot of the knowledge about working the land and traditional foodways."

It takes an abundance mindset to recognize that resisting enclosure—or privatization, as the case may be—creates the opportunity for there to be more for all. This is what Heather McGhee calls the solidarity dividend: the benefit we all receive when we reject zero-sum politics.[5]

The bounds of the inclusive "we" in the Nipmuc language have proven to be elastic, stretching to accommodate more. Ellis drew from Nipmuc history to illustrate their broad concern for both place and people. "It was a Nipmuc named Acquittimaug who saved Boston from famine in the 1600s. And it was grain that came up the Old Connecticut Path . . . to Boston from Nipmuc grain stores. . . . There's long-standing tradition of Nipmuc people helping out this place and helping newcomers."

A long tradition of care and stewardship that includes rather than excludes, in a space sheltered from extractive conceptions of ownership—such is the driving vision at the Black Swamp Commons and in many Indigenous communities. As scholars Eve Tuck and Rubén Gaztambide write, "Our commitments are to what might be called an Indigenous futurity, which does not foreclose the inhabitation of Indigenous land by non-Indigenous peoples, but does foreclose settler colonialism and settler epistemologies. That is to say that Indigenous futurity does not require the erasure of now-settlers in the ways that settler futurity requires of Indigenous peoples."[6] This approach—one of openness and generosity, respect and humility—will flourish as the collective behind it continues to engage in the pragmatic aspects of maintaining a commons within a colonialist, capitalist system.

At the end of our conversation, Ellis was headed back to the Cape, while Wyman drove toward Hull to pick up her daughter. As we walked toward the front door, we passed a wooden cabinet with a sign marking it as the Apothecary. Inside were small, screw-top jars filled with various mixes of herbs concocted to soothe different ailments. They encouraged me to choose a tea to take with me. We all agreed that the anti-anxiety remedy—composed of lemon balm, skullcap, ashwagandha root, and spearmint leaf—would come in handy in the book-writing process.

Wyman and Ellis were also kind enough to leave me behind to roam the land. Ellis had remarked, earlier in the day, "Even when I drive here, I feel like I'm driving to safety." As I walked the wooded paths, past scrubby pine undergrowth and along phragmites-clogged wetlands, through the gap in the low stone wall and under the lone tree in the pasture, dipping my hand into the shallow waters, I too felt safe. It was not the same kind of safety as Ellis's, not her ancestral connection to the land, but rather my sense that their care for this place was already contributing to greater societal safety.

CHAPTER 11

Power and Politics

The absence of security was what prompted twenty tenants in the Residences of West Paseo to gather in their community room on a frigid Tuesday night in Kansas City, Missouri. The behemoth building, located on the city's East Side, is reserved for seniors, and it towers over the more modest homes surrounding it in this historically Black neighborhood. The complex appeared barren as I entered through the back and walked down a gray-carpet corridor. The presence of two leather claw-foot chairs somehow made the space look even more empty. But signs of life hung from a standard-issue bulletin board. A flyer advertising the recurring meeting of the Eastside Tenants Association was pinned to the top left. Hanging off the bottom right was another printed in yellow and red, this one calling on passersby to "Craft the People's Platform with KC Tenants Power."

That call, and the responses, became embodied when I made my way upstairs. Moments after I entered the community room, one of the people assembled there for the tenants meeting began to chant. "In our homes we're staying, staying," the caller howled to the mostly older crowd. They were an organizer known to most as MAK, a Christian Slater look-alike wearing a blue hoodie and white sweatpants. "Eastside tenants ain't playing, playing," the assembled returned. A few rounds of this primed the room for the work that lay ahead.

Many of these residents likely planned to live out the rest of their days at West Paseo. That's the case for most Kansas Citians, said Tara Raghuveer, director of the citywide tenants union known as KC Tenants, of which the Eastside Tenants Association is a part. "One of the most profound things about organizing [in KC] is that the people who live here—whether or not it was their choice—they live here and they're planning to die here. The stakes are very fucking big for the people who live in a place like this." What was once an affordable city is now facing the kind of real estate pressure associated with the US' coastal metropolises. If folks can't afford to stay put in Kansas City, where are they supposed to go?

The many lifers in attendance at the planning meeting may never have legally owned a piece of KC. But the place—its jazz and its barbecue, its ample rail yards and the giant Claes Oldenburg and Coosje van Bruggen shuttlecocks littering the lawn of its premier art museum—was theirs regardless. They are creators and stewards of this commonwealth and thus can be said to have a right to it. In Margaret Kohn's definition, such a right to the city is a "right to share and co-determine the urban commonwealth."[1] This right may be "a logical impossibility in so far as no one can assert a conventional property right to the city,"[2] but articulating it still serves a purpose. The original framer of this right, the Marxist philosopher Henri Lefebvre, intended it to serve as "a 'cry and a demand'; that is, part of social struggle, not an individual legal entitlement." He meant it to inspire struggle against "the hegemonic assumption that the city naturally belongs to those who can pay the high cost of admission, which in most places take the form of high rent or expensive real estate."[3] According to scholars David Madden and Peter Marcuse, the claim of a right to the city is a transformative demand that's realizable through "many routes toward decommodification," from the public provision of housing to "rent controls, more secure tenancies, public ownership of land, public financing, limits on speculation, and the adoption or re-introduction of regulations on home finance mechanisms."[4]

The Residences of West Paseo had recently been acquired by Clemons, a real estate firm focused on urban redevelopment in KC. The purchase had rightfully prompted the residents to wonder about their futures. The East Side, like many Black urban neighborhoods across the country, has seen a wave of real estate purchases; the resultant increase in housing prices has caused the displacement of longtime residents. It's unlikely that Clemons would have shelled out money for a large senior building if it didn't intend to extract profit from it one way or another. The tenants union was there to ensure that the residents' rent remained affordable and their complex properly maintained.

They did what unions do. They organized. The community room was abuzz with chatter about a recent action: delivering a letter of demands to Clemons representatives at a meet and greet. MAK, the organizer, encouraged the tenants to reflect on how it had felt to come together and assert their right to home. The tenants responded:

"They weren't prepared for us."

"They didn't know who they were messing with."

"Their faces were 10 different colors when they saw all the yellow KC Tenants shirts."

"The cookies were 45 minutes late, and who ever heard of cookies and water?"

"Did you feel powerful?" MAK asked. One resident, who'd been quiet until this point, responded, "As soon as I joined, I'm not scared anymore."

In the housing space, a sense of ownership is usually tied to legal status: Are you a homeowner, are you a renter? But as these residents' claim on their building made evident, ownership when constituted by a responsibility to steward rather than a right to profit can transcend all that. They weren't looking to extract from their ownership, like so many landlords or the pro-privatizers at Southbridge and St. James. They just wanted to be. While their short-term interest centered on preventing displacement, their visions for the future indicate that their ability and desire to stay is directly tied to their ability and desire to invest, to steward, their community.

The union spent the rest of the meeting planning their approach for the follow-up meeting that Clemons had agreed to the next week. Residents articulated the tasks and roles—giving testimony, asking questions, reading demands, getting commitments, taking notes, setting up, turning out other residents, standing in solidarity—that would be needed for a successful meeting, which MAK jotted down on a flip chart at the front of the room. One tenant, historically not a rabble-rouser, prompted a debate over what terminology to use when they spoke at the follow-up meeting, what tone to project. They moved through moments of tension and disagreement with grace and used them to strengthen their collective. They talked about how they would know if the follow-up meeting had gone well and what possible next steps might be. MAK made clear that "we'll most likely need to escalate. Why do we escalate? To get what we want. . . . That doesn't mean being spiteful or angry; it means how to hold them accountable." They closed with a political lesson: a quote chosen and delivered by one of the members.

Throughout, I kept thinking back to the beginning of the meeting. After the group had finished its chants and affirmed the baseline community agreements—"Build at the speed of trust," "We don't rat to our landlords or property managers," "We believe that we will win"—one tenant leader asked a simple, probing question: "What's your dream home like?" The answers varied, most rather modest. Some wanted no landlord. Others wanted one who was responsible, who asked after their well-being and worked for the residents. Everyone wanted affordability and proper maintenance. One man dreamt of book and theater clubs, of a food pantry and a community night. MAK had scrawled the responses onto the flip chart in black marker. "You know what this sounds like?" they said. "This sounds like social housing to me!"

WHAT CAN WE DO TODAY?

After the meeting, I asked MAK about their approach to facilitation and how tenant organizing related to a more just housing future.

What I really tried to do is, using the ideas that people bring and put out there, . . . to remind people that what you're talking about is social housing. That's our North Star. We're not going to get that within the next three years. But this little fight that we're picking with Clemons right now, how organized we were tonight, is just heading towards that direction. Because social housing is not just going to be given to us, to communities. They are going to have to gather, are going to have to come together and organize around that as a priority for their community . . . and this is a step towards that direction.

The idea of social housing is just so intimidating and so big and grand, people don't know where to start. But if we can remind people that the work that we're doing every day on these issues is a step towards that direction, and give people confidence to say 'Oh, I just won a rent dropbox and all these things from Clemons at my building' . . . What would it look like if we continue this work? What could I have won in five years? What could I have won in 10 years? So it feels piecemeal, baby steps, and I used to be really against that. But now I actually understand that is part of the long con of it all.

This progression was familiar. When I met with KC Tenants director Raghuveer in the union's stone church headquarters, she peppered our conversation with a quote attributed to liberation theologist Paolo Freire. It asks, "What can we do today so that we can do tomorrow what we cannot do today?" In KC Tenants' case, the answer was: quite a lot. When we met, they were coming off a grueling week: they'd organized and supported the residents of an apartment building that, due to landlord neglect, had lost gas and electricity at the most frigid time of year. They'd hosted a three-day training for tenant organizers from around the country. They'd responded to disappointing White House directives regarding tenant protections, and they'd ratified the platform of a new political organization that would give them a stronger voice in upcoming local elections. Raghuveer now rightfully took the opportunity to put her feet up, literally. Her metallic silver space slippers and a poster of the Freire quote stood out against the off-white walls.

KC Tenants has gained national attention for the power it's been able to amass, no doubt in part due to its breakneck pace and the success of some of its more confrontational actions. One of the most notable was Zero Eviction January, when they managed to shut down housing court in the middle of the pandemic to make sure people could stay in their homes.[5] They also run a hotline to talk tenants through different emergencies, provide resources, and offer emotional support. They've won a campaign for tenants' right to counsel in eviction filings, and they've helped pass a local bond measure to fund a housing trust fund for deeply affordable apartments. They've lost fights, too. Raghuveer advertised herself as the "star witness" of the losing campaign for rent and mortgage cancellation during the worst of the pandemic.

As instrumental as the KC Tenants staff clearly are in the union's success, Raghuveer and MAK were keen to stress that they are not the core. Raghuveer told me, "The main stuff that I'm always anxious about and therefore always looking for in our organizing is just real ownership among leaders in the union. If the union lives and dies by the staff team, that's not a union. That's an advocacy organization, right? The union is a collective of leaders who have decided to do something for their neighborhood, for themselves, for each other. . . . When you asked about stewardship, my mind went to union steward, like what it means to actually steward the interests of a collective." This ethos was clear in the Eastside Tenants meeting, where MAK facilitated but many members led: a "leaderful movement" one of the attendees called it, echoing civil rights legend Ella Baker and those in the Movement for Black Lives who carry on her legacy.

Raghuveer called these neighborhood unions "experiments with infrastructure that we're going to need if we're going to sustain something like a citywide social housing program [in the future]. And so we've got traditions, we've got norms, we've got community agreements, we've got evaluations that happen at the end of every meeting. We tend to be extremely respectful of people's time. So I think noting some of those culture things is important." What ultimately sets KC Tenants apart from other leftist groups, Raghuveer told me, is that their organizing is "really not driven by ideology. It's driven by interest. . . . We're not leading with a critique of racial capitalism. We get there. It doesn't take long. But we're leading with how the fuck are you? And what are you interested in doing with your neighbors?"

This is the key link between organizing against displacement and organizing for the infrastructure that can make the former unnecessary. Raghuveer told me:

We don't knock doors talking to people about social housing, right? We knock doors asking people about how they're living now, which by itself is a very politicizing line of questioning because the people are not living good. And I think from there, there's an arc that we take people on, sometimes in that first conversation but actually often over a much longer period of time, where we call the question on a system that puts profits before people's lives. We localize it, and we do political education about the way that affordability is defined in a place like this, which is really around what's affordable for a developer to build, not what's affordable for a person to live.

All of that actually is not new information for anyone that we're talking to. It's very intuitive. The thing that's not intuitive is, okay, what is the answer to that? What's the solution to this problem? Because by design our imaginations are limited by this conspiracy of the profiteers who have convinced us that there is no possible way that housing could be provided if not by them and in a way that makes them an abundance of money. And what we found is that when we introduce the idea of social housing, people get it immediately. They might think it's a little convoluted or too dreamy, or something like that. But they get the basic premise that . . . like our roads and our public schools, housing should be treated as a public good rather than an investment. And we should be treated like assets to the city and not line items in our landlords' budgets. . . . The people get it.

This approach reminded me of the Concerned Shareholders of St. James. Its organizers led with their interest in stability for current residents, just as the pro-Mitchell-Lama group at Southbridge did. But, unlike the Southbridge stewards, they didn't stop there. With the assistance of CU4ML and local politicians, they extended the narrative to encompass a more systemic view.

That dual-level outlook was also apparent in how Magda Werkmeister, the current hotline coordinator, approached conversations with tenants in crisis.

> I just like to start with, "How does this make you feel?" . . . Nine times out of ten people will readily offer up that they're angry as hell, you know? And they're frustrated. And then that opens the door to talk about who's to blame. . . . I think the hotline is useful in just having a space where people can talk about the issues they're experiencing without being judged, without being blamed. . . . We do tell folks "This isn't your fault, actually." . . . So folks are pretty able to see why these problems are happening; they just haven't been given the space to express that yet. After that we talk about real examples of stuff we have won together because obviously it's not going to do anyone good if you're just angry but don't see any way out of it.

The hotline is often a path for a caller to join the union. They may not do so immediately, or at all, but hotline staffers still invite them, even if their present capacity doesn't allow it. Werkmeister said, "Having these really particular vulnerable conversations with people" at "some of the most traumatic times of their lives" not only provides an important source of support. It also creates an "emotional connection" to KC Tenants, bolstering a caller's understanding of the root causes of their problem. This work can be transformational for the staffers as well. Werkmeister, when we spoke, no longer lived in Kansas City and was in her final year of college back east, but she remained dialed into the hotline. She was committed to returning to Kansas City to continue organizing once she completed her degree. Prior to her work with KC Tenants, she had never considered returning. What's bringing her back? "I was missing out on something that makes life just more joyous, and I think that was just the sense of community . . . and these people that you are able to care about and [who] care about you."

Those are the fundamentals of building power to achieve KC Tenants' North Star: care, political education, community, and a culture that bolsters individuals' stewardship of that community. As Raghuveer told me, "We can't have social housing in Kansas City today, . . . social housing that is publicly backed, publicly managed, democratically controlled, truly and permanently affordable. But we think that we can be the first city in the country to win it. That's our long-term vision." They also understand the need not just to win social housing but to maintain it—the very thing with which Southbridge and St. James struggled.

INFRASTRUCTURE AND INEVITABILITY

Other than the Freire quote, the only adornment in Raghuveer's office was an assortment of Post-it notes arranged along x and y axes, spanning an entire wall. *KC Tenants* was written on one, somewhat lonely on the top left, below the *Kansas City Police Department* Post-it on the right. Throw in a few red strings and grainy photos, and the chart could start to give detective-on-serial-killer's-trail vibes. But as Raghuveer explained it to me, a power map of the city came into focus. It showed KC Tenants' need to support a whole ecosystem of allied organizations should they wish to win and maintain their North Star vision.

"We're always meditating on what feels inevitable, and then what is actually inevitable and what's the difference that organizing can make," Raghuveer told me. "Some of that meditation recently is: it can feel inevitable that . . . 2026 World Cup games will be hosted here, and there will be a downtown stadium, and gentrifying developers like Mac Properties will buy up whole blocks and displace 20 percent of the residents and most of those residents will be Black. All of these things can feel inevitable. And none of it is inevitable, not if we organize." For KC Tenants, creating a sense of inevitability around its own goals is pivotal to its success. Southbridge Rights fostered the same in its successful bid for privatization. Such a sense, and its endurance, can only be built through power.

"To think that introducing a bill is the way that we win social housing—you can popularize the idea that way . . . but that's also how really good ideas get diluted and co-opted and watered down to nothing," Raghuveer noted, expressing not a small amount of frustration with dudes on the Left who regard legislative moves as paramount. "The thing that's going to make social housing is people organized around the demand and then continuing to organize to maintain its legitimacy." Raghuveer pointed to the luminous example of the social housing capital of the world, Vienna: "The thing that people will tell you about Vienna's social housing is that the Social Democrats organized like crazy out of horrible conditions and won social housing. And now, it's still such a tightly organized thing. If any politician in Vienna dared to threaten social housing, they'd be fucking toast! Like, you don't survive, right? But that's predicated on really powerful people organizing around the thing that they need."

Big ideas are nice and to some extent necessary, Raghuveer said, but they're mostly hot air without "the people who are going to create the political will to make it happen and then build the sustaining political will to make sure that it doesn't get co-opted, defunded, privatized in the way that every other major public program in this country always has." Like limited-equity co-ops in New York, the US' premier example of social housing, may be.

Raghuveer explained that KC Tenants thinks about how to do this "by very amateurishly distilling some lessons from Antonio Gramsci's *Prison Notebooks*." She refreshingly acknowledged that she hasn't read the original text, but second-hand commentaries are sufficient. "As I understand it, he writes that the Italian communists had power and had won a lot of big shit. And then all of a sudden, they didn't, and they were all in prison, from where he was writing these notebooks. Part of his assessment is that they had power on one face. They had the power to win material victories but they lacked power on other faces. They lacked the power, the infrastructure, and the ecosystem-level power to sustain the wins. And then they also lacked power to shape ideas and the politics, again, to sustain the material wins."

To create the inevitable, realize it, then make it untouchable means building that infrastructure and shaping political consciousness through education. Such education happens in union meetings, in literature drops at slumlord properties, in one-on-one chats with residents, on the hotline. It brought to mind a Marshall Ganz quote I'd seen in a narrative-strategy evaluation: "Movements have narratives. They tell stories because they are not just about rearranging economics and politics. They also rearrange meaning. And they're not just about redistributing the goods. They're about figuring out what is good."[6]

Raghuveer acknowledged that this was a complicated task, in part due to "people's pretty deep . . . orientation towards homeownership that comes from decades of socialization in that direction. It is really hard to unravel that shit." But key shifts in narrative are powerful. "We have people in our union who are what we call bank tenants. So they're working-class homeowners who don't own their home outright but are tenants of their bank in a way. Many of them are very frustrated with a world that has made it so that their only chance of survival was them figuring out a down payment on a house. . . . They're angry about that as really the only available wealth building tool that we have in this country." KC Tenants includes homeowners with mortgages, and the organization conducts "collective political education about homeownership" as "government subsidized and supported rent control. That's all it is. . . . If you have a fixed rate mortgage, you've just controlled your rent. And the only reason you get to do that, and other people don't is that you have money for a down payment, and you qualify for a mortgage, and they didn't." They are doing their best to win by making their narratives dominant, and reinforcing them until they're regarded as "common sense."

The COVID pandemic has accelerated public interest in social housing and related policies. Raghuveer recalled that just "two or three years ago, rent control was such a third rail. And now it's not. It's being taken seriously in policy conversations." Continuing this momentum requires furthering political education and building more power. That's the impetus behind KC Tenants Power—the political arm of KC Tenants, with a 501(c)4 status that allows it to lobby and engage in electoral campaigns—whose flyer hung in the Residences at West Paseo's barren hallway. KC Tenants Power works to boost its allies on the city council and elect councilors who will engage in what Raghuveer calls co-governance. The union defines co-governance as "the process of consulting with the people most impacted by the issue at hand, ensuring those people are involved in the process every step of the way, amplifying their voices in and out of rooms they are invited into, voting alongside their demands, and giving them recognition, before, during and after, both publicly and directly."[7]

KC Tenants, inspired by their Gramscian readings, has Win goals, Build goals, and Shape goals. While electing political leaders (Win) would be an ideal outcome in the upcoming elections, it's not just about the votes. "The election affords us a massive opportunity to do political education at a scale that we can't access otherwise. And we want to be talking about things like what it looks like to reallocate money from the bloated police budget and put it towards massive public programs that could solve for the root causes of crimes of survival." They are building and shaping as they go, growing their base while also securing power at the top. MAK, in their charismatic and illustrative way, put it like this: "I don't actually think the answer towards revolution is going to be top-down. And I really want to believe it could happen bottom-up. Sometimes you might have to squeeze it out, like a zit."

The cathartic pop that KC Tenants is looking for is still a ways off. Raghuveer acknowledged that "there's a lot politically that needs to shift before we can get there." But politics are in her group's DNA, and politics is what will win and maintain social housing. Most KC Tenants members may not legally be homeowners, but they belong to Kansas City and are taking ownership of its future by doing what they can to steward it.

These politics will necessarily involve affecting higher levels of governance beyond buildings and one city. Raghuveer argued, "There's a massive role for the government to play. And at a certain point, it needs to be the federal government because of the amount of money required for such an infrastructure project." That's one reason she is a leader not just within KC Tenants but also of the national campaign for a federal Homes Guarantee, a suite of policies to ensure everyone in the US has good—and permanently affordable—housing. "Definitely a breakthrough for me as an organizer and campaigner was thinking about how it's just a lie that the federal government doesn't have a role related to housing. But it's a lie that a lot of people, including myself, took as the truth for a long time. And then when you start peeling it back, you're like, wait a second: HUD grants, the Low-Income Housing Tax Credit, Fannie and Freddie, FHFA (Federal Housing Finance Agency)—the federal government is all over our housing system and is actually subsidizing and financing the business models of some of the worst players in an increasingly consolidated market."

Sociologist Brian McCabe writes that "the constellation of tax policies that reward American homeowners, including the mortgage interest deduction, contribute to the politics of exclusion by increasing the investment value of housing and encouraging homeowners to view their housing as a commodity to be bought and sold for a profit."[8] The total value of the mortgage deduction outstrips the combined funding of the two main federal expenditures supporting low-income renters: the budget of Department of Housing and Urban Development and the cost of the federal Housing Choice Voucher program.

A change in priorities is possible, one that favors commonwealth over private wealth. To realize this, we need government and, crucially, its money. As historian John Boughton says, writing in the wake of the UK's 2017 Grenfell tragedy, where seventy-two people died when neglected former social housing, since commodified, caught fire: "We need its regulation and oversight to protect us from commercially driven agendas which value profit over people. We need its investment to provide the safe, secure and affordable housing for all that the market never will. And we need its idealism—that aspiration to treat all its citizens equitably and decently."[9]

Housing will always be political. Any suppositions to the contrary—whether by pro-privatizers at St. James telling council members to stay in their lane or pro-Mitchell-Lama folks at Southbridge avoiding supposedly "ideological" arguments—are rather bogus. Because government is intertwined with housing markets, the decisions around those markets are fundamentally political. What shapes the housing system is the balance of power between political actors. These power dynamics are in no way natural, neutral, inherent, or permanent, should we choose to organize things differently.

The federal level will be a key arena in which the fate of American housing is determined, but the systemic always plays out on the ground. Ordinary communities are influential in their own right, through organizing, decision-making, and mutual care or abandonment. Matt Hern notes, "It is perilous to rely on policy over politics, because what's required is a fundamental shift in social relationships with land, not just a new ordinance here or regulation there."[10] That is possible only if a different way of conceiving of ownership—based on a responsibility to steward—is taken up among the people. The people—like Raghuveer, MAK, Werkmeister, and union members in Kansas City; Pam Ellis and Kristen Wyman on Nipmuc land; Steve Normanton and Ian McSweeney in rural New Hampshire; the resident stewards of St. James and Southbridge—are showing the paths forward.

Their acts of stewardship build our capacity for growing and maintaining the commonwealth, ensuring that its abundance reaches all. And, as we shall see in the next chapter, the diverging paths of St. James and Southbridge show the consequences of either investing in that capacity or letting it wither. What happens when residents renew their sense of solidarity and broaden their universe of obligation? What happens when the commons is no longer?

After Cooperation

Two and a half years after Southbridge's privatization, in 2018, one of its staunchest opponents finally admitted that Southbridge Rights had been right, to a point. Eva Sacks—whose mother had been victorious in breaking the complex's first wave of privatization fever, whose *Just the Facts* newsletters had preached the risks in the gamble, and whose lawsuit had held off the consumption of social housing for a futile year—told me that, "On the economics, we were wrong. More people were selling, and the apartments were selling upwards of $50,000 to $100,000 more than was anticipated. I get a lot of 'I told you so's.'"

Monthly maintenance charges had not increased as of early 2018. The complex had remained affordable for the approximately 1,330 pre-privatization households that had chosen to stay. Around 15 percent of shareholders, some 170 folks, had opted to sell their newly valuable asset by April 2018. Prices exceeded expectations. Southbridge apartments were selling on the open market for more than $1.5 million. Marissa Heine said that those who left "maybe can't live in New York City, but they can certainly go other places." Connecticut for her sister, outside New Orleans for a friend. Some sellers could manage to stick around the city, but they would have to leave Lower Manhattan for neighborhoods farther afield and take on a mortgage, or rent. For those who stayed, Southbridge's maintenance costs continued to be a tremendous deal, and the co-op was keen to tout that deal to prospective buyers. Sacks, though, remained unhappy with the outcome, resigned to her newfound wealth and what it meant for those on the outside looking in. "Great. I have an asset. What am I gonna do with this asset? . . . I still feel like I want to live here until they carry me out in a box. . . . Even being three-quarters of a millionaire, it doesn't feel any different than it did before except that I feel like I can't do with it what I wanted to do, which was let somebody have the opportunities I had." Southbridge was now a very expensive deal to take advantage of, no longer accessible if you weren't already part of the club or wealthy enough to buy your way in.

The high sales prices also made some of the asset-rich residents wealthy in other ways. Jan Naumann, with her real estate license in hand, had "been very active since" the privatization, enjoying the fact that "the place sells itself." Expensive sales also meant more flip tax revenue for the co-op. Harvey Marshall, taking a break from board presidency after his big privatization win, marveled at the tremendous surpluses building up on the co-op's book—a cherry on top of the ample reserves the co-op had squirreled away in its decades of significant public subsidy. Southbridge was still feeding off a nest egg from the state.

Daniel Brampton, even then ruing the flyers he didn't write, observed the pro-privatizers' back-patting with consternation. "I want this financial thing to last because I don't wanna have to move. On the other hand, I don't want it to be too good because then people from other complexes will say 'Oh, AH-HA, well then maybe we should privatize too. . . . For now, the people on the board are taking their bows and saying 'Hey, all these terrible things that people said were gonna happen haven't happened, so what's the problem?'"

Brampton agreed: the terrible things hadn't happened—yet. The whole privatization endeavor hadn't collapsed as quickly as Brampton or Sacks thought it would, but they remained worried about the co-op's future prospects. According to Sacks, "Once the number of sales slows down, the maintenance is going to go up pretty considerably. I have my 403(b), IRA, and Social Security. There's only but a certain amount that all that's gonna last." Brampton was on a similar page: "I think the day will come when we will have to sell and find another place to live that won't be as good as this place. On the other hand, given my age, maybe I won't be around then."

Brampton and Sacks' age-old opponents had begun to acknowledge some downsides as well. Marshall admitted that at some point, the flip tax revenue was going to run out and maintenance would increase. And that "at some point," in his estimation, wasn't actually all that far away—perhaps ten years. Naumann conceded that she'd seen some cases where being asset-rich with a fixed income had resulted in a diminished quality of life: "You do see that certain people, because of the value of their apartment, may not be Medicaid-eligible, and if they have no other assets, the apartment has to go into a trust, and . . . some people don't have the money to put it into a trust. That's something I didn't see or anticipate before I went into it." She also stopped short of recommending privatization to all other Mitchell-Lamas: "It isn't [necessarily] a good deal. I mean, if you have a great low monthly maintenance fee, which is what most of them have, that's a huge plus. Where else are you going to live at that monthly maintenance fee? . . . Maintenance will go up." She was comfortable with the gamble she'd taken, but "other people might not want to risk that, and so depending on where you were, I think that's a real consideration." It was more credence to the pro-Mitchell-Lama side than she'd ever given when the debate was live in her own complex.

That's the funny thing about time: the far-off becomes imminent more quickly than expected. That's especially the case with infrastructure, which, by nature, we often regard as given. Time is the great revealer of whether something that's been called maintenance is actual upkeep or merely a Band-Aid. Like the flip tax's temporary staunching of cost increases, the ability of Southbridge's pre-privatization residents to retain their sense of community had also begun to wither a few years out. That came down to who was moving in and what they'd paid to do so. There were bright spots, as none other than anti-privatization pariah James Szal acknowledged: "What I do see that's promising is that we're getting younger people moving in. And the great thing about young people with children is that they do have a commitment, and it makes for better community. But one of the things we've lost is the diversity, and that we see very clearly." Leo Aria, who'd attempted to heal the wounds of debate with his post-vote letter, was more critical: "I know who's moving in, and who's moving in are people who have no roots in the community and not necessarily family people. They probably are transitory and speculating."

What the new buyers certainly had in common was their sense of what Southbridge was: a speculative co-op in which they'd invested significant funds. They made this clear by their eagerness to understand and enter co-op politics. Naumann mentioned that "a lot of the newer people who are coming in are very interested. They've just plunked down a million dollars for a two-bedroom apartment, and they want to make sure their investment is well protected." Multiple board members mentioned that Southbridge couldn't be picky about buyers the way many other speculative co-ops are, in part because they were reliant on sales to keep their maintenance affordable. The price point itself screened out plenty of people, however. Many of the new arrivals brought financial and legal chops from their jobs in the surrounding Financial District, and they wanted to use them for Southbridge. Tom Goldhaber—who, as treasurer, regarded both his personal and co-op account balances with delight—observed that "you can always see the difference in opinion between the people who came in and spent $1 million for their apartment and those who spent $3,000 for their apartment 25, 30 years ago. It's a transition. It's a process." Tussles over expenditures on aesthetic improvements or funding senior activities had begun with a new dividing line—old vs. new, big spenders vs. lottery winners.

Some residents were in transition, too, as they adjusted to the new normal. Chris Hresko, who'd learned cooperative values as a child at the knees of his parents and grandparents, spoke of how privatization had affected his own outlook on certain matters. It wasn't a wholesale change by any means. He was just beginning to open up, out of resignation or necessity, to how a speculative co-op is run. And yet, he still maintained the same concern for folks to be able to stay in their homes. He also held out hope that maybe, just maybe, there was a way to come back from privatization. As he considered running for a board seat, he dreamed of folks seeing the error of their ways and initiating what would be a unique set-up for a privatized Mitchell-Lama: putting the land on which the buildings rose into a community land trust and using that mechanism to return Southbridge to the social housing sphere.

Hresko, however, knew that this was a pipe dream. "I'm very much a realist when it comes to things, but I also have utopian elements," he told me as we overlooked the East River on Manhattan's Pier 15. It was a balance similar to his fluent deployment of the terms "pedagogy" and "methodological" in a casual conversation that he soon interrupted with a delighted cry of "Frenchies!!" when two French bulldogs waddled by. "Once you let one Frenchie into your heart," he said, it's game over. There wasn't any feasible way back to decommodification for Southbridge, barring some kind of disruptive change. As Hresko and every other cooperator with any history in the co-op knew, though, the place had a record of being near the epicenter of such disruptions. "People don't think about how one of the better benefits of being under the offices of the State or the City is that you have certain protections as a cooperative whereby you can ensure that you're going to get that insurance or you'll be able to get a safe subsidized loan for repairs. . . . My greatest fear now is, God forbid, that next big disaster."

COVID-19 arrived on Lower Manhattan's shores in 2020, almost five years after privatization. It wasn't the type of disaster that Hresko had pictured, but its consequences were. The real estate market suffered, slowing sales and the all-important flip taxes. Businesses shuttered, causing the revenue from some of Southbridge's commercial spaces to dry up. Folks lost jobs, leading some to fall behind on their maintenance. The specter of cooperator departures loomed, born of an inability to keep up with those monthly payments. Hresko himself lost a job he'd been offered but had yet to start when a hiring freeze was imposed.

Through all these changes, though, the co-op's now standard property tax remained at the same high rate. Hresko, for the first time since privatization, became quite concerned with the immediate health of the larger co-op. Sitting on Southbridge's financial services committee, he started "seeing proposals for raising revenue that would have never flown in previous times," among them jacking up the price on parking. "Those kinds of privatized elements are seeping through," he lamented. The eventualities that he and his pro-Mitchell-Lama allies had foretold were starting to come true, with COVID acting as an accelerant. The privatization honeymoon was over, and Hresko now saw the full realization of the co-op's commodified status catch up with its instigators. "There are people still here who expect government and such to come to the beck and call of Southbridge, even though now we're private. That's part of the bargain that was made. You no longer have someone to go and run to. You are in charge of your own destiny now. And you have to deal with the fact that if something is screwed up, it's on you. The onus is on you as a cooperative and no longer as a ward of the state, so to speak."

In 2021, Hresko took the plunge and ran for the board. In May, he won his seat. He remained pro-Mitchell-Lama, assisting in other anti-privatization campaigns around the city—one on the Upper West Side, another on the Lower East. "I'm gonna say [privatization] has gone better than where I was thinking it was gonna go. However, I'm still not going to recommend this to any Mitchell-Lama co-op that exists. I am still going to tell others: stay in the system." He also realized that his new position in his privatized co-op would affect how he saw the world. "I, myself, have changed in so far that I've accepted that this is our fate, and I have to accept that my mindset is going to change."

Time would continue to tell what that change, for the co-op and coop-erators, would look like.

IF WE CAN'T DO IT

As in the aftermaths of 9/11 and Hurricane Sandy, Southbridge pulled together in the face of COVID. Hresko noted that "there was a lot of activism on the part of a lot of our longstanding communities that really got federal help and the State and City to ensure that food and supplies were getting to our elderly or those on fixed incomes. They were mak-ing food packages and things like that distributable through our com-munity room and ensuring that masks and hand sanitizer would also be available to those who needed it." He was surprised and pleased: "That community element is still strong and still vibrant." Hresko had a sense that the wounds of the privatization battle "have healed a lot more than I was actually expecting them to." Time, again, was the key determinant. "There were a lot of people that I know who had argu-ments with people that they previously had long relations with. They were having dinner again; they were going to each other's houses; they had apologized for how they reacted to one another."

But like before, once the immediate threat waned, the divisions came roaring back. When Hresko assumed his board seat and gained its inside perspective on co-op finances, he saw how the lack of maintenance in-creases in previous years had put the co-op in a tenuous position. They were running a deficit, and they could pull only a small percentage of their needed operating costs from their hefty reserves before running afoul of mortgage-lending guidelines set by Fannie Mae and Freddie Mac. If the co-op violated those, prospective buyers would no longer be able to get government-backed mortgages to finance their purchases of the now very expensive Southbridge shares. The resultant loss of flip tax revenue to the co-op would deepen existing deficits. Southbridge was now in a position where it needed to raise money from its cooperators; otherwise, future cost increases would be even higher. Things could spiral.

Hresko recognized that in this new environment, "costs need to in-crease, . . . affordability isn't like a guarantee or an ideal that we can ideate anymore." The wider cooperative body did not seem ready to face this reality, expressed Hresko. "Now, you had all the people who had supported privatization and led the board during the privatization days call in to mention the hardship of the parking spaces, and talk about how the community's affordability is being threatened. And I'm sitting here about to smash my head against the wall. You guys took us [away] from affordability with privatization. And now you're here, putting yourself on the cross, lamenting about losing affordability of parking spaces and saying how we need to bring affordability into play. It was ludicrous. It felt Kafka-esque." In order to plug the co-op's gap, maintenance would likely need to increase by 10 to 30 percent.

With Southbridge's new normal coming into view, its politics were morphing. Pro-privatization and pro-Mitchell-Lama were no longer meaningful designations, and what Hresko and his board allies called "the grievance caucus" began to coalesce. "It's like going back to high school," Hresko said. "It is filled with so much rumormongering, passive aggressiveness, pettiness, backstabbing, betrayal. . . . We're going through the thralls of an experience that's completely unlike anything else compared to past boards." In his estimation, the prevailing animosity was even worse than it had been during the privatization debates.

A co-op listserv was serving up all kinds of takes: that $7 million was missing from co-op accounts due to board corruption, that households without kids shouldn't have to pay for playground maintenance, that the board was undemocratic. It had privatization-debate spice with an even more self-centered twist. As a board member, Hresko was pilloried with bogus claims and unreasonable expectations. The experience caused him to reevaluate his perspective on some board members from years prior. Speaking of one former opponent, Hresko told me that

now I have no qualms working with that individual, because they're sensible, and they have legitimate ideas and concerns for the co-op. And for the longest time when I thought that they were just being jerks for the sake of being jerks, only now am I realizing, he or she is actually thinking from their legal mind of potential consequences and liabilities from certain actions that we're undertaking. So they're actually watching out for us more than they're just being jerks. . . . I'm starting to realize maybe I was on the negative side of doomsaying about what it meant to be a private cooperative these days.

Hresko was considering different options to forestall the coming maintenance increases, ones he'd feared in the lead-up to privatization. "Just projecting in the future, thinking about this fiduciary responsibility you have on the board, . . . and flip tax revenue has run out and maintenance was being increased and arrears were going up. What actual options do you think the co-op has for folks who aren't able to pay? This is the whole thing about the fiduciary nature of things. How compassionate can I be in my role as the head of a corporation?"

Competing considerations abounded. What if listserv gossip made its way onto Zillow or StreetEasy, making potential buyers wary of South-bridge? What if the proposed development atop a long-standing park-ing lot across the street got approved, potentially decreasing the value of Southbridge apartments? Their harbor views would disappear, and there would also be more units with which Southbridge would have to compete. Hresko, once a fan of the inflexible terms that newly privat-ized co-ops got from the State, now even seemed to be advocating for more leniency: "For Mitchell-Lama, if you're going to have an afford-able co-op leave, they cannot pay a property tax that is based on market valuations. Eventually you could do it, but you need a grace period for leaving." Actually, Southbridge had been given a grace period already, its property tax ramping up to the full amount over a few years. That it was hard to pay was the point, and the deal. And Southbridge, with Hresko among its leadership, would have to deal with it. "Ah, yes, you can't have your cake and eat it too," he quipped.

In 2022, Hresko estimated that Southbridge still had a couple of years of flip tax revenue to offset the privatization costs. Despite some financial challenges, the complex remained rich. They had enough mil-lions in their reserves that the finance committee could count on the likes of Goldman Sachs and Morgan Stanley showing up with bound proposals for how to invest this wealth. Those proposals were shared in the same meeting room where, later in the day, struggling cooperators would filter in to dine on cold rice and rotisserie chicken served by a local nonprofit. Only time would tell how those cooperators would fare when the flip tax revenue ran out for good. In the meantime, one cooperator rued that "it seems to me to have gotten more divisive than ever. . . . I love the old stories of hallway parties and everyone leaving their doors open. Those good days are come and gone." Other Mitchell-Lamas seemed to view Southbridge as a cautionary tale, according to Hresko: its "bombastic" privatization had "led towards increasing cooperative consciousness" and "a lot of privatization [campaigns] have actually been met with major resistance."

James Szal, the face of Southbridge's "crazies," was no longer so in-volved in co-op politics. He had been compelled to take up another, more personal fight, against cancer. Even when wearied by chemo, however, he maintained his fire on the issue. "We were blessed . . . but that's going away." His maintenance had already increased from $680 a month to $998 to cover the deficit that Hresko's board had encountered, and that didn't account for new charges for heating and electricity, plus a one-time assessment of $1,000 the year prior. There was no joy in being right, in turning the I-told-you-so's back on the privatizers who had held to "the [supposed] fact that the flip tax would cover any increases in the maintenance, which, of course, by now people have found out is not the case." Hresko, too, was on the receiving end of not a few regrets from those who'd voted in favor of privatization. "If people knew what they know now, I don't think privatization would have gone through. Honestly, God, they had it good before. . . . [People] have come to the realization that if you didn't cut and run from the co-op in the first couple of years after you go private, and you still plan on living here for the long-term, privatization is not a good deal. Privatization is a windfall for those who want to leave but then becomes a hardship for those who want to stay."

One of those who'd wanted to stay, Eva Sacks, had told me years prior, "When I moved in here, I very clearly stated to my friends, the only way I'm leaving is in a body bag." She passed away in June 2022 in New Hampshire in her early eighties, having spent the last months of her life away from Southbridge at her nephew's house. Her comrades mourned her demise and that of the New York she had known. To Leo Aria, New York had "become more of an elitist kind of place, Manhattan, than a place to live." Before privatization, low- and middle-income Southbridgers had been able to live "in the center of the world," in Aria's estimation; they were now succumbing to a self-inflicted wound. Hresko presaged a "major kerfuffle" over the increasing stratification of the city: "I'm not going to say a Marxian revolution, but it's going to come to a real big cultural conflict over those who have and those who have not." As for the co-op, Hresko had said that "if Southbridge can't accomplish a successful transition, no other co-op can."

FROM CO-OP TO COMMONWEALTH

While Southbridge stumbled through the throes of change, the stewards of St. James settled back into the status quo they'd fought to maintain. Graham Hales reported in 2021 that things were "pretty much the same." Wenna Redfern still went to see her movies on Sundays, still talked with Hales about his dog every other day, and occasionally requested his company on her trips to the fish market. Tia Ward refocused on her other campaigns. Seniors like Harriet Brighton kept up their daily routine of heading down to the senior center on Fulton Street. "The scars are still there," Hales said of the privatization battle, but things were a bit duller around St. James, a bit more ordinary. It was a welcome lull for those who had opposed privatization.

At the same time, the relative lack of change wasn't all good news. Many folks went back to taking their social housing for granted. "There is, unfortunately, a fair bit of apathy in the building," Hales told me. "Just trying to get people motivated has been a challenge." He knew that unless pro-Mitchell-Lama cooperators took control of the board, it was very possible that the privatization campaign could return. It had happened at Southbridge. But the anti-privatizers' efforts to win more board seats failed. Wenna kept trying and kept losing. Others didn't care to attempt a run, the commitment too much or board president Deborah Norton too foreboding: "They feel intimidated by her, frankly. I tried to tell them that her bark is worse than her bite." Hales remained the only pro-Mitchell-Lama board member. Ward stood by, understanding many residents' disinterest in carrying forward the campaign: "I have to be ready, because these people aren't equipped. I mean, they're old. . . . Why should they have to be concerned about where they're gonna live now?" "I know I'm getting ready to have a Clash of the Titans war with [board president Deborah Norton] again . . . and you can't build your shield on the battlefield."

In the meantime, more practical co-op matters took precedence, like repairs to the parking lot sinkhole. Rather than tap in to government financing and recommit to Mitchell-Lama, though, the co-op paid for this work by pulling from its reserves, taking out a private loan from the contractor, and assessing a one-time special fee on cooperators. There were also ongoing, routine repairs to the plumbing, the plaster. Then came COVID. While the streets rang with ambulance sirens, St. James remained in pretty good shape. No one's life was easy, but the infrastructure of safe, secure, affordable social housing played its role brilliantly as the most basic form of healthcare. "Before the vaccine, housing was the vaccine," as KC Tenants leader Tara Raghuveer put it. Hales noted that "surprisingly, we haven't had much of an issue in terms of collecting maintenance fees. . . . We really were lucky." Luck may have played its role, but so had the whole conceit of social housing: that housing is a basic need, and that folks should be able to count on living in it at the best of times and, especially, the worst.

Tia Ward, imagining an alternative future in which St. James had privatized, struck a relieved figure when she described how "we went through two years of COVID—what would people have done? Most of the people would have lost their part" in the co-op. She recalled a fellow cooperator approaching her: "She says, Tia, thank you so much. Because you know what, I would probably be homeless now if it wasn't for you." That may have been an overstatement, but the vote and its aftermath clarified that "a lot of people want to keep things as they are in terms of staying Mitchell-Lama," Hales said, "but they're just not willing to make the commitment to fight for it."

Hales, though, remained committed. With a privatization bid now thwarted on his home front, he turned his attention elsewhere. Throughout the city, the larger Mitchell-Lama struggle was still ongoing. Hales took on more duties within CU4ML, engaging with residents at other Mitchell-Lamas debating privatization. Among them was East Midtown Plaza, where Jacob Villa, the well-coifed peer of Chris Hresko at Southbridge, was attempting to add another commodified former social housing unit to his loot. Hales was hopeful: "I think we've really been the silent majority in a sense. . . . The numbers are in our favor."

Contesting individual co-op campaigns was one sphere in which this struggle could be waged. But Hales and CU4ML, having seen the pitfalls of doing so—the allure of quick cash amid a collapsing social safety net, the apathy of cooperators with lots else on their plates—also moved to scale up. Just before the pandemic would set in, the organization joined with two other advocacy groups, the Mitchell-Lama Residents Coalition and the Brooklyn Mitchell-Lama Task Force. Together, they formed the aptly named Mitchell-Lama United. Their goal was to reform the Mitchell-Lama state law to remove the possibility of privatization altogether—to return it to its original state in a sense. Like the organizers at KC Tenants, they understood that broader politics had to be part of their strategy. Their opponent Simon Doran looked on in apparent resignation: "They are organizing, and they are meeting, and we don't have that."

The environment at the state level was different from that in individual co-op battles. Legislators didn't have to denounce pro-privatizers at a specific site like Southbridge and in the process potentially alienate a voting base. In focusing on the rules that governed all Mitchell-Lama co-ops, they paradoxically had more cover. The New York State Legislature had also, as of 2018, come under Democratic control, making more viable the Mitchell-Lama reform bills that had previously stalled in committee. With the housing crisis deepening and made even more stark by the pandemic, a new urgency gripped the State. A full-on privatization ban was off the table, due to concerns that it would spur lawsuits claiming that the change constitutes a seizure, or a taking, of private property. Instead, working with folks at the state and city levels, Mitchell-Lama United crafted a reform bill that would raise the voting thresholds on all steps of privatization, while also making crucial tweaks to make privatization less appealing.

By June 2021, the reform bill had passed both bodies of the New York State Legislature. It mandated that four board meetings a year had to be open to observation by all shareholders, and it restricted the matters for which closed executive sessions of the board could be used. It also required vote records and correspondence regarding financing from the City and State to be available to all cooperators. It outlawed proxy votes, which had led to allegations of vote rigging at Southbridge. Shareholder groups would be entitled to use the community room at their co-ops for free; barring them from doing so would be in violation of the law.

These were all positive steps toward better co-op operations and governance, but the biggest blow to privatization came in changes to the three votes needed to effectuate it. The first vote, the funding of a feasibility study, would now require a two-thirds margin in order to pass, rather than a simple majority. The margin for the second vote, to fund the Red Herring, was raised from two-thirds to 80 percent. So was the margin for the final vote needed to approve the Black Book. The ample funds needed to pay the consultants crafting the privatization plans could no longer be drawn from the co-op's operating budget; they would have to come out of the cooperators' pockets via a special assessment. Should any of the three votes fail, the cooling-off period before a new vote could be scheduled was lengthened from one to five years. Under these rules, Southbridge's privatization would have failed. St. James wouldn't even have made it past the first hurdle.

When long-standing governor Andrew Cuomo was forced to resign in August of 2021 after his penchant for sexual misconduct came to light, the bill was stalled. Lieutenant Governor Kathy Hochul took the reins of the State. Hales hoped to show the new governor that co-ops like St. James were behind the new reform bill: "I feel that a large majority of the population is for the program. I started circulating a petition . . . urging the governor to sign the bill and I got very positive feedback. I got at least 50 signatures. . . . Meanwhile, the board had sent a memo with an attachment of a letter urging the governor not to sign the bill. They only got 20 responses." His organizing—and that of the other members of Mitchell-Lama United—paid off. This time, Christmas came early to the pro-Mitchell-Lama side: on December 21, 2021, Governor Hochul signed the bill.

Backlash to the law was swift and predictable, though hardly widespread. The *New York Post*'s editorial board called the high threshold for privatization a confiscation of cooperators' property rights. It perpetuated the myths that Mitchell-Lamas were always meant to privatize and that "City housing is almost always better in private hands."[1] That the co-ops remained in private hands was immaterial to this ideology, which did its best to paint "public" things as bad and regulation as government takeover. Other critics called the new measures an affront to democratic principles.[2] Just 20 percent of a co-op's shareholders could thwart an attempt to privatize, a minority holding sway over a majority. This is only true, though, if you consider the cooperators as the sole rightful owners of this public good. The reform bill did not fully recognize the broader "we" with a stake in the future of these limited-equity co-ops, but it had empowered a co-op minority to better protect the interests of that much larger majority.

The new law changed the game at St. James. The high voting thresholds needed to even fund a feasibility study dampened the stirrings of a renewed privatization push. "They've just been complaining about that more than anything," Hales reported. St. James was also staring down a roof that needed repair, rising utility costs, and a substantial maintenance increase of between 14 and 36 percent if it chose to borrow the necessary funds from a private lender. If anything, support for staying in Mitchell-Lama had risen among cooperators since 2017. There was really only one way to go, said Hales: "Our best option is to go with the City. . . . We're in a much better position to get money at a . . . much cheaper interest." The board was going to have to finally take the City up on its financing offer and with it take privatization completely off the table for 30 years.

That didn't stop some from feeling coerced. Hales remembered "one board member in particular was complaining that the City's playing a game, because they're offering more free money . . . intimating that the City was trying to trick us to stay in the program. . . . The management company said 'you make a good point. If you don't want to play the game, don't take the money. It is taxpayer-funded money that we're receiving.'" At the time of writing, St. James had yet to actually pull the trigger on this new City debt. But it had begun to look inevitable. Hales was pleased. With privatization increasingly unlikely, the board was functioning better than it had in years. "Some things we may discuss that you may have a different opinion, but overall, we're pretty much in unison," Hales noted. "It's just going private—that's where we get the division. . . . Other than that, we are pretty much cooperative."

The frequency of those privatization discussions has abated and with them the urgency. This stall was a temporary win—wrought through organizing, solidarity, and politics—but it wasn't an end point. There is no finality to this kind of maintenance, that is, unless there's nothing left to maintain. "Maintenance is a drag; it takes all the fucking time," artist Mierle Laderman Ukeles wrote in her manifesto for maintenance art in 1969.[3] The Concerned Shareholders of St. James and the City had bought just a bit of time. They'd kicked the can down the road thirty years, and the kick had largely come from a financial need that could continue to fester as latent commodification, if left unattended. Whether the co-op would be up to defending their, and the wider city's, commonwealth again, only time would tell.

OF GUARDRAILS AND GLIMMERS

Whether to privatize public goods like Southbridge Towers and St. James Towers is ultimately a political question, what theorist Margaret Kohn describes as "a conflict that exposes different understandings of the public good. . . . Politics makes different interests, perspectives, powers, and desires visible and then forces a decision between them. An effective political argument does not assert 'this is good for me' but rather 'this is right for us.' It helps people see their interests in new ways, or to prioritize the needs of others . . . Politics, in this sense, can help us recognize inequality and injustice in practices that would otherwise seem neutral, familiar, or inevitable."[4]

René Moya of the Debt Collective observes that people are sometimes forced into politicization without a framework to understand it. "We can't ignore that kind of economic incentive" present in privatization, he told me. "If anything, I think a politics of liberation has to be founded upon letting people basically understand what their true interests are in a particular situation, but to do so out of solidarity with other people." It calls for organizers from groups like CU4ML and KC Tenants to act as sounding boards, "not by pussyfooting around these issues," said Moya, but "by confronting them head on and challenging people, . . . to speak to them as people who have incipient power in their hands." That means acknowledging the reality that "Black folks in particular, people of color generally, deserve a right to participate in equity-owning society, . . . that you should have a right to possession of the home that you live in. But you don't necessarily deserve the right to make it into a speculative commodity to gin up the value of housing such that in micro it very much enriches me but at the macro level, it literally dismisses others and prevents them from having a shelter over their head at all." It means changing the culture of ownership.

That should leave us a bit uncomfortable, like any good parable does, and there's little doubt that the cooperators at Southbridge and St. James were left discomfited by their whole situation. Their cooperative wounds, individual regrets, and eventual resignation to their respective privatization outcomes illustrate as much. Had these co-ops not been vulnerable to privatization in the first place, this discomfort could have been avoided. Regulations that act as guardrails on the commonwealth may constrain individual decision-making, but they also protect the broader "we" and protect folks from having to make impossible choices. No one should have to choose between paying for eldercare and having a stable, decommodified home; between leaving your children better off and selling out someone on the waitlist who just wants the same opportunity you had.

But making true social housing inevitable isn't enough on its own. Maintaining it is also predicated on broader protections and investments in the commonwealth. There are plenty of indications that our society is moving toward a more sustainable vision of housing. One need look no further than KC Tenants or a new pilot fund for limited-equity co-ops on the South Side of Chicago.[5] You can look to the Debt Collective's Tenant Power Toolkit for Californians, at new social housing policies being advanced at the municipal level in New York City,[6] or the Housing Justice for All coalition fighting for tenant protections across New York State. They, and many others, shine against a dour backdrop of need. The waitlists for Mitchell-Lamas have gotten so long that the

New York State comptroller recently criticized the practice of keeping them open, given that new entrants have almost no chance of getting an apartment.[7]

The idea that owning a home, all by itself, came with a right to profit was once a foreign concept within the cinderblock corridors of Southbridge and along the gingko-blanketed sidewalks of St. James Place. That idea was once outside the norm generally. Preserving our public goods is contingent on moving away from that conception of ownership and toward one based on stewardship.

I think back to Lester Goodyear typing away on the twenty-first floor of St. James, fearful of losing his chance at his American Dream and determined to finally be part of a "we" that had long excluded him and other Black Americans. He wrote: "Ownership of Real Property gives the owner the essential first step in becoming a person of economic substance in American Society." He'd written this sentence as an indictment against anti-privatizers. But there is another way to read it. For me, it serves even better as an assessment of the illness that such a conception of ownership breeds among us.

Goodyear may not know that he, too, is pointing us toward a renewed vision of ownership as stewardship and is teaching us how to get there. So too are the wily campaigners of Southbridge Rights, who in many ways equal the contributions of their tireless opponents in the likes of Eva Sacks and James Szal. For it is in the relationships and organizing of these rather normal folks—the way they answered the political question put before them—that we can understand not just how to win public goods but how to maintain them. From them we can learn how to build an enduring commonwealth together—for our own good.

ACKNOWLEDGMENTS

This is a book about people and their communities, and it would not exist without the generosity and passion of those residents at Southbridge Towers and St. James Towers who were willing to bare their personal lives to me. Thank you. I'm grateful to the many other narrators featured in this book, among them René Moya for his incisive commentary; Ian McSweeney for getting me out of the city; Tara Raghuveer, MAK, and Magda Werkmeister for making KC the model; and especially Pamela Ellis and Kristen Wyman—I've made ample use of the tea and will not forget a healing walk on your land.

I'm spoiled to have an agent and agency who, from the outset, got the import of these stories. Ayla Zuraw-Friedland, a deep thanks for steering this book and me toward publication, and to the entire team at Frances Goldin Literary Agency—I hope I've done your namesake justice. To Catherine Tung, editor extraordinaire, thank you for your deft touch and deep engagement with the text, and to the Beacon Press team for your commitment to books like this one that aim to live in and shape a more just world. I would not have reached Ayla's and Catherine's proverbial doorsteps without the advice, and the occasional shot in the dark email, of so many: Joshua Jelly-Schapiro, Rebecca Solnit, Jacquelyn Hall, Oliver Roeder, Henry Grabar, Nate Storring, Karen Kubey, Ariel Lauren Wilson, Scott Middleton, Jessica Anderson, Zoë Mueller, Pronoy Sarkar, Melissa Flashman, Alice Martell, Alison Lewis, Jessie Kindig, Niels Hooper, Beth Clevenger, and Brandon Proia.

Innumerable people shaped the ideas, arguments, and language of this book over the last decade. Special thanks to Emily Schmidt, Justin Steil, Cassim Shepard, Susanne Schindler, Larry Vale, Carl Adair, and Joseph Terrell—friends and mentors, all. I'm grateful to the support—a heady combination of research, moral, perspectival, connective, and accountability—of Adam Tanaka, Ingrid Gould Ellen, Reed Jordan,

Danya Littlefield, Phoebe Holtzman, Jessica Wolff, Matt Robayna, Garnette Cadogan, Mariana Arcaya, Jeff Chang, Rosalie Genevro, Oksana Mironova, Dick Heitler, Kavita Kulkarni, Peter Munkenbeck, Varick Shute, Andrea Rudner, Caitlin Waickman, Peter Samton, Heather Mc-Ghee, Astra Taylor, and Cristina Fontánez Rodríguez.

Projects like these have many ups and downs; they require leaps of faith and extended stretches of vulnerability. Alexander Stephens, Claire Kane-Boychuck, Katie Byerly, Justin Labeille, Kendra Danowski, Meg Cramer, Erina Keefe, Noah Hoch, Saba Jamaluddin, Salma Mutwafy, and Abby and KC Love offered key nudges and shoulders along the way.

Writing about families divided by privatization made me especially grateful for the resolute unity with which mine supported this endeavor. Thank you to the adults for your belief: Sandy (Mom), Rick (Dad), Dan, Jai, Jessica, Charles, Zach, Sabira (Amma), Navaid (Baba), Tahira (Laloo), Zainab, Muhammad, Junaid, and Anushay. And to my nieces and nephews, for whom we must do better: Lila, Emaan, Noor, Asher, Teal, Ayla, Will, Vera, and Ruby.

To my feline writing companion Kaju—I never took your day-long naps as disinterest.

And last but most, all the love and gratitude to my wife Haleemah Qureshi, who played every role imaginable as this book came into being. You are the vital infrastructure and steward of our common life.

INTRODUCTION: A HOUSE DIVIDED

1. Kriston Capps and Sarah Holder, "The Wolf of Main Street," *Bloomberg*, March 3, 2022, https://www.bloomberg.com/graphics/2022-evictions -monarch-investment-rental-properties.
2. Martine Paris, "US Rents Hit New Record as Parts of NYC Soar Past $4,000 for August," *Bloomberg*, August 29, 2022, https://www.bloomberg .com/news/articles/2022-08-29/most-expensive-us-cities-for-renters-in -august.
3. Brittany Freeman, Sophie Chou, and Mariam Elba, "They Faced Fore-closure Not from Their Mortgage Lender, but from Their HOA," *Pro-Publica*, April 7, 2022, https://www.propublica.org/article/they-faced -foreclosure-not-from-their-mortgage-lender-but-from-their-hoa.
4. Michael Weiner, "Deed Theft in Brooklyn Targets the Most Vulnerable," *Prism*, August 8, 2022, http://prismreports.org/2022/08/08/deed-theft -brooklyn.
5. Debra Kamin, "Home Appraised with a Black Owner: $472,000. With a White Owner: $750,000," *New York Times*, August 18, 2022, https:// www.nytimes.com/2022/08/18/realestate/housing-discrimination -maryland.html.
6. Conor Dougherty and Ben Casselman, "Solving the Housing Crisis Means Building When No One Is Buying," *New York Times*, July 23, 2022, https://www.nytimes.com/2022/07/23/business/housing-market -crisis-supply.html.
7. Emily Badger and Quoctrung Bui, "The Extraordinary Wealth Created by the Pandemic Housing Market," *New York Times*, May 1, 2022, https://www.nytimes.com/2022/05/01/upshot/pandemic-housing-market -wealth.html.
8. D. W. Gibson, "'All Kinds of Discrimination': Inside the Secretive World of New York Housing Co-ops," *The Guardian*, February 8, 2022, https:// www.theguardian.com/lifeandstyle/2022/feb/08/new-york-housing-co-ops -apartments-discrimination.
9. *The 2014 New York City Housing and Vacancy Survey*, https://www .census.gov/data/datasets/2014/demo/nychvs/microdata.html.
10. New York University Furman Center for Real Estate and Urban Policy, *State of New York City's Housing and Neighborhoods in 2022*, 2023, https://furmancenter.org/stateofthecity.

11. National Low Income Housing Coalition, *Out of Reach 2022*, https://nlihc.org/oor.

12. National Oceanic and Atmospheric Administration, "U.S. Coastline to See up to a Foot of Sea Level Rise by 2050," February 15, 2022, https://www.noaa.gov/news-release/us-coastline-to-see-up-to-foot-of-sea-level-rise-by-2050.

13. Conor Dougherty, "The Next Affordable City Is Already Too Expensive," *New York Times*, February 20, 2022, https://www.nytimes.com/2022/02/20/business/economy/spokane-housing-expensive-cities.html.

14. Stephen Menendian, "Deconstructing the 'Housing Crisis,'" Othering & Belonging Institute, November 30, 2022, https://belonging.berkeley.edu/deconstructing-housing-crisis.

15. Mark Paul, "Economists Hate Rent Control. Here's Why They're Wrong," *American Prospect*, May 16, 2023, https://prospect.org/infrastructure/housing/2023-05-16-economists-hate-rent-control.

16. TRD Staff, "Four Decades in Making, East Northport Project Clears Key Hurdle," *Real Deal Tri-State*, August 12, 2022, https://therealdeal.com/tristate/2022/08/12/four-decades-in-making-east-northport-project-clears-key-hurdle.

17. For information on Eugene, see Cole Sinanian, "The Forgotten Answer to the Affordable Housing Crisis," *Eugene Weekly*, February 3, 2022, https://eugeneweekly.com/2022/02/03/the-forgotten-answer-to-the-affordable-housing-crisis. For information on Philadelphia, see Margaret J. Krauss, "How an Old Housing Model Could Help Pittsburgh's Affordability Crisis," 90.5 WESA, May 16, 2022, https://www.wesa.fm/development-transportation/2022-05-16/how-an-old-housing-model-could-help-pittsburghs-affordability-crisis.

18. Amanda Huron, *Carving Out the Commons: Tenant Organizing and Housing Cooperatives in Washington, D.C.* (Minneapolis: University of Minnesota Press, 2018), 139.

19. Albert Amateau, "Southbridge Director Charged in Fraud Case," *AmNY*, sec. Downtown Express, January 12, 2006, https://www.amny.com/news/southbridge-director-charged-in-fraud-case.

20. The terms *privatization, reconstitution, conversion*, and *buyout* are all used interchangeably to refer to erasing the limited-equity nature of these cooperatives, and each is laden with a different political meaning. I prefer "privatization" because rather than just describe the legalistic implications of this act, it also speaks to what the act means on a societal scale.

21. Jennifer Miller, "Investing in Real Estate as Self-Care," *New York Times*, July 29, 2022, https://www.nytimes.com/2022/07/29/realestate/investing-self-care-real-estate-women.html.

22. Celinda Lake, Alysia Snell, and Jesse Kline, *Findings from Focus Groups and a Dial Survey on Housing in the United States*, Funders for Housing and Opportunity, 2020, https://housingnarrative.org/webinar-findings-focus-groups-dial-survey.

23. Paul A. Samuelson, "The Pure Theory of Public Expenditure," *Review of Economics and Statistics* 36, no. 4 (1954): 387–89, https://doi.org/10.2307/1925895.

24. Marc Wuyts, "Deprivation and Public Need," in *Development Policy and Public Action*, ed. Marc Wuyts, Maureen Mackintosh, and Tom Hewitt (Oxford: Oxford University Press, 1993), 31.

25. Jedediah Purdy, *This Land Is Our Land: The Struggle for a New Commonwealth* (Princeton, NJ: Princeton University Press, 2019), xx.

26. Pádraig Ó Tuama, "Philip Metres—One Tree," *Poetry Unbound*, https:// onbeing.org/programs/philip-metres-one-tree, accessed July 4, 2023.

CHAPTER 1: SOCIAL HOMES

1. "'Where Are We to Go?' Ask 1,100 Pratt Area Families," *Brooklyn Daily Eagle*, May 20, 1954, https://www.newspapers.com/image/686539490, accessed November 9, 2022.

2. The term was originally used by James Baldwin in 1963 during a conversation with Dr. Kenneth Clark for public television station WGBH's series *Perspectives: Negro and the American Promise*.

3. Leslie Hanscom, "Ask City OK Slum Clearance in Pratt Institute Area," *Brooklyn Daily Eagle*, July 13, 1953, https://www.newspapers.com /image/53900823, accessed November 9, 2022.

4. New York City Committee on Slum Clearance, *Slum Clearance Plan Under Title I of the Housing Act of 1949: Pratt Institute Area*, 1953, 43, Pratt Institute Archives, https://archives.pratt.edu/repositories/2/archival _objects/436, accessed October 19, 2022.

5. Whittlesey & Conklin Architects & Planners, *Report on Pratt Institute Master Plan*, Pratt Institute, 1962, Appendix G, Pratt Institute Archives, https://archives.pratt.edu/repositories/2/archival_objects/438, accessed October 19, 2022.

6. New York City Committee on Slum Clearance, *Slum Clearance Plan Under Title I of the Housing Act of 1949*, 32.

7. Hilary Botein, "New York State Housing Policy in Postwar New York City: The Enduring Rockefeller Legacy," *Journal of Urban History* 35, no. 6 (September 2009): 833–52, https://doi.org/10.1177/0096144209339558.

8. Kavita Kulkarni, "Co-operatives Within New York's Post-World War II Housing Crisis: Mitchell-Lama and the Promise of Equity over Equality," in *Housing the Co-op: A Micro-Political Manifesto*, ed. Sascha Delz, Rainer Hehl, and Patricia Ventura (Berlin: Ruby Press, 2020).

9. Nicholas Dagen Bloom and Matthew Gordon Lasner, eds., *Affordable Housing in New York: The People, Places, and Policies That Transformed a City* (Princeton, NJ: Princeton University Press, 2015), 144.

10. Annemarie Sammartino, *Freedomland: Co-op City and the Story of New York* (Ithaca, NY: Cornell University Press, 2022).

11. According to journalists Jack Newfield and Paul Dubrul, the fact that the City and State paid for Mitchell-Lama construction meant the developers in charge had no incentive to keep down costs, a situation ripe for exploitation should actual costs be inflated. See Jack Newfield and Paul DuBrul, *The Abuse of Power: The Permanent Government and the Fall of New York* (New York: Viking Press, 1977), and Sammartino, *Freedomland*.

12. Matthew Gordon Lasner, *High Life: Condo Living in the Suburban Century* (New Haven, CT: Yale University Press, 2012), 94.

13. Historic Districts Counsel, "A Guide to Historic New York City Neighborhoods: Sunset Park, Brooklyn," *6 to Celebrate* (blog), 2013, https://6tocelebrate.org/site/alku-and-alku-toinen.
14. Lasner, *High Life*, 94.
15. Principles Committee, *The Guidance Notes to the Cooperative Principles*, International Co-Operative Alliance, 2017, https://ica.coop/sites/default/files/basic-page-attachments/guidance-notes-en-221700169.pdf
16. Rochdale Pioneers Museum, *Introduction to Co-operative Heritage Museum* (Rochdale, England, 2021), https://vimeo.com/ondemand/virtualpioneers2021.
17. Sammartino, *Freedomland*, 6.
18. Historic Districts Counsel, "A Guide to Historic New York City Neighborhoods; Van Cortlandt Village, the Bronx," *6 to Celebrate* (blog), 2012, http://6tocelebrate.org/site/shalom-aleichem-houses.
19. Lasner, *High Life*, 98.
20. Kazan's UHF would, however, end in ignominy as disputes with Co-op City residents over the management and construction of the complex led to their removal from the governance equation and ultimate shuttering. See Sammartino, *Freedomland*.
21. Bloom and Lasner, *Affordable Housing in New York*, 168.
22. New York State Joint Legislative Committee on Housing and Multiple Dwellings, *Report of the Joint Legislative Committee on Housing and Multiple Dwellings 1955*, New York State Legislature, May 25, 1955, New York State Archive, accessed October 12, 2022.
23. Gene Gleason and Fred Cook, "U.S. Rules Flouted by Title 1 Project," *New York World-Telegram*, August 18, 1956, Citizens Housing and Planning Commission Archive, accessed December 2, 2022.
24. Gene Gleason and Fred Cook, "Only Promises Glow at Building Project Site," *New York World-Telegram*, January 17, 1957, Citizens Housing and Planning Commission Archive, accessed December 2, 2022.
25. See Robert A. Caro, *The Power Broker: Robert Moses and the Fall of New York* (New York: Vintage, 1975).
26. City of New York Housing and Redevelopment Board, "Pratt Institute Urban Renewal Area," press release, April 25, 1962, Citizens Housing and Planning Commission Archive.
27. One notable exception is the United Housing Foundation. The UHF maintained a financial and governance interest until it was ousted from some of these arrangements (as with Co-op City) and ultimately folded.
28. New York State, ed., *McKinney's Session Laws of New York 1959* (St. Paul, MN: West Publishing, 1960), 675.
29. Emphasis added. New York State Joint Legislative Committee on Housing and Multiple Dwellings, *Report of the Joint Legislative Committee on Housing and Multiple Dwellings 1960*, New York State Legislature, December 1, 1960, New York State Archive.
30. Botein, "New York State Housing Policy in Postwar New York City."

31. Philip S. Gutis, "Unfettering Mitchell-Lama," *New York Times*, February 23, 1986, https://www.nytimes.com/1986/02/23/realestate/unfettering -mitchell-lama.html, accessed October 21, 2023.
32. Kavita Kulkarni, "Feeling Fort Greene: On Spatial Mediations of Race, Affect, and Collective Being," PhD diss., New York University, 2019, p. 73.
33. Kulkarni, "Feeling Fort Greene," 72.
34. Sammartino, *Freedomland*.
35. Botein, "New York State Housing Policy in Postwar New York City."
36. Margot Gayle, "New York's Changing Scene," *New York Daily News*, October 12, 1975, https://nydailynews.newspapers.com/newspage /395855039/, accessed June 21, 2021.
37. Tishman Speyer, "New York's Newest Middle Income Cooperative Apartments," *New York Amsterdam News*, June 8, 1968, ProQuest Historical Newspapers.
38. "Brooklyn Bridge S.W. Approved," New York City Planning Commission, 1963, Citizens Housing and Planning Commission Archive.
39. Abbott & Adams, *Brooklyn Bridge Southwest Tenant Occupancy and Condition of Structures Survey*, City of New York Housing and Redevelopment Board, 1967, Citizens Housing and Planning Commission Archive.
40. Citizens Housing and Planning Commission, "Brooklyn Bridge Southwest Urban Renewal Area Fact Sheet," n.d., Citizens Housing and Planning Commission Archive, accessed October 25, 2022.
41. Citizens Housing and Planning Commission, "Brooklyn Bridge Southwest (New HRB Proposal)," January 15, 1964, Citizens Housing and Planning Commission Archive.
42. Citizens Housing and Planning Commission, "Brooklyn Bridge Southwest."
43. Citizens Housing and Planning Commission, "Brooklyn Bridge Southwest Support and Opposition Analysis," February 1964, Citizens Housing and Planning Commission Archive.

CHAPTER 2: LIVING COOPERATION

1. Larry Cole, "Residents of Southbridge Find It Hard to Cooperate," *New York Daily News*, September 2, 1973, https://nydailynews.newspapers .com/newspage/465522561/, accessed June 21, 2021.
2. Daniel O'Grady, "Pooch Has Pol in Doghouse on Complex Issue," *New York Daily News*, April 14, 1977, https://nydailynews.newspapers.com/ newspage/482165249/, accessed June 21, 2021.
3. Dolores Acevedo-Garcia, Clemens Noelke, and Nancy McArdle, *The Geography of Child Opportunity: Why Neighborhoods Matter for Equity*, DiversityDataKids.org, 2020, https://www.diversitydatakids.org/sites /default/files/file/ddk_the-geography-of-child-opportunity_2020v2_0.pdf.
4. Matt Hern, *What a City Is For: Remaking the Politics of Displacement* (Cambridge, MA: MIT Press, 2016), 27.
5. Calculated from statistics in Esther Sullivan, *Manufactured Insecurity: Mobile Home Parks and Americans' Tenuous Right to Place* (Oakland: University of California Press, 2018), 15–16.

6. Kristina Borrman, "One Standardized House for All: America's Little House," *Buildings & Landscapes: Journal of the Vernacular Architecture Forum* 24, no. 2 (2017): 37, https://doi.org/10.5749/buildland.24.2.0037.
7. Quoted in Lawrence J. Vale, "The Ideological Origins of Affordable Homeownership Efforts," in *Chasing the American Dream: New Perspectives on Affordable Homeownership*, ed. William M. Rohe and Harry L. Watson (Ithaca, NY: Cornell University Press, 2007), 32.
8. Vale, "The Ideological Origins of Affordable Homeownership Efforts," 24.
9. Quoted in Vale, "The Ideological Origins of Affordable Homeownership Efforts," 27.
10. Vale, "The Ideological Origins of Affordable Homeownership Efforts," 26.
11. Quoted in Vale, "The Ideological Origins of Affordable Homeownership Efforts," 20.
12. Brian McCabe, *No Place Like Home: Wealth, Community & the Politics of Homeownership* (New York: Oxford University Press, 2016), 47.
13. Susanne Schindler, "Housing Beyond and Within the Market, Part 2: Cooperative Conditions in Zurich," *PLATFORM*, April 5, 2021, https://www.platformspace.net/home/housing-beyond-and-within-the-market-part-2-cooperative-conditions-in-zurich.
14. Francesca Mari, "Lessons from a Renters' Utopia," *New York Times Magazine*, May 23, 2023, https://www.nytimes.com/2023/05/23/magazine/vienna-social-housing.html.
15. Cassim Shepard, "Land Power," *Places Journal*, July 26, 2022, https://placesjournal.org/article/community-land-trusts-and-civic-empowerment.
16. Shepard, "Land Power."
17. David J. Madden and Peter Marcuse, *In Defense of Housing: The Politics of Crisis* (New York: Verso, 2016), 142.
18. Annemarie Sammartino, *Freedomland: Co-op City and the Story of New York* (Ithaca, NY: Cornell University Press, 2022), 70.

CHAPTER 3: LET'S EXPLORE OUR OPTIONS

1. Untruthbusters for Mitchell-Lama, "One Small Step for a Mitchell-Lama, One Giant Step for Privatization!" *UNTRUTHBUSTERS for MITCHELL-LAMA* (blog), May 12, 2008, http://untruthbusters4ml.blogspot.com/2008/05/one-small-step-for-mitchell-lama.html.
2. Thomas P. DiNapoli, *Enforcement of the Mitchell-Lama Surcharge Provisions*, Office of the New York State Comptroller, 2018, 18.
3. Jack Newfield and Paul DuBrul, *The Abuse of Power: The Permanent Government and the Fall of New York* (New York: Viking Press, 1977), 298.
4. Noah Goldberg, "Handbags for Housing: Coney Island Women Accused of Bribery Scam," *Brooklyn Eagle*, May 21, 2019, https://brooklyneagle.com/articles/2019/05/21/handbags-for-housing-coney-island-women-accused-of-bribery-scam.
5. David Cruz, "Tracey Towers Residents Wonder How Their Complex Became 'Little Ghana,'" *Norwood News*, January 6, 2020, https://www.norwoodnews.org/tracey-towers-residents-wonder-how-their-complex-became-little-ghana.

6. The change is not immediate but is gradually implemented over five years.
7. Amanda Huron, *Carving Out the Commons: Tenant Organizing and Housing Cooperatives in Washington, D.C.* (Minneapolis: University of Minnesota Press, 2018), 132.
8. Lynne Goodman, "The Mitchell-Lama Debate: Buying Out or Selling Out?" *Cooperator News New York*, November 2001, https://cooperator news.com/article/the-mitchell-lama-debate.
9. Josh Rogers, "Big Bucks at Southbridge—Residents Will Be Rich, Study Says," *AmNY*, sec. Downtown Express, October 12, 2006, https://www .amny.com/news/big-bucks-at-southbridge-residents-will-be-rich-study -says.
10. New York City Department of Housing Preservation and Development, "Mitchell-Lama Program," https://www.nyc.gov/site/hpd/services -and-information/mitchell-lama-program.page, accessed December 1, 2022.
11. Nancy Wu, "Most NYC Buyers Are First-Timers, but Don't Want Starter Home," *StreetEasy* (blog), March 27, 2019, https://streeteasy.com/blog /most-nyc-buyers-are-first-timers.
12. See Nicholas Dagen Bloom, Fritz Umbach, and Lawrence J. Vale, eds., *Public Housing Myths: Perception, Reality, and Social Policy* (Ithaca, NY: Cornell University Press, 2015).
13. New York City Housing Authority, *Resident Data Summary*, 2021, https://www1.nyc.gov/assets/nycha/downloads/pdf/Resident-Data-Book -Summary-2021.pdf.
14. Personal correspondence with the New York City Department of Housing Preservation and Development, June 18, 2021.
15. Alfred Lubrano, "Blowup over Possible Buyout," *New York Daily News*, August 20, 1989, https://www.newspapers.com/image/467008632.
16. David Freund, "Marketing the Free Market," in *The New Suburban History*, ed. Kevin M. Kruse and Thomas J. Sugrue (Chicago: University of Chicago Press, 2006).
17. Richard Rothstein, *The Color of Law: A Forgotten History of How Our Government Segregated America* (New York: Liveright, 2017).
18. Josh Rogers, "Southbridge Privatizers Win Control of the Board," *AmNY*, sec. Downtown Express, May 24, 2007, https://www.amny.com /news/southbridge-privatizers-win-control-of-the-board, accessed November 24, 2022.
19. Charles V. Bagli, *Other People's Money: Inside the Housing Crisis and the Demise of the Greatest Real Estate Deal Ever Made* (New York: Plume, 2013).
20. Rogers, "Big Bucks at Southbridge—Residents Will Be Rich, Study Says."
21. Annemarie Sammartino, *Freedomland: Co-op City and the Story of New York* (Ithaca, NY: Cornell University Press, 2022).

CHAPTER 4: AN OFFERING
1. Jeff Chang et al., *A Future for All of Us*, Butterfly Lab, Race Forward, 2022, 21, https://www.raceforward.org/system/files/pdf/reports/2022 /ButterflyLab-Y1-FullReport_15.pdf.

2. Narrative Initiative, *Toward New Gravity*, 2017, 14, https://narrative initiative.org/wp-content/uploads/2019/08/TowardNewGravity-June 2017.pdf.
3. Narrative Initiative, *Toward New Gravity*, ii.
4. John Guyton et al., "Tax Evasion at the Top of the Income Distribution: Theory and Evidence," National Bureau of Economic Research Working Paper Series (March 2021), https://doi.org/10.3386/w28542.
5. Paul Kiel, "Has the IRS Hit Bottom?" *ProPublica*, June 30, 2020, https://www.propublica.org/article/has-the-irs-hit-bottom?token=kRdWvK9Ne Qw5o9MUlMvTQZvMtYHYiaOB.
6. Victor Nee and Richard Swedberg, eds., *The Economic Sociology of Capitalism* (Princeton, NJ: Princeton University Press, 2005).
7. Suleiman Osman, *The Invention of Brownstone Brooklyn: Gentrification and the Search for Authenticity in Postwar New York* (New York: Oxford University Press, 2012).
8. Emphasis added. N.Y. Comp. Codes R. & Regs. tit. 9, § 1725–2.1.
9. Amanda Huron, *Carving Out the Commons: Tenant Organizing and Housing Cooperatives in Washington, D.C.* (Minneapolis: University of Minnesota Press, 2018), 150.
10. Maja Hojer Bruun, "Communities and the Commons: Open Access and Community Ownership of the Urban Commons," in *Urban Commons: Rethinking the City*, ed. Christian Borch and Martin Kornberger (New York: Routledge, 2015), 153–70.
11. J. G. Ballard, *High-Rise* (New York: Liveright, 2012).
12. Jessica Dailey, "FiDi's Affordable Southbridge Towers Will Go Market-Rate," *Curbed NY*, October 1, 2014, https://ny.curbed.com/2014/10/1/10040686/fidis-affordable-southbridge-towers-will-go-market-rate.
13. nonstopid, "Q&A Flyer Pt. 1 & 2," *Southbridge Towers* (blog), September 25, 2014, https://southbridgetowers.wordpress.com/2014/09/25/qa-flyer-pt-1.
14. Herman Schwartz, "Housing, the Welfare State, and the Global Financial Crisis: What Is the Connection?" *Politics & Society* 40, no. 1 (March 1, 2012): 35–58, https://doi.org/10.1177/0032329211434689.

CHAPTER 5: A RIGHT TO PROFIT

1. Amy Starecheski, *Ours to Lose: When Squatters Became Homeowners in New York City* (Chicago: University of Chicago Press, 2016), 42–46.
2. Starecheski, *Ours to Lose*, 18.
3. Starecheski, *Ours to Lose*, 219.
4. John Locke and Mark Goldie, *Second Treatise of Government; and a Letter Concerning Toleration* (Oxford: Oxford University Press, 2016).
5. David Orrell and Roman Chlupatý, *The Evolution of Money* (New York: Columbia University Press, 2016), 140–41.
6. David Freund, "Marketing the Free Market," in *The New Suburban History*, ed. Kevin M. Kruse and Thomas J. Sugrue (Chicago: University of Chicago Press, 2006).
7. Susan Saegert et al., "The Promise and Challenges of Co-ops in a Hot Real Estate Market," *Shelterforce*, July 1, 2005, https://shelterforce.org

/2005/07/01/the-promise-and-challenges-of-co-ops-in-a-hot-real-estate
-market, accessed July 12, 2023.
8. Amy Chan et al., *Predatory Equity: The Survival Guide*, Making Policy
Public, Center for Urban Pedagogy, 2009, http://cup.linkedbyair.net
/Projects/MakingPolicyPublic/PredatoryEquity, accessed June 4, 2021.
9. nonstopid, "Beginning of the End," *Southbridge Towers* (blog), October
1, 2014, https://southbridgetowers.wordpress.com/2014/10/01/beginning
-of-the-end.
10. Joan Lobis, SBT Cooperators for Mitchell-Lama and SBT Shareholders
Association v. New York State Division of Housing and Community Renewal and Southbridge Towers, Inc., No. 100297/15, Supreme Court of
the State of New York, August 11, 2015.
11. David Graeber, "'Consumption,'" *Current Anthropology* 52, no. 4 (August 2011): 491, https://doi.org/10.1086/660166, accessed May 14,
2021.
12. In its final year as a Mitchell-Lama property, Southbridge owed the City
a shelter-rent tax of $676,000. Had it not benefited from the shelter-rent
tax arrangement provided to Mitchell-Lamas, it would have owed
$8,170,800 in property tax. (Note that both figures do not account for
other, unrelated tax exemptions.) See New York City Department of
Finance records.

CHAPTER 6: A PIECE OF THE ROCK
1. The address of the townhouse is 304 Lafayette Avenue. Sales information access via New York City's Automated City Register Information
System (ACRIS).
2. Amanda Huron, *Carving Out the Commons: Tenant Organizing and
Housing Cooperatives in Washington, D.C.* (Minneapolis: University of
Minnesota Press, 2018), 122.
3. Huron, *Carving Out the Commons*, 80.
4. Brian McCabe, *No Place Like Home: Wealth, Community & the Politics
of Homeownership* (New York: Oxford University Press, 2016), 36.
5. James Carr, Katrin Anacker, and Ines Hernandez, *The State of Housing in Black America 2013*, National Association of Real Estate Brokers
(NAREB), 2013, https://www.nareb.com/site-files/uploads/2020/10/2013
-SHIBA-REPORT-Small.pdf.
6. Sarah Burd-Sharps and Rebecca Rasch, *Impact of the US Housing Crisis
on the Racial Wealth Gap Across Generations*, American Civil Liberties
Union, 2015, https://www.aclu.org/wp-content/uploads/publications
/discrimlend_final.pdf
7. Keeanga-Yamahtta Taylor, *Race for Profit: How Banks and the Real Estate Industry Undermined Black Homeownership* (Chapel Hill: University of North Carolina Press, 2019), 2.
8. Nick Estes, *Our History Is the Future: Standing Rock Versus the Dakota
Access Pipeline, and the Long Tradition of Indigenous Resistance* (New
York: Verso, 2019), 210.
9. Susan Berfield and Jordyn Holman, "What Happened When Evanston Became America's First City to Promise Reparations," *Bloomberg*, May 28,

2021, https://www.bloomberg.com/news/features/2021-05-28/reparations
-for-black-residents-in-chicago-evanston-illinois-s-hard-reality
10. Taylor, *Race for Profit*, 31.
11. Emily Badger, "Why a Housing Scheme Founded in Racism Is Making a
Resurgence Today," *Washington Post*, November 24, 2021, https://www
.washingtonpost.com/news/wonk/wp/2016/05/13/why-a-housing
-scheme-founded-in-racism-is-making-a-resurgence-today.
12. Taylor, *Race for Profit*, 146.
13. Taylor, *Race for Profit*, 170.
14. Taylor, *Race for Profit*, 58.
15. Taylor, *Race for Profit*, 231.
16. Samuel Stein, *Capital City: Gentrification and the Real Estate State*
(New York: Verso, 2019).
17. Norman Oder, "When 'Affordable' Rents Push $3,000," *BKLYNR*,
August 21, 2014, https://www.bklynr.com/when-affordable-rents-push
-3000.
18. "A Kibbutz in the Bronx," *Newsweek*, October 5, 1970, https://archive.org
/details/newsweek76octnewy/page/n9/mode/2up, accessed July 12, 2023.
19. Julie Besonen, "Clinton Hill, Brooklyn, a Neighborhood in Transition,"
New York Times, December 2, 2015, https://www.nytimes.com/2015/12
/06/realestate/clinton-hill-brooklyn-a-neighborhood-in-transition.html.

CHAPTER 7: KEEPING THE FAITH
1. Emphasis in the original.
2. Kavita Kulkarni, "Feeling Fort Greene: On Spatial Mediations of Race, Affect, and Collective Being," PhD diss., New York University, 2019, p. 155.
3. Charles Tilly, "Do Unto Others," in *Identities, Boundaries and Social
Ties* (Boulder, CO: Routledge, 2006), 49.
4. Debra Kamin, "Discrimination Seeps into Every Aspect of Home Buying
for Black Americans," *New York Times*, November 29, 2022, https://
www.nytimes.com/2022/11/29/realestate/black-homeowner-mortgage
-racism.html.
5. Michael McAfee and Vanice Dunn, *Governing for All: An Equity Narrative Playbook for Policy-Makers*, PolicyLink, 2022, p. 10, https://www
.policylink.org/sites/default/files/Governing%20for%20All%20-%20
Mini%20Playbook.pdf.
6. L. T. Greene, "Emmanuel Baptist Church Hosts Summit on Black Involvement in Billion Dollar Cannabis Industry," *PoliticsNY*, February 27,
2019, https://politicsny.com/2019/02/27/emmanuel-baptist-church-hosts
-summit-on-black-involvement-in-billion-dollar-cannabis-industry.

CHAPTER 8: A RESPONSIBILITY TO STEWARD
1. City of New York, "NYC Community Boards," https://www.nyc.gov/site
/communityboards/index.page, accessed May 26, 2023.
2. Lauren Gill, "Mitchell-Drama! Clinton Hill Co-op at War over Whether
to Cash In," *Brooklyn Paper*, February 23, 2017, https://www.brooklyn
paper.com/mitchell-drama-clinton-hill-co-op-at-war-over-whether-to
-cash-in.

3. As it appears in the comments to Gill.

4. David J. Madden and Peter Marcuse, *In Defense of Housing: The Politics of Crisis* (New York: Verso, 2016), 9.

5. Madden and Marcuse, *In Defense of Housing*, 11.

6. Madden and Marcuse, *In Defense of Housing*, 12.

7. Christopher Jencks, "Varieties of Altruism," in *Beyond Self-Interest*, ed. Jane J. Mansbridge (Chicago: University of Chicago Press, 1990), 54.

8. Charles Tilly, "Do Unto Others," in *Identities, Boundaries and Social Ties* (Boulder, CO: Routledge, 2006), 66.

9. Tilly, "Do Unto Others," 66.

10. Madden and Marcuse, *In Defense of Housing*, 117.

11. Rebecca Solnit, "The Ideology of Isolation," *Harper's Magazine*, July 2016, https://harpers.org/archive/2016/07/the-ideology-of-isolation.

12. Maja Hojer Bruun, "Communities and the Commons: Open Access and Community Ownership of the Urban Commons," in *Urban Commons: Rethinking the City*, ed. Christian Borch and Martin Kornberger (New York: Routledge, 2015).

13. Robin Wall Kimmerer, "Returning the Gift," *Minding Nature* 14, no. 2 (Spring–Summer 2021), Centers for Humans and Nature, https://humansandnature.org/wp-content/uploads/2022/02/MindingNature_Spring21_webfinal.pdf.

14. Editorial Board, "When Housing Policy Is Personal, Politicians Should Butt Out," *Crain's New York Business*, February 27, 2017, https://www.crainsnewyork.com/article/20170228/OPINION/170229889/editorial-when-housing-policy-is-personal-politicians-should-butt-out.

15. Bill de Blasio, "Transcript: Mayor de Blasio Announces New Program to Save City's Remaining Affordable Mitchell-Lama," City of New York, October 26, 2017, https://www.nyc.gov/office-of-the-mayor/news/690-17/transcript-mayor-de-blasio-new-program-save-city-s-remaining-affordable-mitchell-lama.

16. Amanda Huron, *Carving Out the Commons: Tenant Organizing and Housing Cooperatives in Washington, D.C.* (Minneapolis: University of Minnesota Press, 2018), 127.

17. Matt Hern, *What a City Is For: Remaking the Politics of Displacement* (Cambridge, MA: MIT Press, 2016), 23.

CHAPTER 9: LAND AND TRUST

1. Eula Biss, "The Theft of the Commons," *New Yorker*, June 8, 2022, https://www.newyorker.com/culture/essay/the-theft-of-the-commons.

2. Amanda Huron, *Carving Out the Commons: Tenant Organizing and Housing Cooperatives in Washington, D.C.* (Minneapolis: University of Minnesota Press, 2018), 55.

3. Huron, *Carving Out the Commons*, 55.

4. Margaret Kohn, *The Death and Life of the Urban Commonwealth* (New York: Oxford University Press, 2016), 2.

5. Kohn, *The Death and Life of the Urban Commonwealth*, 6.

6. Agrarian Trust, "Principles," https://www.agrariantrust.org/principles, accessed May 26, 2023.

7. Agrarian Trust, "Agrarian Commons Frequently Asked Questions," https://agrariantrust.org/wp-content/uploads/2021/09/Agrarian-Trust -FAQ-Agrarian-Commons-2021.pdf, accessed May 26, 2023.
8. Agrarian Trust, "How Does Agrarian Trust Relate to Land Return?" https://www.agrariantrust.org, accessed August 16, 2022.
9. Matt Hern, *What a City Is For: Remaking the Politics of Displacement* (Cambridge, MA: MIT Press, 2016), 99.
10. Agrarian Trust, *Our First Impact Report 2020-2022*, https://www .agrariantrust.org/wp-content/uploads/2024/01/Agrarian-Trust-Impact -Report-2020-2022.pdf.

CHAPTER 10: ABUNDANCE AND RETURN
1. Eastern Woodlands Rematriation, "About Rematriate," https://rematriate .org, accessed May 26, 2023.
2. The word is often rendered as P8gwaso, with the numeral 8 standing for the bilabial resonant consonant that sounds somewhat like a *b* in English.
3. Matt Hern, *What a City Is For: Remaking the Politics of Displacement* (Cambridge, MA: MIT Press, 2016), 124.
4. Amanda Huron, *Carving Out the Commons: Tenant Organizing and Housing Cooperatives in Washington, D.C.* (Minneapolis: University of Minnesota Press, 2018), 159.
5. Heather McGhee, *The Sum of Us: What Racism Costs Everyone and How We Can Prosper Together* (New York: One World, 2022).
6. As quoted in Hern from Eve Tuck and Rubén A. Gaztambide-Fernández, "Curriculum, Replacement, and Settler Futurity," *Journal of Curriculum Theorizing* 29, no. 1 (June 18, 2013), https://journal.jctonline.org/index .php/jct/article/view/411, accessed June 7, 2023.

CHAPTER 11: POWER AND POLITICS
1. Margaret Kohn, *The Death and Life of the Urban Commonwealth* (New York: Oxford University Press, 2016), 63.
2. Kohn, *The Death and Life of the Urban Commonwealth*, 188.
3. Kohn, *The Death and Life of the Urban Commonwealth*, 191.
4. David J. Madden and Peter Marcuse, *In Defense of Housing: The Politics of Crisis* (New York: Verso, 2016), 201.
5. KC Tenants, "Could We End Evictions?" *Hammer & Hope*, February 15, 2023, https://hammerandhope.org/article/issue-1-article-3.
6. Jennifer E. Cossyleon, *"It Just Makes Us More Powerful": A Participatory Evaluation of the Housing Justice Narrative Fellowship*, Community Change, 2022, p. 22, https://bayareaequityatlas.org/sites/default/files /Housing%20Narrative-Draft.pdf.
7. Jared Brey, "What If City Renters Had More Political Power?" *Governing*, March 23, 2023, https://www.governing.com/community/what-if -city-renters-had-more-political-power.
8. Brian McCabe, *No Place Like Home: Wealth, Community & the Politics of Homeownership* (New York: Oxford University Press, 2016), 122.

9. John Boughton, *Municipal Dreams: The Rise and Fall of Council Housing* (New York: Verso, 2019), 6.
10. Matt Hern, *What a City Is For: Remaking the Politics of Displacement* (Cambridge, MA: MIT Press, 2016), 169.

EPILOGUE: AFTER COOPERATION

1. Editorial Board, "Albany Needs to Correct the 'Affordable Housing' Mistake It Just Made," *New York Post*, January 2, 2022, https://nypost .com/2022/01/02/albany-needs-to-correct-affordable-housing-mistake.
2. Bill Morris, "New Law Raises Bar for Opting Out of Mitchell-Lama Program," *Habitat Magazine*, January 7, 2022, https://www.habitatmag.com /Publication-Content/Legal-Financial/2022/2022-January/New-Law -Raises-Bar-for-Opting-Out-of-Mitchell-Lama-Program.
3. Mierle Laderman Ukeles, *MANIFESTO FOR MAINTENANCE ART, 1969! Proposal for an Exhibition: "CARE,"* October 1969, four typewritten pages, each 8½ x 11 in., https://feldmangallery.com/exhibition /manifesto-for-maintenance-art-1969, accessed July 4, 2023.
4. Margaret Kohn, *The Death and Life of the Urban Commonwealth* (New York: Oxford University Press, 2016), 126.
5. Grace Del Vecchio, Sonal Soni, and City Bureau, "Affordable Housing Advocates Push for Housing Co-ops," *City Bureau*, December 8, 2022, https://www.citybureau.org/newswire/2022/12/7/affordable-housing -advocates-push-for-housing-co-ops.
6. Oksana Mironova et al., *Pathways to Social Housing in New York*, Community Service Society, 2022, https://www.cssny.org/pages/pathways-to -social-housing-in-new-york.
7. Caroline Spivack, "Mitchell-Lama Applicants Pay Thousands, with 'Virtually No Chance' at Getting Apartments," *Curbed NY*, December 23, 2019, https://ny.curbed.com/2019/12/23/21032008/mitchell-lama -affordable-housing-program-dinapoli-audit.

on, 64. *See also* BIPOC farmers; racial covenants; racism; White residents; *names of specific people*
Black Swamp Commons, 196, 197–205
blockbusting, 67. *See also* housing discrimination; racism; redlining
Borch, Christian, 190
Boston, 203, 204
Boughton, John, 217
Brampton, Daniel, 32, 60, 70–71, 76–78, 80, 90, 129
Brighton, Harriet, 159–60, 228
Brooklyn Bridge Southwest Urban Renewal Area, 29, 105
Brooklyn Girl, 173–74
Brooklyn Mitchell-Lama Task Force, 229
Brown, Jared, 54–55
Brown, Ron, 33
brownstones, 27, 88, 144
Brunn, Maja Hojer, 95
Bui, Quoctrung, 6
Bullet Space (cooperative), 112
Butterfly Lab (Race Forward), 81
buyout, 238n20. *See also* privatization

Cadman Towers, 165
California, 233
cannabis industry, 164
capitalist ideologies, 87–89, 113, 133, 189
Carpenter, Whitney, 188, 194
Carving Out the Commons (Huron), 190. *See also* Huron, Amanda
Chalamet, Timothée, 17
Charles, Herbert, 18
Chicago, 233
Chisholm, Shirley, 152
citizenship, 35, 38, 39, 41, 141–42, 157, 183, 195. *See*

also homeownership, as concept
Clemons (firm), 207
Codes, Rules, and Regulations of the State of New York (publication), 89
co-governance, 215. *See also* governance
collective ownership model, 4. *See also* community land trusts; limited-equity co-ops; shared equity models
Colón, Mark, 54, 72
Committee on Slum Clearance (New York City), 15
commodification of housing, 5, 6–11, 18, 42, 54–56, 79–80, 122–24, 177, 183. *See also* affordability debates; decommodification of housing; home equity; privatization
commodification of land, 198
commons, 14, 183, 189–205. *See also* stewardship; togetherness
commonwealth, 217–18, 227–32
communism, 22, 39, 79
Community Change, 81
community land trusts, 8, 13, 41. *See also* collective ownership model
Concerned Shareholders for Transparency (group), 84
Concerned Shareholders of St. James (group), 152, 154, 156–57, 162–64, 177–79, 201, 212, 232. *See also* St. James Towers
Coney Island, 17–18, 55
Confessions of an Economic Hit Man (Perkins), 137
consumption, as concept, 122–23
conversion, 238n20. *See also* privatization

United Housing Federation
(UHF), 18, 22, 24, 166,
240n20, 240n27
unity, 31–32, 90, 224
University Terrace, 15–16
Urban Homesteading Assistance
Board (UHAB), 76
urban renewal, 4, 15–16, 18, 24,
29–30, 34, 52, 136. *See also*
forced relocation
use value *vs.* exchange value,
8–9. *See also* value-creation
ideology

Vale, Lawrence, 39
value-creation ideology, 8–9,
70–71, 112–14. *See also* use
value *vs.* exchange value
Vernon, Jeremiah, 194
Vienna, Austria, 40, 214
Villa, Jacob, 80, 84–87, 89, 106,
114–15, 128–29
Vladeck Houses, 64
voting and voting rights: activist organizations on, 41,
215–16; DHCR on, 55, 110;
familial wealth building and,
102–3; final vote on Southbridge Towers privatization,
108–10, 116–18; Honest
Ballot Association on, 94,
100, 175

Wagner, Robert, 17, 29
waitlists of co-op housing:
elimination of, 57, 62, 66; in
Mitchell-Lama programs, 4,
7, 10, 53, 63, 233; of Southbridge Towers, 55–56, 84–85,

95, 102, 105, 109, 119; of St.
James Towers, 136
Wald Houses, 64
Wall Street, 87–88
Ward, Tia: on community benefits, 158–60, 161; description of, 151–52, 228; distrust
of co-op board by, 156–57,
162, 164, 168; eldercare by,
34, 140; on privatization,
149, 150–51, 154, 175; public
events by, 172–74
Washington, DC, 59, 183
Waterview Towers, 44–45
Werkmeister, Magda, 212
West Paseo, 206
White middle class, 11, 113, 114,
124, 142. *See also* gentrification; middle class
White residents: blockbusting
and, 67; property control by,
26; public housing statistics
of, 64; return to city of, 4; in
suburbia, 4, 17, 113, 124, 147.
See also Black residents; White
middle class
Willoughby Walk, 136
Wolfson, Jody, 10, 54–55
working class, 22, 27, 111, 148,
215. *See also* middle class
World Trade Center, 87–88
Wyman, Kristen, 197–205, 217

Yang, K. Wayne, 195
Yiddish culture, 22
YIMBY (Yes In My Backyard), 8

Zero Eviction January, 210
Zurich, Switzerland, 40